# Mini Mickey

## THE POCKET-SIZED *unofficial* GUIDE®
## ᵀᴼ Walt Disney World®

**6TH EDITION**

# Mini Mickey

## THE POCKET-SIZED *unofficial* GUIDE®
## TO Walt Disney World®

**6TH EDITION**

BOB SEHLINGER

**\*Walt Disney World is officially known as
the Walt Disney World Resort®**

WILEY

Please note that prices fluctuate in the course of time, and travel information changes under the impact of many factors that influence the travel industry. We therefore suggest that you write or call ahead for confirmation when making your travel plans. Every effort has been made to ensure the accuracy of information throughout this book, and the contents of this publication are believed correct at the time of printing. Nevertheless, the publishers cannot accept responsibility for errors or omissions or for changes in details given in this guide or for the consequences of any reliance on the information provided by the same. Assessments of attractions and so forth are based upon the author's own experience, and therefore, descriptions given in this guide necessarily contain an element of subjective opinion, which may not reflect the publisher's opinion or dictate a reader's own experience on another occasion. Readers are invited to write the publisher with ideas, comments, and suggestions for future editions.

Published by:
John Wiley & Sons, Inc.
111 River Street
Hoboken, NJ 07030

Produced by Menasha Ridge Press

Cover design by Michael J. Freeland

Interior design by Vertigo Design

For information on our other products and services or to obtain technical support please contact our Customer Care Department within the United States at 800-762-2974, outside the United States at 317-572-3993 or fax 317-572-4002.

John Wiley & Sons, Inc. also publishes its books in a variety of electronic formats. Some content that appears in print may not be available in electronic formats.

ISBN 0-7645-8823-0

Manufactured in the United States of America

5  4  3  2

# CONTENTS

# LIST *of* MAPS

# WHY *this* POCKET GUIDE?

THE OPTIMUM STAY AT WALT DISNEY WORLD is seven days, but many visitors don't have that long to devote to Disney attractions. Some are on business with only a day or two available for Disney's enticements. Others are en route elsewhere or want to sample additional attractions in Orlando and central Florida. For these visitors, efficient, time-effective touring is a must. They can't afford long waits in line for rides, shows, or meals. They must determine as far in advance as possible what they really want to see.

This guide distills information from the comprehensive *Unofficial Guide to Walt Disney World* to help short-stay or last-minute visitors decide quickly how best to spend their limited hours. It will help these guests answer questions vital to their enjoyment: What are the rides and attractions that appeal to me most? Which additional rides and attractions would I like to experience if I have any time left? What am I willing to forgo?

## DECLARATION OF INDEPENDENCE

THE AUTHOR AND RESEARCHERS OF THIS guide are totally independent of Walt Disney Co. Inc., Disneyland Inc., Walt Disney World Inc., and all other members of the Disney corporate family. We represent and serve the consumer. The material in this guide originated with the author and researchers and hasn't been reviewed or edited by the Walt Disney Co., Disneyland, or Walt Disney World. Ours is the first comprehensive critical appraisal of Walt Disney World. It aims to provide the information necessary to tour Walt Disney World with the greatest efficiency and economy.

## HOW THIS GUIDE WAS RESEARCHED AND WRITTEN

LITTLE WRITTEN ABOUT DISNEY WORLD has been comparative or evaluative. Many guides parrot Disney's promotional material. In preparing this guide, however, we took nothing for granted. Each theme park was visited at different times throughout the year by trained observers. They conducted detailed evaluations and rated each park, with its component rides, shows, exhibits, services, and concessions, according to a formal, pretested rating method. Interviews were conducted to determine what tourists—of all ages—enjoyed most and least during their Disney World visit.

The essence of this guide consists of individual critiques and descriptions of each feature of the Magic Kingdom, Epcot, Disney-MGM Studios, and the Animal Kingdom, along with detailed touring plans to help you avoid bottlenecks and crowds. Also included are descriptions for Typhoon Lagoon, Blizzard Beach, and Pleasure Island.

# WALT DISNEY WORLD: *an* OVERVIEW

THERE'S NOTHING ON EARTH LIKE Walt Disney World. Incredible in its scope, genius, beauty, and imagination, it's a joy and wonder for all ages. Disney attractions are a quantum leap beyond most man-made entertainment we know. We can't understand how anyone could visit Florida and bypass Walt Disney World.

## WHAT WALT DISNEY WORLD ENCOMPASSES

WALT DISNEY WORLD ENCOMPASSES 43 square miles, an area twice as large as Manhattan Island. In this expanse are the Magic Kingdom, Epcot, Disney-MGM Studios, and the Animal Kingdom theme parks, two water parks, two nightlife areas, a sports complex, golf courses, hotels and campgrounds, more than 100 restaurants, four interconnected lakes, a shopping complex, three convention venues, a nature preserve, and a transportation system.

The formal name is Walt Disney World, but most tourists refer to the entire Florida Disney facility simply as Disney

World. The Magic Kingdom, Epcot, Disney-MGM Studios, and the Animal Kingdom are thought of as being "in" Disney World.

## THE MAJOR THEME PARKS

### The Magic Kingdom

The Magic Kingdom is the heart of Disney World. It's the collection of adventures, rides, and shows symbolized by the Disney cartoon characters and Cinderella Castle. The Magic Kingdom is divided into seven subareas or "lands," six of which are arranged around a central hub. First encountered is Main Street, U.S.A. Moving clockwise around the hub, other lands are Adventureland, Frontierland, Liberty Square, Fantasyland, and Tomorrowland. Mickey's Toontown Fair, the first new land in the Magic Kingdom since the park opened, is along the Walt Disney Railroad on three acres between Fantasyland and Tomorrowland. Access is through Fantasyland, Tomorrowland, or via the railroad. The Contemporary Resort, Polynesian Resort, and Grand Floridian Beach Resort are close to the Magic Kingdom and connected to it by monorail and boat. Shades of Green and the Wilderness Lodge Resort and Villas are nearby but not served by the monorail.

### Epcot

Epcot opened in October 1982. Divided into two major areas, Future World and World Showcase, it's twice as big as the Magic Kingdom. Future World consists of pavilions relating to human creativity and technological advancement. The World Showcase, arranged around a 41-acre lagoon, presents the architectural, social, and cultural heritages of 11 nations, each represented by famous landmarks and local settings. Epcot is more educational than the Magic Kingdom and has been characterized as a sort of permanent World's Fair.

Epcot has seven hotels: the Beach Club, Yacht Club, Beach Club Villas, BoardWalk Inn and Villas, Swan, and Dolphin. All are within a 5- to 15-minute walk of the International Gateway entrance to Epcot. The hotels are also linked by canal and tram. The monorail links Epcot to the Magic Kingdom and its hotels.

### Disney-MGM Studios

This $300 million, 100-plus-acre attraction opened in 1989 and has two areas. The first is a theme park relating to the past, present, and future of the movie and television industries. It contains movie-theme rides and shows and covers about half the complex. The remaining half is a working motion-picture and television production facility made up of three soundstages, a backlot of streets and sets, and creative support services.

Disney-MGM is connected to other Disney World areas by highway and canal but not by monorail. Guests can park in the Studios lot or commute by bus. Epcot resort guests can arrive by boat.

## Disney's Animal Kingdom

More than five times the size of the Magic Kingdom, the Animal Kingdom combines zoological exhibits with rides, shows, and live entertainment. A lush rain forest funnels visitors to centrally located Discovery Island, dominated by the 14-story-tall, hand-carved Tree of Life. The island encompasses guest services, shopping, and dining. From here you can access the theme areas of Africa, DinoLand U.S.A., Asia, and Camp Minnie-Mickey. The 100-acre Africa has herds roaming in a re-creation of the Serengeti Plain.

Animal Kingdom has its own pay parking lot and is connected to other Disney World destinations by the Disney bus system. Although it has no hotels, the All-Star, Animal Kingdom Lodge, and Coronado Springs Resorts are nearby.

## WATER THEME PARKS

DISNEY WORLD HAS TWO WATER THEME parks: Typhoon Lagoon and Blizzard Beach. Typhoon Lagoon has a wave pool capable of producing six-foot waves; Blizzard Beach features more slides. Typhoon Lagoon and Blizzard Beach have their own parking lots. River Country, a third water park (and Disney's first) closed in 2002.

## OTHER DISNEY WORLD VENUES

### Downtown Disney

Downtown Disney is a large shopping, dining, and entertainment complex encompassing Downtown Disney Marketplace on the east, six-acre Pleasure Island nighttime entertainment venue (tickets required) in the middle, and Disney's West Side on the west. The Marketplace has the world's largest Disney-merchandise store. Pleasure Island includes eight nightclubs and several upscale restaurants and shops. The West Side combines nightlife, shopping, dining, and entertainment. It includes a permanent showplace for the extraordinary Cirque du Soleil show *La Nouba;* DisneyQuest, a high-tech interactive virtual reality and electronic games venue; and a 24-screen cinema.

You can access Downtown Disney by bus from most Disney World locations.

## Disney's BoardWalk

Near Epcot, the BoardWalk is an idealized replication of an East Coast turn-of-the-century waterfront resort. Open all day, it features restaurants, shops, and galleries; a brew pub; an ESPN Sports Bar; a nightclub with dueling pianos; and a dance club. Clubs levy a cover charge at night. Also on-site are a 378-room deluxe hotel and a 532-unit time-share development.

The BoardWalk is within walking distance of Epcot's resorts and International Gateway. Boats link it to Disney-MGM Studios, and buses run to other Disney World locations.

## Disney's Wide World of Sports

The 200-acre Wide World of Sports is a competition and training facility consisting of a 7,500-seat ballpark; a field house; and venues for baseball, softball, tennis, track and field, beach volleyball, and 27 other sports. It's the spring training home for the Atlanta Braves, and it hosts numerous professional and amateur competitions. Spectators must pay. Guests may not use the facilities unless they're in one of the competitions.

## Walt Disney World

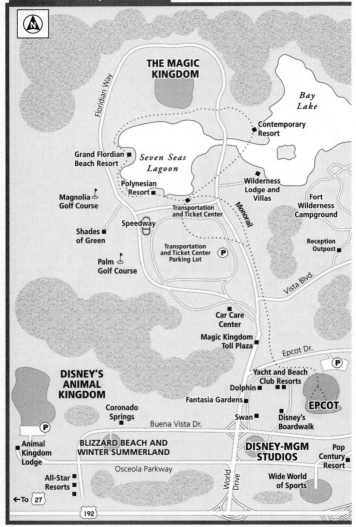

THE MAGIC KINGDOM

Bay Lake

Contemporary Resort

Floridian Way

Grand Flordian Beach Resort

Seven Seas Lagoon

Polynesian Resort

Wilderness Lodge and Villas

Fort Wilderness Campground

Magnolia Golf Course

Shades of Green

Speedway

Transportation and Ticket Center

Monorail

Reception Outpost

Transportation and Ticket Center Parking Lot

Palm Golf Course

Vista Blvd.

Car Care Center

Magic Kingdom Toll Plaza

Epcot Dr.

DISNEY'S ANIMAL KINGDOM

Yacht and Beach Club Resorts

Dolphin

Fantasia Gardens

EPCOT

Coronado Springs

Buena Vista Dr.

Swan

Disney's Boardwalk

Animal Kingdom Lodge

BLIZZARD BEACH AND WINTER SUMMERLAND

DISNEY-MGM STUDIOS

Pop Century Resort

Osceola Parkway

World Drive

Wide World of Sports

All-Star Resorts

← To 27

192

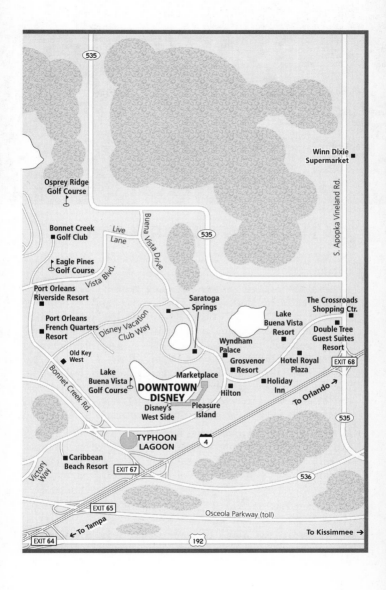

535

Winn Dixie
Supermarket

Osprey Ridge
Golf Course

S. Apopka Vineland Rd.

Bonnet Creek
Golf Club

Live
Lane

Buena Vista Drive

535

Eagle Pines
Golf Course

Vista Blvd.

Port Orleans
Riverside Resort

The Crossroads
Shopping Ctr.

Saratoga
Springs

Lake
Buena Vista
Resort

Port Orleans
French Quarters
Resort

Disney Vacation
Club Way

Double Tree
Guest Suites
Resort

Wyndham
Palace

Old Key
West

Grosvenor
Resort

Hotel Royal
Plaza

EXIT 68

Lake
Buena Vista
Golf Course

Marketplace

DOWNTOWN
DISNEY

Holiday
Inn

Hilton

Bonnet Creek Rd.

Disney's
West Side

Pleasure
Island

To Orlando ↗

535

TYPHOON
LAGOON

4

Caribbean
Beach Resort

EXIT 67

536

Victory Way

EXIT 65

Osceola Parkway (toll)

EXIT 64

← To Tampa

To Kissimmee →

192

# PART ONE

# PLANNING *before* YOU LEAVE HOME

# ▌ GATHERING INFORMATION

IN ADDITION TO THIS GUIDE, WE RECOMMEND that you obtain:

**1. THE WALT DISNEY TRAVEL COMPANY FLORIDA VACATIONS BROCHURE AND VIDEO/DVD** This video and brochure describe Walt Disney World in its entirety, lists rates for all Disney resort hotels and campgrounds, and describes Disney World package vacations. It's available from most travel agents or by calling the Walt Disney Travel Company at ☎ 407-828-8101 or 407-934-7639. Be prepared to hold; you may have a long wait. When you get a live representative on the line, tell them you want the video or DVD vacation planner that lists the benefits and costs of the various packages.

**2. THE DISNEY CRUISE LINE BROCHURE AND DVD** This brochure provides details on vacation packages that combine a cruise on the Disney Cruise Line with a stay at Disney World. Disney Cruise Line also offers a free DVD that tells all you need to know about Disney cruises and then some. To obtain a copy, call ☎ 800-951-3532 or order at **www.disney cruise.disney.go.com/disneycruiseline.**

**3. THE UNOFFICIAL GUIDE TO WALT DISNEY WORLD WEB SITE** Our Web site, **www.touringplans.com,** offers a free online trip organizer, 50 touring plans, and updates on changes at Walt Disney World, among other features. The site is described more fully later in this chapter.

**4. ORLANDO MAGICARD** If you're considering lodging outside Walt Disney World or if you think you might patronize attractions and restaurants outside of Disney World, it's worthwhile to obtain an Orlando MagiCard, a Vacation Planner, and the *Orlando Official Accommodations Guide* (all free) from the Orlando Visitors Center. The Orlando Magicard can be conveniently downloaded from a new Web site, **www.orlandoinfo.com/magicard.** To order the accommodations guide, call ☎ 800-643-9492. For additional information and materials, call ☎ 407-363-5872 or visit **www.go2orlando.com.** Phones are staffed during weekday business hours; allow four weeks for delivery.

**5. FLORIDA TRAVELER DISCOUNT GUIDE**  Another good source of discounts on lodging, restaurants, and attractions throughout the state is the *Florida Traveler Discount Guide,* published by Exit Information Guide. The guide is free, but you will be charged $3 ($5 shipped to Canada) for handling. Call ☎ 352-371-3948, Monday–Friday, 8 a.m.–5 p.m. EST or go to **www.travelerdiscountguide.com.** Similar guides to other states are available at the same number. It's sometimes difficult to get through on the phone, however. Also, their **www.roomsaver.com** Web site has hotel coupons you can print off your computer for free.

**6. KISSIMMEE–ST. CLOUD TOUR & TRAVEL SALES GUIDE**  This full-color directory of hotels and attractions is one of the most complete available and is of particular interest to those who intend to book lodging outside of Disney World. In addition to hotels and motels, the directory lists rental houses, time-shares, and condominiums. To receive a copy, call the Kissimmee–St. Cloud Convention and Visitors Bureau at ☎ 800-327-9159 or check out **www.floridakiss.com.**

**7. GUIDEBOOK FOR GUESTS WITH DISABILITIES**  If you have disabled individuals in your family or group, check out each park's *Guidebook for Guests with Disabilities,* available online at **www.disneyworld.com.**

## WALT DISNEY WORLD ON THE WEB

DISNEY'S OFFICIAL WEB SITE, **www.disney.com,** offers much of the same information as the Walt Disney Travel Company's vacation guidebook, but the guidebook has better pictures. Though the Web site is supposedly updated daily, we frequently find errors. Now you can purchase theme-park admissions and make resort and dining reservations on the Internet. The Web site also offers online shopping, weather forecasts, and information on renovations and special events.

## Other Recommended Web Sites

Len Testa, Internet guru and *Unofficial Guide* researcher, has combed the Web looking for the best Disney sites. Here are Len's picks:

**BEST OFFICIAL THEME-PARK SITE** For the second consecutive year, the official Walt Disney World Web site (**www.disney world.com**) gets the nod over the official Universal Studios site (**www.universalorlando.com**) and the official SeaWorld Web site (**www.seaworld.com**). Each contains information on ticket options, park hours, attraction height requirements, disabled guest access, and the like. Disney's site is more comprehensive, providing downloadable color maps of each park, plus lists of attractions closed for refurbishment. As of this writing, Disney was beginning to test a free online vacation planner on its Web site, but we still like ours better (and it's free, too). On the minus side, however, the Disney site is so loaded with high-tech gimmickry (music, video, pop-up images, etc.) that it takes much longer to bring up each screen.

**BEST GENERAL UNOFFICIAL SITE** The Walt Disney World Information Guide (**www.allearsnet.com**) is the first Web site we recommend to friends interested in going to Disney World. It contains information on virtually every hotel, restaurant, and activity in the World. Want to know what the rooms look like at the Disney resorts before you book a reservation? This site has photos of rooms at every resort— sometimes for each floor of a particular resort. The Web site is updated several times per week, and includes menus from Disney restaurants, ticketing information, maps, driving directions, and more.

**UNOFFICIAL GUIDE WEB SITES** The *Unofficial Guide to Walt Disney World* Web site can be found at **www.touringplans. com**. The official Web site of the *Unofficial Guide* Travel and Lifestyle Series, providing in-depth information on all the *Unofficial Guides* in print, is at **www.theunofficialguides.com**.

**BEST MONEY-SAVING SITE** We humbly suggest that Mary Waring's **www.mousesavers.com** is the kind of Web site for which the Internet was invented. The site keeps an updated list of discounts and reservation codes for use at Disney resorts. The codes are separated into categories such as "For anyone," "For residents of certain states," and so on. The site also lists discount codes for rental cars and non-Disney hotels in the Orlando area.

**BEST DISNEY DISCUSSION BOARDS** The best online discussions of all things Disney can be found at **www.disboards.com.** With almost 70,000 members and 7 million posts, the discussion boards are the most active and popular on the Web. Posting a question on any aspect of an upcoming trip is likely to get you helpful responses from lots of folks who've been in the same situation. For discussion boards that feel more familiar than your neighborhood bar, try **www.disneyecho.emuck.com.** Disney visitors living in the United Kingdom can say "cheerio" to one another on the boards at **www.wdisneyw.com/forums,** where tips on transatlantic airfare discounts, visa requirements, American customs, and more can be found.

**BEST SITE FOR WDW LIVE ENTERTAINMENT SCHEDULES** Orlando resident Steve Soares posts the daily performance schedule a week in advance for every live show in Walt Disney World. This information is invaluable if you're trying to integrate these shows into your touring plans. Visit **http:// pages.prodigy.net/stevesoares** for the details.

**BEST SITE FOR BREAKING NEWS AND RUMORS** We try to check **www.wdwmagic.com** every few days for the latest news and rumors on Disney World. The site is popular with Disney fans and park cast members, who often provide insider information on upcoming attractions and developments. WDWMagic also has pages dedicated to major rides, parades, and shows in each park, including audio and video. User forums allow you to read and post messages to other Disney fans. A close second is **www.screamscape.com.** Lance and crew continue to do an excellent job of uncovering the very latest on Disney projects still in development. Years after its debut, Screamscape is one of the sites we check a couple of times per week.

**BEST "THEME PARK INSIDER" SITE** If the folks at "E! True Hollywood Stories" ever did an episode on theme park development, they'd end up with something like **www.jimhillmedia.com.** Well-researched and supplied with a seemingly limitless amount of inside information, Jim's columns will guide you through the internal squabbles, budget compromises, and outside competition that made (and continue to make) Walt Disney World what it is today. Runners-up: Greg Maletic's columns found on **www.laughingplace.com** are excellent; we also enjoy Mike Scopa's writings at **www.mouseplanet.com.**

**BEST TRIVIA SITES** Lou Mongello's excellent *The Walt Disney World Trivia Book* has an equally good Web site: **www. disneyworldtrivia.com,** with message boards, park news, and more. Lou hosts live Internet "chats" via his site, usually on Tuesdays. We've been known to pop in occasionally.

At long last, fans of Steve Barrett's *Hidden Mickeys* book now have an online destination to keep updated on the latest tri-circle sightings at **www.hiddenmickeysguide.com.**

**BEST ORLANDO WEATHER INFORMATION** The Weather Channel offers printable ten-day forecasts for the Orlando area at **www.weather.com.** We find this site to be especially useful in the winter and spring months, when temperatures can vary dramatically. During summer, the ultraviolet index forecasts will help you choose between a tube and a keg of sunscreen.

**BEST WEB SITE FOR TRAFFIC, ROADWORK, AND CONSTRUCTION INFORMATION** Visit **www.expresswayauthority.com** for the latest information on road work and construction in the Orlando and Orange County areas. The site also contains detailed maps, driving directions, and toll-rate information for the most popular tourist destinations.

**BEST DRIVING DIRECTIONS** The printable directions available at **www.mapquest.com** are accurate and efficient. We especially like the feature that allows you to get driving directions for the return drive with the click of a button. Perhaps future maps will be able to flag every Stuckey's roadside stand along your route, too.

There are hundreds of other Disney sites, as well as sites that rate and contrast thrill rides in theme parks in the United States and all over the world. Start with the sites listed above and follow the links.

## DISNEY WORLD INFORMATION BY MAIL

INFORMATION ABOUT WALT DISNEY WORLD is also available at the public library, travel agencies, AAA, or by contacting any of the following:

### Important Walt Disney World Addresses

**Walt Disney World Info/Guest Letters/Letters to Mickey Mouse**
P.O. Box 10040
Lake Buena Vista, Florida 32830-0040

**Walt Disney World**
Central Reservations
P.O. Box 10100
Lake Buena Vista, Florida 32830-0100

**Convention and Banquet Information**
Walt Disney World Resort South
P.O. Box 10000
Lake Buena Vista, Florida 32830-1000

## More Walt Disney World Addresses

**Walt Disney World Educational Programs**
P.O. Box 10000
Lake Buena Vista, Florida 32830-1000

**Merchandise Mail Order**
**(Guest Service Mail Order)**
P.O. Box 10070
Lake Buena Vista, Florida 32830-0070

**Walt Disney World Ticket Mail Order**
P.O. Box 10100
Lake Buena Vista, Florida 32830-0140

**Compliments, Complaints, and Suggestions**
Walt Disney World Guest Communications
P. O. Box 10040
Lake Buena Vista, Florida 32830-1000

## IMPORTANT DISNEY WORLD TELEPHONE NUMBERS

WHEN YOU CALL THE MAIN INFORMATION number, you will be offered a menu of options for recorded information on theme-park operating hours, recreation areas, shopping, entertainment complexes, tickets and admissions, resort reservations, and directions by highway and from the airport. If you are using a rotary telephone, your call will be forwarded to a Disney information representative. If you are using a Touch-Tone phone and have a question not covered by recorded information, press eight (8) at any time to speak to a Disney representative.

| | |
|---|---|
| General Information | ☎ 407-824-4321 |
| Accommodations/Reservations | ☎ 407-934-7639 |
| | or ☎ 407-824-8000 |
| Convention Information | ☎ 407-828-3200 |
| Dining Advance Reservation | ☎ 407-939-3463 |
| Disabled Guests Special Requests | ☎ 407-939-7807 |
| Lost and Found | ☎ 407-824-4245 |
| Merchandise Guest Services Department | ☎ 407-363-6200 |
| Resort Dining and Recreational Information | ☎ 407-939-3463 |
| Telecommunication for the Deaf | |
|    Reservations | ☎ 407-939-7670 |
|    WDW Information | ☎ 407-939-8255 |
| Walt Disney Travel Company | ☎ 407-828-3232 |

# WHEN *to* GO *to* WALT DISNEY WORLD

## SELECTING THE TIME OF YEAR FOR YOUR VISIT

WALT DISNEY WORLD IS BUSIEST CHRISTMAS day through New Year's Day. Thanksgiving weekend, the week of Washington's birthday, Martin Luther King holiday weekend, spring break for colleges, and the two weeks around Easter are also extremely busy. What does "busy" mean? As many as 92,000 people have toured the Magic Kingdom alone on a single day in these peak times! While this level of attendance isn't typical, it is possible, and only those who absolutely cannot go at any other time should challenge the Disney parks at their peak periods.

The least busy time is from after the Thanksgiving weekend until the week before Christmas. The next slowest times are November through the weekend preceding Thanksgiving, January 4 through the first week of February, and the week after Easter through early June. Late February, March, and early April are dicey. Though crowds have grown markedly in September and October as a result of special promotions aimed at locals and the international market, these months continue to be good for weekday touring at the Magic Kingdom, Disney-MGM Studios, and the Animal Kingdom, and for weekend visits to Epcot.

### The Downside of Off-Season Touring

Though we strongly recommend going to Walt Disney World in the fall, winter, or spring, there are trade-offs. The parks often open late and close early during the off-season. When they open as late as 9 a.m., everyone arrives about the same time, which makes it hard to beat the crowd. A late opening coupled with an early closing drastically reduces the hours available to tour. Even when crowds are small, it's difficult to see a big park like the Magic Kingdom or Epcot between 9 a.m. and 6 p.m. Early closing (before 8 p.m.) also usually means that evening parades or fireworks are eliminated. And, because these are slow times at Disney World, some rides and attractions may be closed for maintenance or renovation. Finally, central Florida temperatures fluctuate wildly during the late fall, winter, and early spring; daytime lows in the 40s and 50s are not uncommon.

Given the choice, however, small crowds, bargain prices, and stress-free touring are well worth risking a little cold weather or a couple of closed attractions. So much easier is touring in the fall and other "off" periods that our research team, at the risk of being blasphemous, would advise taking children out of school for a week at those times rather than battling the summer crowds.

## EXTRA MAGIC HOURS

"EXTRA MAGIC HOURS" IS A PERK FOR families staying at a Walt Disney World resort, including the Swan, Dolphin, and Shades of Green, and the Hilton in the Downtown Disney resort area. On selected days of the week, Disney resort guests will be able to enter a Disney theme park one hour earlier, or stay in a selected theme park up to three hours later than the official park-operating hours. Theme park visitors not staying at a Disney resort may stay in the park for Extra Magic Hour evenings, but cannot experience any rides, attractions, or shows. In other words, they can shop and eat.

**CROWD CONDITIONS AND THE BEST AND WORST PARKS TO VISIT FOR EACH DAY OF THE YEAR** Each year we receive more than 1,000 e-mails and letters inquiring about crowd conditions on specific dates throughout the year. Readers also want to know which park is best to visit on each day of their stay. To make things easier for you (and us!), we provide a calendar on our Web site, **www.touringplans.com,** covering the last five months of 2005 and all of 2006. For each date, we offer a crowd-level index based on a scale of 1 to 10, with 1 being least crowded and 10 being most crowded. Our calendar takes into account all holidays, special events, and more, as described below. The same calendar lists the best and worst park(s) to visit in terms of crowd conditions on any given day. All you have to do is look up the days of your intended visit on the calendar.

**SUMMER AND HOLIDAYS** If you visit on a nonholiday midsummer day, arrive at the turnstile 30 minutes before the stated opening on a non-early-entry day. If you visit during a major holiday period, arrive 40 to 60 minutes ahead of the official opening time. Hit your favorite rides early using one of our touring plans, and then return to your hotel for lunch, a swim, and perhaps a nap. Don't forget to have your hand stamped for re-entry when you exit. If you are interested in the special parades and shows, return to the park in the late afternoon or early evening. Work under the assumption that, unless you use FASTPASS, early morning will be the only time you can experience the attractions without long waits. Finally, do not wait until the last minute in the evening to leave the park. The exodus at closing is truly mind-boggling.

Epcot is usually the least crowded park during holiday periods. Expect the other parks to be mobbed. To save time in the morning, purchase your admission in advance. Also, consider bringing your own stroller or wheelchair instead of renting one of Disney's. If you are touring Epcot or the Magic Kingdom and plan to spend the day, try exiting the park for lunch at one of the nearby resort hotels. Above all, bring your sense of humor and pay attention to the morale of your party. Bail out when it gets to be more work than fun.

# PART TWO

# MAKING *the* MOST *of* YOUR TIME *and* MONEY

## ■ ALLOCATING MONEY

HOW MUCH YOU SPEND DEPENDS ON HOW long you stay at Walt Disney World. But even if you only stop by for an afternoon, be prepared to drop a bundle. In Part Three, we'll show you how to save money on lodging, and in Part Eight, you'll find lots of tips for economizing on meals. This section will give you some sense of what you can expect to pay for admission, as well as which admission option will best meet your needs.

### WALT DISNEY WORLD ADMISSION OPTIONS

IN AN EFFORT TO ACCOMMODATE VACATIONS of various durations and activities, Disney offers a number of different admission options to its theme parks. These options range from the basic "One Day, One Park" ticket, good for a single entry into any one of Disney's theme parks, to the top of the line Premium Annual Pass, good for 365 days of admission into every theme and water park Disney operates, plus DisneyQuest and Pleasure Island.

The sheer number of ticket options available makes it difficult and, yes, daunting, for a family to sort out which option represents the least expensive way to see and do everything they want. Finding the optimum admission, or combination of admissions, however, could save the average family a nice chunk of change.

### HELP IS ON THE WAY!

TO SIMPLIFY THINGS, WE TRIED TO DEFINE guidelines to help you choose the best ticket options for your vacation.

After a day or so, we realized that a handful of general guidelines was an impossible task, so we wrote a computer program to figure it out. You can use the program to determine the best ticket options for you by visiting our Web site at **www.touringplans.com.** The program takes into account discounts for Florida residents, members of the military, and families able to take advantage of advance-purchase tickets. All you have to do is answer a few simple questions relating to the theme parks you intend to visit, whether you intend to stay at a Disney or non-Disney hotel, etc. (nothing personal). The program will then identify the four least-expensive ticket options for your vacation.

## MAGIC YOUR WAY

IN JANUARY 2005 WALT DISNEY WORLD pretty much chunked its entire panoply of admission options and introduced a completely new array of theme-park tickets in a program called "Magic Your Way." The new scheme applies to both one-day and multiday passports and begins with a "Base Ticket" (also referred to in some Disney literature as a "Starter Pass"). Features that were previously bundled with certain tickets, such as the ability to visit more than one park per day ("park hopping"), or the inclusion of admission to Disney's minor venues (Typhoon Lagoon, Blizzard Beach, Pleasure Island, DisneyQuest, etc.) are now available as individual add-ons to the Base Ticket.

As before, there is a volume discount. The more days of admission you purchase, the lower the cost per day. Base Tickets can be purchased from one to up to ten days. The Base Ticket admits you to exactly one Disney theme park per day. Unlike Disney's previous multiday tickets, you cannot use a Base Ticket to visit more than one park per day.

Under the old system, unused days on multiday passports were good indefinitely. Now passes expire 14 days from the first day of use. If you purchase a four-day Base Ticket on June 1 and use it that day for admission to the Magic Kingdom, you'll be able to visit a single Walt Disney World theme park on any of your three remaining days between June 2 and June 15. After that, the ticket expires and any unused days will be lost. Through another add-on, however, you can avoid the 14-day expiration and wind up with a ticket that's valid forever. More on that later.

## BASE TICKET ADD-ON OPTIONS

THREE ADD-ON OPTIONS ARE OFFERED with the Base Ticket, each at an additional cost:

**PARK HOPPING** Adding this feature to your Base Ticket allows you to visit more than one theme park per day. The cost is a flat $37.28 (tax included) on top of the Base Ticket price and covers the total number of days' admission you buy. It's an exorbitant price for one or two days but becomes more affordable the longer your stay. As an add-on to a Seven-Day Base Ticket, the $37.28 flat fee would work out to $5.33 per day for park-hopping privileges. If you want to visit the Magic Kingdom in the morning and dine at Epcot in the evening, this is the feature to request.

**NO EXPIRATION DATE** Adding this option to your ticket means that unused admissions to the major theme parks and the swimming parks, as well as other minor venues, never expire. If you added this option to a Ten-Day Base Ticket and used only four days this year, the remaining six days could be used for admission at any date in the future. The No Expiration option ranges from $10.65 with tax for a two-day ticket, to $58.57 for tickets with seven or more days. This option is not available on one-day tickets.

*unofficial* **TIP**
With the No Expiration option, any admissions you don't use are good forever, including your visits to the minor parks of your choice (water parks, Pleasure Island, and the sports complex).

**"PLUS PACK"** A "plus" is a single admission to one of Disney's water parks (Blizzard Beach and Typhoon Lagoon), DisneyQuest, or Pleasure Island. The cost is a flat $47.93, and the number of pluses per ticket is tied to the number of days' admission you buy. One-, two-, and three-day tickets come with two pluses; four- and five-day tickets get three pluses; six-day tickets merit four pluses; and five pluses are accorded to seven-through ten-day tickets. The number of pluses is fixed. You cannot, for example, purchase a Ten-Day Base Ticket with only two pluses or a Three-Day Base Ticket with four pluses. You can, however, skip the Plus Pack entirely and buy an individual admission to any of these minor parks.

**PREMIUM PASSES** A Premium Pass is simply a Base Ticket bundled with the Park Hopping and Plus Pack features. The price of a Premium Pass is the same as that of a Base Ticket with Plus Pack and Park Hopping add-ons. In other words, there is no discount for purchasing the bundled pass. The No Expiration add-on can also be purchased for Premium Passes.

The forgoing add-ons are available for purchase in any combination (except for no expiration add-on on one-day tickets). If you buy a Base Ticket and decide sometime later that you want one or more of the options, you can, at full price, upgrade the Base Ticket to add the feature(s) you desire.

**MAGIC YOUR WAY ADMISSION CHART**

| TICKET TYPE | | | | | | |
|---|---|---|---|---|---|---|
| 7-Day | 6-Day | 5-Day | 4-Day | 3-Day | 2-Day | 1-Day |
| **BASE TICKET ADULTS** | | | | | | |
| $212 | $209 | $206 | $197 | $182 | $127 | $64 |
| $30/day | $35/day | $41/day | $49/day | $60/day | $63/day | $64/day |
| **BASE TICKET CHILDREN (ages 9 and under)** | | | | | | |
| $170 | $167 | $165 | $158 | $146 | $102 | $51 |
| $24/day | $28/day | $33/day | $39/day | $49/day | $51/day | $51/day |
| **PARK HOPPER ADD-ON** | | | | | | |
| $37 | $37 | $37 | $37 | $37 | $37 | $37 |
| $5/day | $6/day | $7/day | $9/day | $12/day | $19/day | $37/day |
| **PLUS PACK ADD-ON** | | | | | | |
| $48 for 5 visits | $48 for 4 visits | $48 for 3 visits | $48 for 3 visits | $48 for 2 visits | $48 for 2 visits | $48 for 2 visits |
| $10/visit | $12/visit | $16/visit | $16/visit | $24/visit | $24/visit | $24/visit |
| **PREMIUM TICKET ADULTS** | | | | | | |
| $297 | $294 | $291 | $282 | $267 | $212 | $149 |
| $42/day | $49/day | $58/day | $71/day | $89/day | $106/day | $149/day |
| **PREMIUM TICKET CHILDREN (ages 9 and under)** | | | | | | |
| $256 | $252 | $250 | $243 | $231 | $187 | $136 |
| $37/day | $42/day | $50/day | $61/day | $77/day | $94/day | $136/day |
| **NO EXPIRATION ADD-ON** | | | | | | |
| $59 | $48 | $37 | $16 | $11 | $11 | N/A |

*All prices include tax and are rounded to the nearest dollar.*

## Annual Passes

An Annual Pass provides unlimited use of the major theme parks for one year. An add-on is available to provide unlimited use of the minor parks. Annual Pass holders also get perks, including free parking and seasonal offers such as room-rate discounts at Disney resorts. Tax included, Annual Passes run $421 for adults and $358 for children ages 3 to 9. A Premium Annual Pass, at $548 for adults and $466 for children ages 3 to 9, is also available. The Premium Annual Pass provides unlimited admission to Pleasure Island, Blizzard Beach, Typhoon Lagoon, DisneyQuest, and the Wide World of Sports complex, in addition to the four major theme parks.

*unofficial* **TIP**
The longer your Disney vacation, of course, the more you save with the Annual Pass.

## HOW TO GET THE MOST
## FROM THE NEW TICKETS

FIRST, HAVE A REALISTIC IDEA OF WHAT you want out of your vacation. As with anything, it doesn't make sense to pay for options you'll never use. A seven-day theme-park ticket with five plusses might seem like a wonderful idea, but actually trying to visit all those parks in a week in July might end up feeling more like Navy SEAL training. If you're going to make only one visit to a water park, DisneyQuest, or Pleasure Island, you're almost always better off purchasing that admission separately, rather than in a Plus Pack.

Next, think carefully about paying for the No Expiration option. An inside source reports that fewer than one in ten admission tickets with unused days are ever reused at a Disney theme park. The rest are misplaced, discarded, or forgotten. Unless you are absolutely certain you'll be returning to Walt Disney World within the next year and have identified a safe place to keep those unused tickets, we don't think the additional cost is worth the risk. (We've lost a few of these passes ourselves.) And we'd avoid altogether the No Expiration option on Base Tickets of fewer than five days.

## WHERE TO PURCHASE
## MAGIC YOUR WAY TICKETS

YOU CAN BUY YOUR ADMISSION PASSES on arrival at Walt Disney World or purchase them in advance. Admission passes are available at Walt Disney World resorts and theme parks. Passes are also available at some non-Disney hotels, certain Walt Disney World–area grocery stores, and through independent ticket brokers. Offers of free or heavily discounted tickets abound, but they generally require you to attend a timeshare sales presentation.

Disney offers discounts of around $7–$12 on certain multiday tickets if you buy them in advance from their Web site. Visit **www.disneyworld.com** for more details.

If you're trying to keep costs to an absolute minimum, consider using an online ticket wholesaler, such as **www.maple leaftickets.com** or **www.theofficialticketcenter.com,** especially for trips with five or more days in the theme parks. All tickets sold are brand new, and savings can range from $7 to more than $25, depending on the ticket and options chosen.

The Official Ticket Center and Maple Leaf Tickets offer discounts on tickets for almost all central Florida attractions, including Disney, Universal, SeaWorld, and Cirque du

Soleil. Discounts for the major theme parks are about 6%. Tickets for other attractions are more deeply discounted.

Finally, if all this is too confusing, our Web site will help you navigate all of the new options and find you the least-expensive ticket options for your vacation. Visit **www.touringplans.com** for more details.

### For Additional Information on Passes

If you have a question or concern regarding admissions that can be addressed only through a person-to-person conversation, call Disney Ticket Services at ☎ 407-827-4166. If you need current prices or routine information, you're better off calling ☎ 407-824-4321 for recorded admission info or visit **www.disneyworld.com.**

### Special Passes

Walt Disney World offers a number of special and situational passes that are not known to the general public and are not sold at any Disney World ticket booth. The best information we've found on these passes is available on the Internet at **www.mousesavers.com.**

# ALLOCATING TIME

## WHICH PARK TO SEE FIRST?

THIS QUESTION IS LESS ACADEMIC THAN it appears, especially if there are children or teenagers in your party. Children who see the Magic Kingdom first expect more of the same type of entertainment at the other parks. At Epcot, they're often disappointed by the educational orientation and more serious tone (many adults react the same way). Disney-MGM offers some pretty wild action, but the general presentation is educational and more adult. Though most children enjoy zoos, animals can't be programmed to entertain. Thus, children may not find the Animal Kingdom as exciting as the Magic Kingdom or Disney-MGM.

First-time visitors especially should see Epcot first; you will be able to enjoy it fully without having been preconditioned to think of Disney entertainment as solely fantasy or adventure. See the Animal Kingdom second. Like Epcot, it has an educational thrust, but it provides a change of pace because it features live animals. Next, see Disney-MGM Studios, which helps all ages make a fluid transition from the educational Epcot and Animal Kingdom to the fanciful Magic Kingdom. Also, because Disney-MGM Studios is smaller, you won't walk as much or stay as long. Save the Magic Kingdom for last.

## OPERATING HOURS

DISNEY CAN'T BE ACCUSED OF BEING inflexible regarding operating hours at the parks. They run a dozen or more schedules each year, making it advisable to call ☎ 407-824-4321 for the exact hours before you arrive. In the off-season, parks may be open for as few as eight hours (from 9 a.m. to 5 p.m.). By contrast, at busy times (particularly holidays), they may be open from 8 a.m. until 2 a.m. the next morning.

### Official Opening vs. Real Opening

Operating hours you're quoted when you call are "official hours." Sometimes, the parks actually open earlier. If the official hours are 9 a.m.–9 p.m., for example, Main Street in the Magic Kingdom might open at 8:30 a.m. and the remainder of the park will open at 9 a.m.

Disney publishes hours of operation well in advance but allows the flexibility to react daily to gate conditions. Disney traffic controllers survey local hotel reservations, estimate how many visitors to expect on a given day, and open the theme parks early to avoid bottlenecks at parking facilities and ticket windows and to absorb the crowds as they arrive.

At day's end, rides and attractions shut down at approximately the official closing time. Main Street in the Magic Kingdom remains open 30 minutes to one hour after the rest of the park has closed.

## THE CARDINAL RULES FOR SUCCESSFUL TOURING

EVEN THE MOST TIME-EFFECTIVE TOURING plan won't allow you to cover two or more major theme parks in one day. Plan to allocate at least an entire day to each park (an exception to this rule is when the parks close at different times, allowing you to tour one park until closing and then proceed to another park).

### One-Day Touring

A comprehensive, one-day tour of the Magic Kingdom, the Animal Kingdom, Epcot, or Disney-MGM Studios is possible, but requires knowledge of the park, good planning, and plenty of energy and endurance. One-day touring doesn't leave much time for sit-down meals, prolonged browsing in shops, or lengthy breaks. One-day touring can be fun and rewarding, but allocating two days per park, especially for the Magic Kingdom and Epcot, is always preferable.

Successful touring of the Magic Kingdom, the Animal Kingdom, Epcot, or Disney-MGM Studios hinges on *three rules:*

### 1.  Determine in Advance What You Really Want to See

To help you set your touring priorities, we describe the theme parks and every attraction in detail in this book. In each description, we include the author's evaluation of the attraction and the opinions of Walt Disney World guests expressed as star ratings. Five stars is the best possible rating.

Finally, because attractions range from midway-type rides and horse-drawn trolleys to colossal, high-tech extravaganzas, we have developed a hierarchy of categories to pinpoint an attraction's magnitude:

**SUPER HEADLINERS**  The best attractions the theme park has to offer. Mind-boggling in size, scope, and imagination. Represents the cutting edge of modern attraction technology and design.

**HEADLINERS**  Full-blown, multimillion-dollar, themed adventures and theater presentations. Modern in technology and design and employing a full range of special effects.

**MAJOR ATTRACTIONS**  Themed adventures on a more modest scale, but incorporating state-of-the-art technologies. Or, larger-scale attractions of older design.

**MINOR ATTRACTIONS**  Midway-type rides, small "dark" rides (cars on a track, zig-zagging through the dark), small theater presentations, transportation rides, and walk-through attractions.

**DIVERSIONS**  Exhibits, both passive and interactive. Includes playgrounds, video arcades, and street theater.

### 2.  Arrive Early! Arrive Early! Arrive Early!

Have breakfast before you arrive so you won't waste prime touring time sitting in a restaurant. The earlier a park opens, the greater your potential advantage. This is because most vacationers won't make the sacrifice to rise early and get to a theme park before it opens. Fewer people are willing to be on hand for an 8 a.m. opening than for a 9 a.m. opening. On those rare occasions when a park opens at 10 a.m., almost everyone arrives at the same time, so it's almost impossible to get a jump on the crowd. If you are visiting during mid-summer, arrive at the turnstile 40 minutes before official opening time. During holiday periods, arrive at the parks 45–60 minutes before official opening.

**3. Avoid Bottlenecks**

We provide touring plans for the Magic Kingdom, the Animal Kingdom, Epcot, and Disney-MGM Studios to help you avoid bottlenecks. In addition, we provide detailed information on all rides and performances, enabling you to estimate how long you may have to wait in line and allowing you to compare rides for their capacity to accommodate large crowds. Touring plans for the Magic Kingdom begin on page 157; Epcot, on page 202; the Animal Kingdom, on page 236; and Disney-MGM Studios, on page 261.

## TOURING PLANS EXPLAINED

OUR TOURING PLANS ARE STEP-BY-STEP guides for seeing as much as possible with a minimum of standing in line. They're designed to help you avoid crowds and bottlenecks on days of moderate-to-heavy attendance. On days of lighter attendance (see "Selecting the Time of Year for Your Visit," pages 14–15), the plans will still save time but won't be as critical to successful touring.

### What You Can Expect from the Touring Plans

Though we present one-day touring plans for each of the theme parks, you should understand that the Magic Kingdom and Epcot have more attractions than you can reasonably see in one day, even if you never wait in line. If you must cram your visit into a single day, the one-day touring plans will allow you to see as much as is humanly possible. Under certain circumstances you may not complete the plan, and you definitely won't be able to see everything. For the Magic Kingdom and Epcot, the most comprehensive, efficient, and relaxing touring plans are the two-day plans. Although Disney-MGM Studios has grown considerably since its 1989 debut, you should have no problem seeing everything in one day. Likewise, the Animal Kingdom is a one-day outing.

### Variables that Affect the Success of Touring Plans

How quickly you move from one ride to another; when and how many refreshment and restroom breaks you take; when, where, and how you eat meals; and your ability to find your way around will all have an impact on the success of the plans. Smaller groups almost always move faster than larger groups, and parties of adults generally can cover more ground than families with young children. Switching off (see page 75), among other things, inhibits families with little ones from moving expeditiously among attractions. Plus, some children simply cannot conform to the "early-to-rise" conditions of the touring plans.

Finally, if you have young children in your party, be prepared for character encounters. The appearance of a Disney character is usually sufficient to stop a touring plan dead in its tracks. What's more, while some characters continue to stroll the parks, it is becoming more the rule to assemble characters in some specific venue (like the Hall of Fame at Mickey's Toontown Fair) where families must queue up for photos and autographs. If your kids are into collecting character autographs, you will need to anticipate these interruptions to the touring plan and negotiate some understanding with your children about when you will follow the plan and when you will collect autographs.

While we realize that following the touring plans is not always easy, we nevertheless recommend continuous, expeditious touring until around noon. After noon, breaks and diversions won't affect the plans significantly. If unforeseen events interrupt a touring plan, skip one step on the plan for every 20 minutes you're delayed. If you lose your billfold, for example, and spend an hour finding it, skip three steps and pick up from there.

## Custom Touring Plans Are Now Available

The new *Unofficial Guide* Touring Plan program allows us to offer our readers customized touring plans to all of the Disney theme parks. If you want to arrive at the park at 11 a.m. instead of at park opening (as called for by the one-day touring plans in this guide), or if you want to commence touring at 3 p.m., a customized touring plan will guarantee the least time waiting in line. *If you plan to arrive when the park opens, as prescribed by the touring plans in the* Unofficial Guide, *you will not need a customized touring plan.*

*unofficial* **TIP**
Because Disney changes its park operating hours without advance notice, the best time to request your custom touring plan is two to four weeks before leaving home.

In response to readers urging us to create additional touring plans, we've posted on our Web site, **www.touringplans.com,** more than 50 of the most requested custom plans. These are one- and two-day touring plans that cover all four Walt Disney World theme parks and a whole array of special situations: plans for senior citizens, Disney Cruise guests, holiday touring, and much more. While the plans in this guide emphasize efficient touring and seeing as much as possible, the Web site's touring plans offer rather laid-back itineraries allowing guests to tour in a more relaxed fashion. By making the plans available online, we're able to reflect changes in park operating hours, parade and show times, as well as closing of attractions for maintenance.

Allow us to underscore that the most efficient touring plans are those included in this guide. They allow you to see more attractions with less waiting because they require you to be on hand when the parks open. If you can't get the kids up and out early, or if you want to take a morning off, or if you prefer attractions different from those included in our touring plans, a custom plan is a good option for you.

## FASTPASS

YOUR HANDOUT PARK MAP, AS WELL AS signage at respective attractions, will tell you which attractions are included in the FASTPASS program. Attractions operating FAST-PASS will have a regular line and a FASTPASS line. A sign at the entrance will tell you how long the wait is in the regular line. If the wait is acceptable to you, hop in line. If the wait seems too long, you can insert your park admission pass into a special FASTPASS machine and receive an

*unofficial* **TIP**
Obtain FASTPASSes for all members of your party, including those who are too short, too young, or simply not interested in riding.

appointment time (for sometime later in the day) to come back and ride. When you return at the appointed time, you will enter the FASTPASS line and proceed directly to the attraction's preshow or boarding area with no further wait. There is no extra charge to use FASTPASS.

FASTPASS doesn't eliminate the need to arrive at the theme park early. Because each park offers a limited number of FASTPASS attractions, you still need to get an early start if you want to see as much as possible in a single day. Plus, as we'll discuss later, there is a limited supply of FAST-PASSes available for each attraction on a given day. If you don't arrive until the middle of the afternoon, you might find that all the FASTPASSes have been distributed to other guests. FASTPASS does make it possible to see more with less waiting than ever before, and it's a great benefit to those who like to sleep late or who enjoy an afternoon or evening at the theme parks on their arrival day at Walt Disney World. It also allows you to postpone wet rides, like Kali River Rapids at the Animal Kingdom or Splash Mountain at the Magic Kingdom, until the warmer part of the day.

**UNDERSTANDING THE FASTPASS SYSTEM** When you insert your admission pass into a FASTPASS time clock, the machine spits out a small slip of paper about two-thirds the size of a credit card—small enough to fit in your wallet but also small enough to lose easily. Printed on the paper is the name of the attraction and a specific one-hour time window, for example 1:15–2:15 p.m., during which you can return to enjoy the ride.

When you report back to the attraction during your one-hour window, you'll enter a line marked "FASTPASS Return" that will route you more or less directly to the boarding or preshow area. Each person in your party must have his or her own FASTPASS and be ready to show it to the Disney cast member at the entrance of the FASTPASS Return line. Before you enter the boarding area or theater, another cast member will collect your FASTPASS.

You can obtain a FASTPASS anytime after a park opens, but the FASTPASS Return lines do not begin operating until 45–90 minutes after opening. Thus, if the Magic Kingdom opens at 9 a.m., the FASTPASS time clock machines will also be available at 9 a.m., and the FASTPASS Return line will begin operating at about 9:45 a.m.

**WHEN TO USE FASTPASS** Except as discussed below, there's no reason to use FASTPASS during the first 30–40 minutes a park is open. Lines for most attractions are quite manageable during this period, and this is the only time of day when FASTPASS attractions exclusively serve those in the regular line. Regardless of time of day, however, if the wait in the regular line at a FASTPASS attraction is 25–30 minutes or less, we recommend joining the regular line.

**FASTPASS RULES** Disney amended the rules so that now you can obtain a second FASTPASS two hours or less from the time the first one was issued. Rules aside, the real lesson here is to check out the posted return time before obtaining a FASTPASS. If the return time is hours away, forgo the FAST-PASS. Especially in the Magic Kingdom, there will be a number of other FASTPASS attractions where the return time is only an hour or so away.

**FASTPASS Guidelines**

- Don't mess with FASTPASS unless it can save you 30 minutes or more.
- If you arrive after a park opens, obtain a FASTPASS for your preferred FASTPASS attraction first thing.
- Do not obtain a FASTPASS for a theater attraction until you have experienced all the FASTPASS rides on your itinerary (using FASTPASS at theater attractions usually requires more time than using the standby line).
- Always check the FASTPASS return period before obtaining your FASTPASS.
- Obtain FASTPASSes for Rock 'n' Roller Coaster at MGM-Studios; Mission: Space and Test Track at Epcot; and Winnie the Pooh, Peter Pan's Flight, Space Mountain, and Splash Mountain at the Magic Kingdom as early in the day as practicable.
- Don't depend on FASTPASSes being available for rides after 2 p.m. during busier times of year.
- Make sure everyone in your party has their own FASTPASS.
- Be mindful that you can obtain a second FASTPASS as soon as you enter the return period for your first FASTPASS or after two hours from issuance, whichever comes first.

**TRICKS OF THE TRADE** In the final days of 2002, Disney wisely chose to demystify the rules for acquiring a second FASTPASS. Now when a FASTPASS is issued, the time when you can obtain another FASTPASS is printed on the bottom of the front of the FASTPASS. This specified time on the FASTPASS is consistent with the beginning of your return time slot. Thus if your return window to come back and ride is 11 a.m. to 12 noon, your FASTPASS will indicate that you can acquire a second FASTPASS anytime after 11 a.m.

When obtaining FASTPASSes, it's faster and more considerate of other guests if one person obtains passes for your entire party. This means entrusting one individual with both your valuable park-admission passes and your FASTPASSes, so choose wisely.

Though you can't use your FASTPASS until the return window begins, Disney is usually not strict when it comes to the end of the return window. About 85% of the time you'll be able to use your FASTPASS after the return window expires.

# PART THREE

# ACCOMMODATIONS

## ■ THE BASIC CONSIDERATIONS

### BENEFITS OF STAYING IN THE WORLD

WALT DISNEY WORLD RESORT HOTEL and campground guests have privileges and amenities unavailable to those staying outside the World. Though some of these perks are only advertising gimmicks, others are real and potentially valuable:

**1. CONVENIENCE** If you don't have a car, the commute to the theme parks is short via the Disney Transportation System. This is especially advantageous if you stay in one of the hotels connected by the monorail or boat service. If you have a car, however, there are dozens of hotels outside Disney World that are within 5 to 10 minutes of theme-park parking lots.

**2. EXTRA MAGIC HOURS AT THE THEME PARKS** Disney World lodging guests (excluding guests at the independent hotels of Downtown Disney Resort Area, except for the Hilton) are invited to enter a designated park one hour earlier than the general public each day or to enjoy a designated theme park for three hours after it closes to the general public in the evening. Disney guests are also offered specials on admission, including discount tickets to the water parks. These benefits are subject to change without notice.

**3. BABYSITTING AND CHILDCARE** A number of options for babysitting, childcare, and children's programs are offered to Disney hotel and campground guests. Each of the resort hotels connected by the monorail, as well as several other Disney hotels, offer "clubs," or themed childcare centers, where potty-trained children ages 3–12 can stay while the adults go out.

**4. GUARANTEED THEME-PARK ADMISSIONS** On days of unusually heavy attendance, Disney resort guests are guaranteed admission to the theme parks. In practice, no guest is ever turned away until a theme park's parking lot is full. When this happens, that park most certainly will be packed to the point of gridlock. You would have to lack the common sense of an amoeba to exercise your guaranteed-admission privilege under such conditions. The privilege, by the way, doesn't extend to the Blizzard Beach or Typhoon Lagoon water parks.

**5. CHILDREN SHARING A ROOM WITH THEIR PARENTS** There is no extra charge per night for children younger than 18 sharing a room with their parents. Many hotels outside Disney World also observe this practice.

**6. FREE PARKING** Disney resort guests with cars don't have to pay for parking in the theme-park lots. This privilege saves about $8 per day.

**7. RECREATIONAL PRIVILEGES** Disney resort guests get preferential treatment for tee times at the golf courses.

## STAYING IN OR OUT OF THE WORLD: WEIGHING THE PROS AND CONS

**1. COST** If cost is a primary consideration, you'll lodge much less expensively outside Disney World. Our ratings of hotel quality and cost (pages 61–68) compare specific hotels both in and out of the World.

**2. EASE OF ACCESS** Even if you stay in Disney World, you're dependent on some mode of transportation. It may be less stressful to use the Disney transportation system, but with the single exception of commuting to the Magic Kingdom, the fastest, most efficient, and most flexible way to get around is usually a car. Walt Disney World is so large that some destinations within the World can be reached more quickly from off-property hotels than from Disney hotels. For example, guests at hotels and motels on US 192 (near the so-called Walt Disney World main entrance) are closer to Disney-MGM Studios, the Animal Kingdom, and Blizzard Beach water park than guests at many hotels inside Disney World.

**3. YOUNG CHILDREN** Although the hassle of commuting to most non-World hotels is only slightly (if at all) greater than that of commuting to Disney hotels, a definite peace of mind results from staying in Walt Disney World. The salient point, regardless of where you stay, is to make sure you get your young children back to the hotel for a nap each day.

**4. SPLITTING UP**  If you're in a party that probably will split up to tour (as frequently happens in families with children of varying ages), staying in the World offers more transportation options and, thus, more independence. Mom and Dad can take the car and return to the hotel for a relaxed dinner and early bedtime while the teens remain in the park for evening parades and fireworks.

**5. FEEDING THE ARMY OF THE POTOMAC**  If you have a large crew that chows down like cattle on a finishing lot, you may do better staying outside the World, where food is far less expensive.

**6. VISITING OTHER ORLANDO-AREA ATTRACTIONS**  If you will visit SeaWorld, Kennedy Space Center Visitor Complex, Universal Orlando, or other area attractions, it may be more convenient to stay outside the World.

## HOW TO GET DISCOUNTS ON LODGING AT WALT DISNEY WORLD

THERE ARE SO MANY GUEST ROOMS IN and around Walt Disney World that competition is brisk, and everyone, including Disney, wheels and deals to keep them filled. This has led to a more flexible discount policy for Disney World hotels. Here are tips for getting price breaks:

**1. SEASONAL SAVINGS**  You can save from $15 to $50 per night on a Walt Disney World hotel room by scheduling your visit during the slower times of the year. However, Disney uses so many adjectives (regular, holiday, peak, value, etc.) to describe its seasonal calendar that it's hard to keep up without a scorecard. To confuse matters more, the dates for each "season" vary from resort to resort. If you're set on staying at a Disney resort, obtain a copy of the Walt Disney Travel Company Walt Disney World Florida Vacations video/brochure, described on page 8. The Disney seasonal calendar can also be found at **www.mousesavers.com.**

**2. ASK ABOUT SPECIALS**  When you talk to Disney reservationists, inquire specifically about special deals. Ask, for example, "What special rates or discounts are available at Disney hotels during the time of our visit?"

**3. "TRADE-UP" OR "UPSELL" RATES**  If you request a room at a Disney value resort and none are available, you may be offered a room in the next category up (moderate resorts, in this example) at a discounted price. Similarly, if you ask for a room in a moderate resort and none are available, Disney will usually offer a good deal at a Home-Away-From-Home rooms or a Deluxe resort. You can angle for a trade-up rate by asking for a resort category that is more likely to be sold out.

**4. KNOW THE CODE** The folks at **www.mousesavers.com** keep an updated list of discounts and reservation codes for use at Disney resorts. The codes are separated into categories such as "For anyone," "For residents of certain states," "For annual passport holders," and so on. For example, the site listed code "CVZ," published in an ad in some Spanish-language newspapers and magazines, offering a rate of $65 per night for Disney's All-Star resorts from April 22 through August 8 and $49 per night from August 9 through October 3. Anyone calling the Disney central reservations office (call ☎ 407-W-DISNEY) can use a current code and get the discounted rate. Two other sites, **www.allearsnet.com** and **www.wdwinfo.com,** have discount codes we've used to get up to 50% off rack rates at the Swan and Dolphin.

*unofficial* **TIP**
Dozens of discounts are usually listed on the Mousesavers site, covering almost all Disney resort hotels.

**5. EXPEDIA** Online travel seller Expedia (**expedia.com**) has established an active market in discounting Disney hotels. Most discounts are in the 15–25% range but can go as deep as 45%.

**6. WALT DISNEY WORLD WEB SITE** Disney has become more aggressive about offering deals on its Web site. Go to **www.disneyworld.com** and look for the icon marked "Vacation Savings." If there, click on it to see what deals are available. Note that the "Vacation Savings" icon does not appear consistently on the site. It comes up periodically or seasonally when Disney needs to boost its resort occupancy numbers. You must click on the "Vacation Savings" box to get the discounts. If you click on "Reservations & Tickets" in the upper right corner you'll be charged full rack rate with never a mention of available discounts.

**7. ANNUAL PASSHOLDER DISCOUNTS** Annual Passholders are eligible for a broad range of discounts on dining, shopping, and lodging. If you visit Walt Disney World once a year or more, of if you plan to visit for five or more days, you might save money overall by purchasing annual passes. During the past year we saw resort discounts as deep as 35% for annual passholders. It doesn't take long to recoup the extra bucks for an annual pass when you're saving that kind of money on lodging. Discounts in the 10–25% range are more the norm.

**8. RENTING DISNEY VACATION CLUB POINTS** The Disney Vacation Club (DVC) is Disney's time-share condominium program. DVC resorts at Walt Disney World include Old

Key West, Saratoga Springs, the Beach Club Villas, Villas at Wilderness Lodge, and the BoardWalk Villas.

*unofficial* **TIP**
Because the program is designed to snare uncommitted travelers, you must reserve your room in person at the center. If you call in advance and tell staffers you're on your way down, however, they usually will tell you what's available and at what discount.

DVC members receive a number of "points" annually that they use to pay for their Disney accommodations. Sometimes members elect to "rent" (sell) their points instead of using them in a given year. Though Disney is not involved in the transaction, it allows DVC members to make these points available to the general public. You can potentially save a considerable amount of money by renting points rather than booking through the Disney Reservation Center.

When you rent points, you deal with the selling DVC member and pay him or her directly. Arrangements vary widely, but some trust is required from both parties. You should always insist on receiving the confirmation before making more than a one-night deposit.

Disboards, **www.disboards.com,** the popular Disney discussion boards site, has a specific board that deals with DVC rentals, and the unofficial discount Web site, **www.mouse savers.com,** has a page with tips on renting DVC points: see **www.mousesavers.com/disneyresorts.html#rentpoints.**

**9. TRAVEL AGENTS** Once ineligible for commissions on Disney bookings, travel agents now are active players and particularly good sources of information on time-limited special programs and discounts. In our opinion, a good travel agent is the best friend a traveler can have.

**10. ORGANIZATIONS AND AUTO CLUBS** Eager to sell rooms, Disney has developed time-limited programs with some auto clubs and other organizations. Recently, for example, AAA members were offered a 10–20% savings on Disney hotels, preferred parking at the theme parks, and discounts on Disney package vacations. Such deals come and go, but the market suggests there will be more in the future. If you're a member of AARP, AAA, or any travel or auto club, ask whether the group has a program before shopping elsewhere.

**11. ROOM UPGRADES** Sometimes, a room upgrade is as good as a discount. If you're visiting Disney World during a slower time, book the least expensive room your discounts will allow. Checking in, ask very politely about being upgraded to a "water-view" or "pool-view" room. A fair percentage of the time, you'll get one at no additional charge.

| COSTS PER NIGHT OF DISNEY RESORT HOTEL ROOMS | |
| --- | --- |
| Grand Floridian | $349–$870 |
| Polynesian Resort | $304–$720 |
| Swan (Westin) | $259–$409 |
| Dolphin (Sheraton) | $259–$409 |
| Beach Club Resort | $294–$675 |
| Beach Club Villas | $294–$449 |
| Yacht Club Resort | $294–$680 |
| BoardWalk Inn | $294–$625 |
| BoardWalk Villas | $294–$459 |
| Wilderness Lodge | $199–$490 |
| Wilderness Lodge Villas | $284–$449 |
| Saratoga Springs | $259–$379 |
| Old Key West Resort | $259–$379 |
| Contemporary Resort | $244–$560 |
| Fort Wilderness Resort | $234–$339 |
| Animal Kingdom Lodge | $199–$620 |
| Coronado Springs Resort | $134–$209 |
| Caribbean Beach Resort | $134–$209 |
| Port Orleans Resort | $134–$209 |
| All-Star Resorts | $77–$119 |
| Pop Century Resorts | $77–$119 |

| WHAT IT COSTS TO STAY IN THE DOWNTOWN DISNEY RESORT AREA | |
| --- | --- |
| DoubleTree Guest Suites Resort | $118–$328 |
| Hilton | $134–$345 |
| Wyndham Palace | $149–$299 |
| Hotel Royal Plaza | $82–$220 |
| Holiday Inn at Walt Disney World | $99–$180 |
| Grosvenor Resort | $79–$220 |
| Lake Buena Vista Resort | $89–$259 |

**12. MILITARY DISCOUNTS** The Shades of Green Armed Forces Recreation Center, located near the Grand Floridian Resort, offers luxury accommodations at rates based on the serviceman's rank. Shades of Green completed an extensive renovation and expansion in 2003 that doubled the number of guest rooms and upgraded most of the public areas. For rates and other information see **www.shadesofgreen.org** or call ☎ 888-593-2242.

## CHOOSING A WALT DISNEY WORLD HOTEL

IF YOU WANT TO STAY IN WALT DISNEY WORLD but don't know which hotel to choose, consider:

**1. COST** First, look at your budget. Rooms start at about $77 a night at the All-Star and Pop Century resorts and top out near $870 at the Grand Floridian. Suites are more expensive.

The BoardWalk Villas, Wilderness Lodge Villas, Old Key West Resort, Saratoga Springs, and Beach Club Villas offer condo-type accommodations with one-, two-, and three-bedroom units complete with kitchens, living rooms, VCRs, and washers and dryers. Prices range from about $259 per night for a one-bedroom villa at the Beach Club to more than $2,400 per night for a three-bedroom villa at the Board-Walk Villas. Fully equipped cabins at Fort Wilderness Resort and Campground cost $234–$339 per night. A limited number of suites are available at the more expensive Disney resorts, but they don't have kitchens.

Also at Disney World are the seven hotels of the Downtown Disney Resort Area (DDRA), also known as the DisneyVillage Hotel Plaza. Accommodations range from fairly luxurious to Holiday Inn quality. Though not typically good candidates for bargains, these hotels surprised us with some great deals during 2005. While the DDRA is technically part of Disney World, staying there is like visiting a colony rather than the motherland. Free parking at theme parks isn't offered—nor is early entry, with one exception, the Hilton—and hotels operate their own buses rather than use Disney transportation. See our profiles of the Hilton Walt Disney World and the Wyndham Palace in the section beginning on page 46.

**2. LOCATION** If you intend to use your own car, the location of your Disney hotel isn't especially important unless you plan to spend most of your time at the Magic Kingdom. (Disney transportation is always more efficient than your car in this case because it bypasses the Transportation and Ticket Center and deposits you at the theme-park entrance.)

Most convenient to the Magic Kingdom are the three resorts linked by monorail: the Grand Floridian, Contemporary, and Polynesian. Commuting to the Magic Kingdom via monorail is quick and simple, allowing visitors to return to their hotel for a nap, swim, or meal.

The Contemporary Resort, in addition to being on the monorail, is only a 10–15 minute walk to the Magic Kingdom. Contemporary Resort guests reach Epcot by monorail but must transfer at the Transportation and Ticket Center. Buses connect the Contemporary to Disney-MGM Studios and the Animal Kingdom. No transfer is required, but the bus makes several stops before heading to either destination.

The Polynesian Resort is served by the Magic Kingdom monorail and is an easy walk from the Transportation and Ticket Center, Disney World's transportation hub. At the transportation center you can catch an express monorail to Epcot. This makes the Polynesian the only Disney resort with direct monorail access to both Epcot and the Magic Kingdom. To minimize your walk to the transportation center, book a room in the Pago Pago, Moorea, or Oahu guest buildings.

Most convenient to Epcot and Disney-MGM Studios are the BoardWalk Inn, BoardWalk Villas, Yacht and Beach Club resorts, Beach Club Villas, and Swan and Dolphin. Though all are within easy walking distance of Epcot's International Gateway, boat service is also available. Vessels also connect Epcot hotels to Disney-MGM Studios. Epcot hotels are best for guests planning to spend most of their time at Epcot or Disney-MGM Studios.

Though not centrally located, the All-Star, Coronado Springs, and Animal Kingdom Lodge Resorts have very good bus service to all Disney World destinations and are closest to the Animal Kingdom theme park. Wilderness Lodge and Villas, Old Key West, and Fort Wilderness Campground have the most convoluted transportation service.

If you plan to golf, book the Old Key West Resort or the Saratoga Springs Resort. The resorts are built around golf courses. Shades of Green, the military-only resort, is adjacent to two golf courses. Located near but not on a golf course are the Grand Floridian, Polynesian, and Port Orleans resorts. For boating and water sports, try the Polynesian, Contemporary, or Grand Floridian resorts or Wilderness Lodge and Villas. The Lodge is also the best hotel for hikers, bikers, and joggers.

**3. ROOM QUALITY** Few Walt Disney World guests spend much time in their hotel rooms, though they're among the best designed and most well appointed anywhere. Plus, they're meticulously maintained. Top of the line are the spacious and luxurious rooms of the Grand Floridian. Bringing up the rear are the small, garish rooms of the All-Star

Resorts. But even these are sparkling clean and livable. Check our hotel table on pages 61–68 for ratings of all Disney and non-Disney hotels.

**4. THE SIZE OF YOUR GROUP** Larger families and groups may be interested in how many persons can be accommodated in a Disney resort room, but only Lilliputians would be comfortable in a room filled to capacity. Groups requiring two or more guest rooms should consider condo/villa accommodations, either in or out of Walt Disney World. The most cost-efficient lodging in Walt Disney World for groups of five or six persons are the cabins at Fort Wilderness Campground. Both sleep six adults plus a child or toddler in a crib. For detailed room schematics that show the maximum number of persons per room as well as the rooms' relative size and configuration, consult *The Unofficial Guide to Walt Disney World*.

> *unofficial* **TIP**
> If there are more than six in your party, you will need either two hotel rooms, a suite, or a condo.

**5. THEME** All of the Disney hotels are themed. Each is designed to make you feel you're in a special place or period of history.

Some resorts carry off their themes better than others, and some themes are more exciting. The Wilderness Lodge and Villas, for example, is extraordinary. The lobby opens eight stories to a timbered ceiling supported by giant columns of bundled logs. One look eases you into the Northwest-wilderness theme. Romantic and isolated, the lodge is a great choice for couples and seniors, and is heaven for children.

The Animal Kingdom Lodge replicates the grand safari lodges of Kenya and Tanzania and overlooks its own private African game preserve. By far the most exotic of the Disney resorts, it's made to order for couples on a romantic getaway as well as for families with children. The Polynesian, likewise dramatic, conveys the feeling of the Pacific Islands. It's great for romantics and families. Many waterfront rooms offer a perfect view of Cinderella Castle and the Magic Kingdom fireworks across Seven Seas Lagoon.

Grandeur, nostalgia, and privilege are central to the Grand Floridian and Yacht and Beach Club resorts and the Board-Walk Inn and Villas. Although modeled after Eastern Seaboard hotels of different eras, the resorts are amazingly similar. Thematic distinctions are subtle and are lost on many guests.

The Port Orleans Resort lacks the mystery and sultriness of the New Orleans French Quarter, but it's hard to replicate the Big Easy in a sanitized Disney version. Old Key West Resort, however, hits the mark with its Florida Keys theme.

The Caribbean Beach Resort's theme is much more effective at night, thanks to creative lighting. By day, the resort looks like a Miami condo development, albeit a nice one, and is arrayed around a large lake.

Coronado Springs Resort offers several styles of Mexican and Southwestern American architecture. Though the lake setting is lovely and the resort is attractive and inviting, the theme (with the exception of the main swimming area) isn't especially stimulating. Coronado Springs feels more like a Scottsdale, Arizona, country club than a Disney resort.

The All-Star Resorts encompass 30 three-story, T-shaped hotels with almost 6,000 guest rooms. There are 15 themed areas: five celebrate sports (surfing, basketball, tennis, football, and baseball), five recall Hollywood movie themes, and five have musical motifs. The resort's design, with entrances shaped like giant dalmatians, Coke cups, footballs, and the like, is pretty adolescent, sacrificing grace and beauty for energy and novelty. Guest rooms are small, with décor reminiscent of your teenage son's bedroom. Despite the theme, there are no sports, music, or movies at the All-Star Resorts. The new Pop Century Resort is nearly a clone of the All-Star Resorts, only this time the giant icons are symbolic of particular decades of the 20th century. Expect giant Big Wheels, 45 rpm records, silhouettes of people doing period dances, etc.

Pretense aside, the Contemporary, Swan, and Dolphin are essentially themeless though architecturally interesting. The Contemporary is a 15-story, A-frame building with monorails running through the middle. Views from guest rooms in the Contemporary Tower are among the best at Disney World. The Swan and Dolphin resorts are massive yet whimsical. Designed by Michael Graves, they're excellent examples of "entertainment architecture." The guest rooms of both hotels, originally avant garde, were completely redecorated. While well designed and visually interesting, the rooms are now more restful and easier on the eye.

**6. DINING** The best resorts for quality and selection in dining are the Epcot resorts: Swan, Dolphin, Yacht, and Beach Club resorts, Beach Club Villas, and BoardWalk Inn and Villas. Each has good restaurants and is within easy walking distance of the others and of the 11 ethnic restaurants in the World Showcase section of Epcot. If you stay at an Epcot resort, you have 21 of Walt Disney World's finest restaurants within a 5- to 12-minute walk.

The only other place in Disney World where restaurants and hotels are similarly concentrated is at the Downtown Disney Resort Area. In addition to restaurants in the hotels themselves, the Hilton, Holiday Inn at Walt Disney World, Grosvenor Resort, and Wyndham Palace are within walking distance of restaurants at Downtown Disney.

Guests at the Contemporary, Polynesian, and Grand Floridian can eat in their hotel, or they can commute to restaurants in the Magic Kingdom (not recommended) or in other monorail-linked hotels. Riding the monorail to another hotel or to the Magic Kingdom takes about ten minutes each way, not counting the wait for the train.

All of the other Disney resorts are somewhat isolated. This means you're stuck dining at your hotel unless (1) you have a car and can go anywhere you like or (2) you eat your meals at the theme parks or Downtown Disney.

**7. AMENITIES AND RECREATION** Disney resorts offer a staggering variety of amenities and recreational opportunities. All provide elaborate swimming pools, themed shops, restaurants or food courts, bars or lounges, and access to the five Disney golf courses. Predictably, the more you pay for your lodging, the more amenities and opportunities you have. The Grand Floridian, Animal Kingdom Lodge, Yacht and Beach Club resorts, and Swan and Dolphin, for example, offer concierge floors.

*unofficial* **TIP**
Tennis is available at all of the deluxe and Home Away from Home resorts, as well as at the Swan and Dolphin Resorts.

For sunning and swimming, the Contemporary, Polynesian, Wilderness Lodge and Villas, and Grand Floridian offer both pools and white-sand beaches on Bay Lake or Seven Seas Lagoon. The Caribbean Beach Resort also provides both pools and beaches. Though lacking a beach, the Animal Kingdom Lodge, Yacht and Beach Club, Port Orleans, Saratoga Springs, and Coronado Springs resorts and the BoardWalk Inn and Villas have exceptionally creative pools.

Bay Lake and the Seven Seas Lagoon are the best venues for boating. Resorts fronting these lakes are the Contemporary, Polynesian, Wilderness Lodge and Villas, Grand Floridian, and Fort Wilderness Campground. Though on smaller bodies of water, the Caribbean Beach, Old Key West, Port Orleans, Coronado Springs, Saratoga Springs, and Yacht and Beach Club resorts also rent watercraft.

Most convenient for golf are Saratoga Springs, Shades of Green, Old Key West, Contemporary, Polynesian, Grand Floridian, and Port Orleans resorts.

While there are many places you can bike or jog at Disney World (including golf-cart paths), the best biking and jogging is at the Fort Wilderness Resort and Campground and the adjacent Wilderness Lodge and Villas. The Caribbean Beach Resort offers a lovely hiking, biking, and jogging trail around the circumference of the lake. Also good for biking and jogging is the area along Bonnet Creek extending through Port Orleans and the Old Key West resorts toward Downtown Disney. The Epcot resorts offer a lakefront promenade and bike path, as well as a roadside walkway suitable for jogging.

Eight Disney resorts offer evening childcare programs on-site: the Grand Floridian, Animal Kingdom Lodge, Yacht and Beach Club, Polynesian, Wilderness Lodge and Villas, and BoardWalk Inn and Villas. All others offer in-room babysitting. For more information on babysitting options, see pages 87–88.

**8. NIGHTLIFE** The boardwalk at BoardWalk Inn and Villas has an upscale dance club, a club with dueling pianos and sing-alongs, a brew pub, and a sports bar. BoardWalk clubs are within easy walking distance of all the Epcot resorts. Most of the non-Disney hotels in Walt Disney World Hotel Plaza, as well as the Saratoga Springs Resort, are within walking distance of the Downtown Disney nightspots. Nightlife at other Disney resorts is limited to lounges that stay open late. The best are Mizner's Lounge at the Grand Floridian, Kimono's at the Swan, and the California Grill Lounge on the 15th floor of the Contemporary Resort. At the California Grill Lounge, you can relax over dinner and watch the fireworks at the nearby Magic Kingdom.

## CAMPING AT WALT DISNEY WORLD

FORT WILDERNESS CAMPGROUND IS A spacious resort campground for tent and RV camping. Sites are priced according to utilities furnished. Sites with water and electric go for only $34–$65 per night, depending on the season. Sites with water, electric, and sewer run $39–$76. If you add cable, the price is $47–$80. All sites are arranged on loops accessible from one of three main roads. There are 28 loops altogether, with loops 100–2,000 dedicated to tent and RV campers, and loops 2,100–2,800 offering prefab log cabin accommodations. All sites are level and provide a picnic table, a waste container, and a grill. No fires are permitted except in the grills. RV sites are roomy by eastern U.S. standards, but tent campers will probably feel a little cramped. On any given day, about 90% or more of the campers will be RVers.

Fort Wilderness Campground arguably offers the most recreational facilities and activities of any Disney resort. Among other things, there are two video arcades, nightly campfire programs, Disney movies, a dinner theater, two swimming pools, a beach, walking paths, bike, boat, canoe, golf cart, and water ski rentals, a petting zoo, horseback riding, hay rides, fishing, and tennis, basketball, and volleyball courts. There are two convenience stores, a restaurant, and a tavern. Comfort stations with toilets, showers, pay phones, ice machine, and laundry facilities are within easy walking distance of all campsites.

Access to the Magic Kingdom is by boat from Fort Wilderness Landing and by bus with a transfer at the Ticket and Transportation Center. Transportation to all other Walt Disney World destinations is by bus. Motor traffic within the campground is permitted only when entering or exiting. Options for getting around within the campground include bus, golf cart, or bike, the latter two of which are available for rent.

# HOTELS *outside*
# WALT DISNEY WORLD

## SELECTING AND BOOKING A HOTEL OUTSIDE WALT DISNEY WORLD

THERE ARE THREE PRIMARY out-of-the-World areas to consider:

**1. INTERNATIONAL DRIVE AREA** This area, about 15–20 minutes east of Walt Disney World, parallels I-4 on its southern side and offers a wide selection of both hotels and restaurants. Accommodations range from $40 to $320 per night. The chief drawbacks of the International Drive area are its terribly congested roads, countless traffic signals, and inadequate access to westbound I-4. While the biggest bottleneck is the intersection with Sand Lake Road, the mile of International Drive between Kirkman Road and Sand Lake Road stays in near-continuous gridlock. It's common to lose 25–35 minutes trying to navigate this stretch.

Hotels in the International Drive area are listed in the *Orlando Official Accommodations Guide* published by the Orlando/Orange County Convention and Visitors Bureau. For a copy, call ☎ 800-255-5786 or ☎ 407-363-5872.

**2. LAKE BUENA VISTA AND THE I-4 CORRIDOR** A number of hotels are situated along FL 535 and north of I-4 between Walt Disney World and I-4's intersection with the Florida Turnpike. These properties are easily reached from the interstate and are near a large number of restaurants, including

*Hotel Concentrations around Walt Disney World*

those on International Drive. Most hotels in this area are listed in the *Orlando Official Accommodations Guide*.

**3. US 192** This is the highway to Kissimmee, southeast of Walt Disney World. In addition to a number of large, full-service hotels are many small, privately owned motels that are often a good value. Several dozen properties on US 192 are closer to the Disney theme parks than are the more expensive hotels in Walt Disney World Village and the Disney Village Hotel Plaza. The number and variety of restaurants on US 192 has increased markedly in the past several years, easing the area's primary shortcoming.

Hotels on US 192 and in Kissimmee can be found in the *Kissimmee–St. Cloud Visitor's Guide;* call ☎ 800-327-9159 or check **www.floridakiss.com.**

## GETTING A GOOD DEAL ON A ROOM OUTSIDE WALT DISNEY WORLD

**1. ORLANDO MAGICARD** Orlando MagiCard is a discount program sponsored by the Orlando/Orange County Convention and Visitors Bureau. Cardholders are eligible for discounts of 20–50% at approximately 50 participating hotels. The MagiCard is also good for discounts at area attractions, including SeaWorld, the Universal parks, several dinner theaters, and Disney's Pleasure Island. Valid for up to six persons, the card isn't available for groups or conventions.

To obtain an Orlando MagiCard and a list of participating hotels and attractions, call ☎ 800-255-5786 or ☎ 407-363-5874. Anyone older than 18 is eligible, and the card is free. If you miss getting a card before you leave home, you can get one at the Convention and Visitors Bureau at 8723 International Drive in Orlando. When you call for a MagiCard, also request the *Orlando Official Accommodations Guide* and the *Orlando Vacation Planner.*

**2. EXIT INFORMATION GUIDE** Exit Information Guide publishes a book of discount coupons for bargain rates at hotels statewide. The book is free in many restaurants and motels on main highways leading to Florida. Because most travelers make reservations before leaving home, picking up the coupon book en route doesn't help much. If you call and use a credit card, EIG will send the guide first class for $3 ($5 U.S. for Canadian delivery). Contact:

Exit Information Guide
4205 N.W. Sixth Street
Gainesville, Florida 32609
☎ 352-371-3948

**3. HOTEL SHOPPING ON THE INTERNET** Web sites we've found most dependable for Walt Disney Area hotel discounts are:

| | |
|---|---|
| **www.mousesavers.com** | Best site for hotels in Disney World. |
| **www.dreamsunlimitedtravel.com** | Excellent for both Disney and non-Disney hotels |
| **www.2000orlando-florida.com** | Comprehensive hotel site |

| | |
|---|---|
| **www.valuetrips.com** | Specializes in budget accommodations |
| **www.travelocity.com** | Multi-destination travel superstore |
| **www.roomsaver.com** | Provides discount coupons for hotels |
| **www.floridakiss.com** | Primarily US 192/Kissimmee area hotels |
| **www.orlandoinfo.com** | Good for hotel info; not user friendly for booking |
| **www.orlandovacation.com** | Great rates for a small number of properties, including condos and home rentals |
| **www.expedia.com** | Largest of the multi-destination travel sites |
| **www.hotels.com** | Largest Internet hotel-booking service; many other sites link to **www.hotels.com** and its subsidiary, **www.hoteldiscounts.com** |

Another tool in the hotel-hunting arsenal is **www.travelaxe. com.** Travelaxe offers free software you can download on your PC (won't run on Macs) that will scan an assortment of the better hotel discount sites and find the cheapest rate (from among the sites scanned) for each of more than 200 Disney-area hotels. The site offers various filters such as price, quality rating, and proximity to a specific location (Walt Disney World, SeaWorld, the convention center, airport, etc.) to allow you to more narrowly define your search. As you'll see when you visit the Travelaxe site, the same software scans for best rates in cities throughout the United States and around the world.

**4. IF YOU MAKE YOUR OWN RESERVATION** Always call the hotel in question, not the hotel chain's national toll-free number. Often, reservationists at the toll-free number are unaware of local specials. Don't hesitate to bargain, but do it before you check in. If you're buying a hotel's weekend package, for example, and want to extend your stay, you can often obtain at least the corporate rate for the extra days.

*unofficial* **TIP**
Always ask about specials before you inquire about corporate rates.

**5. CONDOMINIUM AND VACATION HOME DEALS** A large number of condo resorts, time-shares, and all-suite properties in the Kissimmee/Orlando area rent to vacationers for a week or less. Look for bargains, especially during off-peak periods. Reservations and information can be obtained from:

| | |
|---|---|
| Condolink | ☎ 800-733-4445 |
| East and West of Disney Condo | ☎ 800-633-7108 |

| | |
|---|---|
| Holiday Villas | ☎ 800-344-3959 |
| Kissimmee–St. Cloud Reservations | ☎ 800-333-5477 |
| Vistana Resort | ☎ 800-877-8787 |
| Ramada Suites by SeaWorld | ☎ 800-633-1405 |
| Holiday Inn Family Suites | ☎ 877-387-KIDS |
| Vacation Homes at Disney | ☎ 800-288-6608 |

A majority of rental condos are listed with travel agents. Condo owners often pay an enhanced commission to agents who rent the units for reduced consumer rates.

## THE BEST HOTELS FOR FAMILIES OUTSIDE WALT DISNEY WORLD

### Zone 1: International Drive

**DoubleTree Castle Hotel**
**8629 International Drive, Orlando; ☎ 407-345-1511 or 800-952-2785; www.doubletreecastle.com**

**Rate per night** $150. **Pool** ★★★. **Fridge in room** Yes. **Shuttle to parks** Yes (Disney, Universal, SeaWorld). **Maximum persons per room** 4. **Special comments** Add $10 to room rate and up to four people receive continental breakfast; two signature chocolate-chip cookies come with every room.

DESCRIPTION AND COMMENTS You can't miss this one—it's the only castle on I-Drive. Inside you'll find royal colors (purple dominates), opulent fixtures, European art, Renaissance music, and, of course, a mystical Castle Creature at the door. The 216 guest rooms also receive the royal treatment when it comes to décor, and some may find them on the gaudy side; however, they are fairly large and well equipped with TV with PlayStation, fridge, three phones, coffeemaker, iron and board, hair dryer, and safe. Guests can enjoy full or continental breakfast in the Castle Cafe located off the lobby. A court jester appears at breakfast four days a week to entertain with juggling and balloon sculptures. For lunch or dinner, you might walk next door to either Vito's Chop House or Café Tu Tu Tango (an *Unofficial* favorite). The heated circular pool is five feet deep and features a fountain in the center, a poolside bar, and a whirlpool. There is no separate kiddie pool. Other on-site amenities include a fitness center, arcade, gift shop, lounge, valet laundry service and facilities, and guest services desk with park passes for sale and babysitting recommendations. A nice security feature: all elevators require an electronic guest card key.

## Hard Rock Hotel
**5800 Universal Boulevard, Orlando; ☎ 407-503-2000 or 888-273-1311; www.universalorlando.com**

**Rate per night** $264. **Pool** ★★★★. **Fridge in room** No, but available for $10 per day. **Shuttle to parks** Yes (Universal, SeaWorld, Wet n' Wild). **Maximum persons per room** 4. **Special comments** Microwaves available for $15 per day.

**DESCRIPTION AND COMMENTS** Located on the Universal property, the 650-room Hard Rock Hotel is nirvana for any kid over age 8, especially those interested in music. The hotel's architecture is California mission–style, and rock memorabilia is displayed throughout. If you're planning to spend at least a few days at the Universal parks, this is an excellent upscale option. Hotel guests receive special theme-park privileges such as early theme-park admission on select days and all-day access to the Universal Express line-breaking program, plus delivery of packages to their hotel room and advance reservation at select Universal restaurants. The music-filled pool area is a big draw with a white-sand beach, water slide, underwater audio system, and ultrahip pool bar. You'll also find two restaurants, including the world-renowned Palm Restaurant, a chic lounge, a fitness center, and a Hard Rock merchandise store (watch your teens closely here). Guest rooms are ultrahip too, of course, with cutting-edge contemporary décor, a CD sound system, TV with pay-per-view movies and video games, coffeemaker, iron and board, robes, hair dryer, and two phones. There's also a supervised children's activity center for kids ages 4–14.

## Nickelodeon Family Suites by Holiday Inn
**14500 Continental Gateway, Orlando ☎ 407-387-5437 or 866-GO2-NICK**

**Rate per night** $137–$250. **Pools** ★★★★★. **Fridge in room** Yes. **Shuttle to parks** Yes (Disney only). **Maximum persons per room** 7. **Special comments** Complimentary hot breakfast buffet.

**DESCRIPTION AND COMMENTS** Spongebob, eat your heart out. This recently revamped resort is as kid-friendly as they come. Decked out in all themes Nickelodeon, the hotel is sure to please any fan of TV shows the likes of "Rugrats," "Jimmy Neutron, Boy Genius," or the "Fairly Oddparents," to name a few. Nickelodeon characters from the channel's many shows hang out in the resort's lobby and mall area, greeting kids while parents check in. Guests can choose from among 777 one-, two-, and three-bedroom Kid Suites executed in a number of different themes—all very brightly and creatively decorated. All suites include a kitchenette with microwave, fridge, coffeemaker, TV and DVD player, iron and board, two hair dryers, and a safe. Kid Suites feature a semiprivate kids' bedroom with bunk beds, pull-out sleeper bed, 36-inch TV and DVD player, Nintendo 64 (you can rent games for a small fee at the hotel's video arcade), CD/cassette player, and activity table. The master bedroom offers ample storage space that the kids' bedroom lacks. Additional amenities include high-tech video arcade, Studio Nick—a game-show studio that will host six game shows a night for the entertainment of a live studio audience, a buffet (kids 12 and younger eat free with a paying adult), food court offering Pizza Hut and A&W Root Beer, the Nick@Night Cafe coffeehouse, convenience store, lounge, gift shop, fitness center, washer and dryer in each courtyard, and guest activities desk (buy Disney tickets and get recommendations on babysitting). Not to be missed (don't worry, your kids won't let you) are the resort's two pools, Oasis and Lagoon. Oasis features a water park complete with water cannons, rope ladders, geysers, and dump buckets, as well as two hot tubs for adults (with a view of the rest of the pool to keep an eye on little ones) and a smaller play area for younger kids. Kids will love the huge, zero-depth-entry Lagoon Pool, replete with a 400-gallon dump bucket, plus nearby basketball court and nine-hole mini-golf course. Pool activities for kids are scheduled several times a day, seasonally; some games feature the infamous green slime. "Dive-in" movies, family-friendly films shown on a giant screen on the deck, are in the works. Whatever you do, avoid letting your kids catch you saying the phrase, "I don't know" while you're here—trust us.

## Portofino Bay Hotel
**5601 Universal Boulevard, Orlando; ☎ 407-503-1000 or 888-273-1311; www.universalorlando.com**

**Rate per night** $284. **Pools** ★★★★. **Fridge in room** Minibar; fridge available for $10 per day. **Shuttle to parks** Yes (Universal, SeaWorld, Wet n' Wild). **Maximum persons per room** 4. **Special comments** Character dinner on Monday and Friday.

**DESCRIPTION AND COMMENTS** Also located in Universal, the 750-room Portofino Bay Hotel is themed like a seaside village on the Italian Riviera. Like at the Hard Rock Hotel, Portofino guests receive special theme-park privileges such as early theme-park admission on select days and all-day access to the Universal Express line-breaking program, plus delivery of packages to their hotel room and advance reservation at select Universal restaurants. The guest rooms are ultraluxurious by any standard, with Italian furnishings, opulent baths, and soothing neutral hues. Standard guest-room amenities include minibar, coffeemaker, iron and board, hair dryer, safe, umbrella, and TV with pay-per-view movies. Microwaves are available ($15 a day). Camp Portofino offers supervised activities (movies, video games, crafts, etc.) from 5 to 11:30 p.m. for children ages 4 to 14. The cost is $45 per child and $35 for each additional child in the same family; dinner is included. Trattoria del Porto, one of the Portofino's casual-dining restaurants, offers a character dinner from 6 until 9 p.m. on Friday. Characters such as Scooby Doo and Woody Woodpecker attend. The cost is $19.50 for adults, $12.75 for 12 and younger. Portofino has four other Italian restaurants (each with a children's menu), an Italian bakery (also serves gelato), and two bars. Three elaborate pools, gardens, jogging trails, pet friendly rooms, and a spa and fitness center round out major amenities. If you have the bank account to pay for it and plan to spend time at Universal, you can't go wrong here.

## Sheraton World Resort
**10100 International Drive, Orlando; ☎ 407-352-1100 or 800-327-0363; www.sheratonworld.com**

**Rate per night** $130–$150. **Pools** ★★★★. **Fridge in room** Yes. **Shuttle to parks** Yes (Disney only). **Maximum persons per room** 4. **Special comments** A good option if you're visiting SeaWorld.

DESCRIPTION AND COMMENTS Set on 28 acres, the Sheraton World Resort offers plenty of room for kids to roam. And with three heated pools, two kiddie pools, a small playground, an arcade, and a complimentary minigolf course (very mini, indeed), this resort offers more than enough kid-friendly diversions. The main pool is especially pleasant, with fountains, lush landscaping, and a poolside bar. Other on-site amenities and services include fitness center, massage therapy, gift shop, guest services desk, and lounge. A golf club is located one mile away. We recommend booking a room in the new tower if possible, even though it's set away from the kiddie pools and playground. The tower rooms are a bit larger and more upscale than the low-rise rooms, some of which could use a renovation. All 1,102 guest rooms include fridge, coffeemaker, TV with Nintendo, iron and board, hair dryer, and safe. The Sheraton has one restaurant and a deli with a Pizza Hut. If your family loves SeaWorld, you're in luck here—Shamu and friends are within walking distance.

## Zone 2: Lake Buena Vista and I-4 Corridor

### Hilton Walt Disney World
**1751 Hotel Plaza Boulevard, Lake Buena Vista;**
☎ **407-827-4000 or 800-782-4414; www.hilton-wdwv.com**

**Rate per night** $209. **Pools** ★★★★. **Fridge in room** Minibar. **Shuttle to parks** Yes (Disney theme and water parks only). **Maximum persons per room** 4. **Special comments** Sunday character breakfast and Disney early-entry program.

DESCRIPTION AND COMMENTS Located in the Disney Village, the Hilton offers 814 guest rooms and suites set on 23 landscaped acres. Since it's an official Walt Disney World hotel, guests can take advantage of the Disney early-entry program, which allows hotel guest to enter a selected Disney park one hour before official opening time. At press time, the Hilton was the only hotel in the Disney Village to offer this privilege. Hilton guest rooms are spacious, luxurious, and tasteful. Decorated in earth tones and complete with marble baths, all standard rooms are equipped with iron and board, hair dryer, two phones, desk, minibar, coffeemaker, and cable TV with pay-per-view movies and video games. One family amenity offered by the Hilton is its character breakfast. Offered on Sunday only from 8:30 to 11 a.m., the food is served buffet-style, and four characters attend but only two are present at a time. When we visited, the characters were Minnie Mouse, Brer Bear, Donald Duck, and Pluto. Reservations are not accepted for the character breakfast. Other important family amenities include the Hilton Vacation Station, where kids ages 4–12 can take part in supervised activities; babysitting services; an arcade and pool table; and two beautifully landscaped and heated swimming pools, as well as a kiddie pool. Adults and older children can blow off steam after a long day at the parks in the fitness center. And nine on-site restaurants, including Benihana, add to the hotel's convenience.

### Holiday Inn SunSpree Resort
**13351 FL 535, Lake Buena Vista;** ☎ **407-239-4500 or 800-366-6299; www.kidsuites.com**

**Rate per night** $120. **Pool ★★★. Fridge in room** Yes. **Shuttle to parks** Yes (Disney only). **Maximum persons per room** 4–6. **Special comments** The first hotel in the world to offer Kidsuites.

**DESCRIPTION AND COMMENTS** Put on your sunglasses—you'll know you're there when the hot pink, bright blue, green, and yellow exterior comes into view. Once inside, kids get into the action from the very beginning at their own check-in counter, where they'll receive a free goody bag. Max, Maxine, and the Kidsuite Gang, the character mascots here, come out to play with the kids at scheduled times during the day. But the big lure is the Kidsuites, which are 405-square-foot rooms with a separate area for kids. Themes include a tree house, circus tent, jail, space capsule, igloo, fort, and many more. The kids' area sleeps three to four children and has either two sets of bunk beds or one bunk bed and a twin, plus a cable TV and VCR, Nintendo, radio/cassette or CD player, fun phone, and game table and chairs. The separate adult area has its own TV and VCR, safe, hair dryer, and a mini kitchenette with fridge, microwave, sink, and coffeemaker. Standard guest rooms are also available and offer the same amenities found in the adult areas of the Kidsuites. Other kid-friendly amenities include free bedtime tuck-in service by a member of the Kidsuite Gang (reservations required); the tiny Castle Movie Theater, which shows continuous movies daily and clown and magic shows nightly; a playground; a state-of-the-art arcade with Sega games and air hockey among many other games; a basketball court; and Camp Holiday, a free supervised activities program for kids ages 3–12. Held every day in Max's Magic Castle, Camp Holiday activities might include movies and cartoons, clown and magic shows, bingo, face-painting, karaoke, and computer and arcade games. There's also a large, attractive free-form pool, complete with kiddie pool and two whirlpools, and a fitness center ($6 hour, per child, 10 a.m–10 p.m.). You won't go hungry with Maxine's Food Emporium on site. Open 7 a.m.–10 p.m., it includes Little Caesars, A&W Restaurant, Otis Spunkmeyer Cookies and Muffins, TCBY, and more. There's also a mini-mart. Another perk: kids ages 12 and under eat free from a special menu when dining with one paying adult; there's a maximum of four kids per paying adult.

## Hyatt Regency Grand Cypress
**One Grand Cypress Boulevard, Lake Buena Vista; ☎ 407-239-1234 or 888-591-1234; www. hyattgrandcypress.com**

**Rate per night** $219. **Pool ★★★★★. Fridge in room** Minibar; fridge available on request. **Shuttle to parks** Yes (Disney only).

**Maximum persons per room** 4. **Special comments** Wow, what a pool!

**DESCRIPTION AND COMMENTS** There are myriad reasons to stay at this 1,500-acre resort, but in our book, the pool ranks as number one. It's a sprawling, 800,000-gallon tropical paradise with a 125-foot water slide, ubiquitous waterfalls, caves and grottoes, and a suspension bridge. The only problem is that your kids may never want to leave the pool to visit the theme parks. The Hyatt is also a golfer's paradise. With a 45-hole championship Jack Nicklaus–designed course, an 18-hole course, a 9-hole pitch-and-putt course, and a golf academy, there's something for golfers of all abilities. Other recreational perks include a racquet facility with hard and clay courts, a private lake complete with beach, a fitness center, and miles of nature trails for biking, walking or jogging, and horseback riding. The 750 standard guest rooms are 360 square feet and provide a casual but luxurious Florida ambience, with green and reddish hues, touches of rattan, and private balconies. In-room amenities include minibar, iron and board, safe, hair dryer, ceiling fan, and cable TV with pay-per-view movies and video games. Suite and villa accommodations offer even more amenities. Camp Hyatt provides supervised programs for kids, and in-room babysitting is also available. Five restaurants provide plenty of dining options, and four lounges offer nighttime entertainment. If outdoor recreation is high on your family's list, the Hyatt is an excellent high-end choice.

## Marriott Village Fairfield Inn
**8623 Vineland Avenue, Lake Buena Vista; ☎ 407-938-9001 or 877-682-8552; www.marriottvillage.com**

**Rate per night** $79–$119. **Pools** ★★★. **Fridge in room** Yes. **Shuttle to parks** Yes (Disney, Universal, SeaWorld, Wet n' Wild). **Maximum persons per room** 4. **Special comments** Complimentary continental breakfast at Fairfield Inn and SpringHill Suites.

**DESCRIPTION AND COMMENTS** This gated community includes a 388-room Fairfield Inn, a 400-suite Spring Hill Suites, and 312-room Courtyard. Whatever your travel budget, you'll find a room to fit it here. For a bit more space, book the Spring Hill Suites; if you're looking for a good value, try the Fairfield Inn; and if you need limited business amenities, reserve at the Courtyard. In-room amenities at all three properties include fridge, cable TV with PlayStation, iron and board, and hair dryer. Additionally, the Spring Hill Suites have microwaves in all suites, and all Courtyard rooms feature Web TV. Cribs and rollaway beds are available at no extra charge at all locations. Pools at all three hotels are attractive and medium-sized with children's interactive splash zones and whirlpools, and all properties have their own fitness center. An incredibly convenient feature here is the Village Marketplace food court, which includes Pizza Hut, TCBY Yogurt, Oscar Mayer Hot Dog Construction Company, Oscar Mayer 1883 Deli, Village Grill, Gourmet Bean Coffee and Pastry Shop, and a 24-hour convenience store. And if you're looking for a full-service restaurant experience, Bahama Breeze, Fish Bones, and Golden Corral restaurants are adjacent and within walking distance of the compound. Each hotel also features its own Kids Club. For kids ages 4–8, Kids Clubs have a theme (backyard, tree house, and library) and feature a big-screen TV, computer stations, and three educational centers (math and science, reading, and creative activities). They operate approximately six hours per day with a staff member on duty at all times. And best of all, there's no extra charge to participate in the Kids Club program. Marriott Village also offers a Kids Night Out program (for ages 4–10), which runs on select nights from 6 to 10 p.m. Cost is $35 per child and includes activities and dinner. The program is supervised by two staff members. A Disney planning station and attraction ticket sales, an arcade, and a Hertz car rental desk complete the Marriott Village services and amenities. And last but not least, shoppers in the family will be pleased to know that Marriott Village is adjacent to the Orlando Premium Outlets. You'll get a lot of bang for your buck at Marriott Village.

### Sheraton Safari Hotel
**12205 Apopka-Vineland Road, Lake Buena Vista;**
☎ **407-239-0444 or 800-423-3297; www.sheraton.com**

**Rate per night** $150. **Pool** ★★★. **Fridge in room** In safari suites only. **Shuttle to parks** Yes (Disney complimentary; other parks for a fee). **Maximum persons per room** 4–6. **Special comments** Cool python water slide.

DESCRIPTION AND COMMENTS The Sheraton Safari offers a more lowkey theme experience. The safari theme is nicely executed throughout the property—from the lobby dotted with African artifacts and native décor to the 79-foot python water slide dominating the pool. The 393 guest rooms and 90 safari suites also sport the safari theme with tasteful animal-print soft goods in brown, beige, and jewel tones and African-inspired art. Inroom amenities include cable TV with PlayStation, coffeemaker, iron and board, hair dryer, and safe. The safari suites are a good option for families since they provide added space with a separate sitting room and a kitchenette with a fridge, microwave, and sink. The first thing your kids will probably want to do is hit the pool and take a turn on the python water slide. It's pretty impressive, but as one *Unofficial Guide* researcher pointed out, it's somewhat of a letdown that the python doesn't actually spit you out of its mouth. Instead, you're deposited below the snake's chin. Details, details. Other on-site amenities include a restaurant (children's menu available), deli, lounge, arcade, and fitness center. Should you want to escape for a night of strictly adult fun, babysitting services are available.

### Sheraton Vistana Resort
**8800 Vistana Center Drive, Lake Buena Vista; ☎ 866-208-0003; www.starwoodvo.com**

**Rate per night** $184. **Pools** ★★★★. **Fridge in room** Minibar. **Shuttle to parks** Yes (Disney, Universal, SeaWorld). **Maximum persons per room** 6. **Special comments** Though actually time-shares, the villas are rented nightly as well.

**DESCRIPTION AND COMMENTS** The Sheraton Vistana is deceptively large, stretching as it does across either side of Vistana Center Drive. Since Sheraton's sales emphasis is on ownership of the time-shares, the rental angle is a small secret in local lodging. But it's worth considering for visiting families, as the Vistana is one of the best off-Disney properties in Orlando. If you want to have a serene retreat from your days in the theme parks, this is an excellent home base. You may even have difficulty prying yourself out of here to go to the parks. The spacious "villas" come in one-bedroom, two-bedroom, and two-bedroom-with-lockoff combinations. All are cleanly decorated in simple pastels, but the main emphasis is on the profusion of amenities. Each villa comes with full kitchen (including fridge with freezer, microwave, oven/range, dishwasher, toaster, and coffeemaker, with an option to pre-stock with groceries), washer and dryer, TVs in the living room and each bedroom (one with VCR), stereo with CD player, separate dining area, and private patio or balcony in most. The grounds themselves have resort amenities close at hand, with seven swimming pools (four with poolside bars), four playgrounds, three restaurants, game rooms, fitness centers, a mini-golf course, sports equipment rental (including bikes), and courts for basketball, volleyball, tennis, and shuffleboard. The resort organizes a mind-boggling array of activities for kids (and adults) of all ages, from arts and crafts to a variety of games and sports tournaments. Of special note is the fact that the Vistana is extremely secure, with locked gates bordering all guest areas, so children can have the run of the place without parents worrying about them wandering off.

## Wyndham Palace Resort & Spa
**1900 Buena Vista Drive, Lake Buena Vista;** ☎ **407-827-2727 or 800-WYNDHAM; www.wyndhampalaceresort.com**

**Rate per night** $150. **Pools** ★★★★. **Fridge in room** Minibar. **Shuttle to parks** Yes (Disney only). **Maximum persons per room** 4. **Special comments** Sunday character breakfast available.

**DESCRIPTION AND COMMENTS** Located in the Disney Village, the Wyndham Palace is an upscale and convenient choice for your Disney vacation headquarters. Surrounded by a man-made lake and plenty of palms, the attractive and spacious pool area contains three heated pools, the larger of which is partially covered by a pool house (nice for when you're ready for a little shade), a whirlpool, and a sand volleyball court. Plus, there's even a pool concierge who will fetch your favorite magazine or fruity drink. On Sunday, the Wyndham offers a character breakfast at the Watercress Cafe. Cost is $23 for adults and $13 for children. Minnie Mouse, Pluto, and Goofy were in attendance when we visited. The 1,014 guest rooms are posh and spacious, and each comes with a desk, coffeemaker, hair dryer, cable TV with pay-per-view movies, iron and board, and minibar. There are also 112 suites. Children ages 4–12 can participate in supervised programs through the Wyndy Harbour Kids' Klub, and in-room babysitting is available through the All about Kids child-care service. Three lighted tennis courts, a European-style spa offering 60 services, a fitness center, an arcade, a playground, and a beauty salon round out the hotel's amenities. You won't have a problem finding a decent meal with three restaurants and a mini-market on site. And if you're not wiped out after spending time in the parks, you might consider the Laughing Kookaburra Good Time Bar for live entertainment and dancing. Note: all these amenities and services come at a price—a $10 per night resort fee will be added to your bill.

## Zone 3: US 192

## Comfort Suites Maingate Resort
**7888 West US 192, Kissimmee;** ☎ **407-390-9888 or 888-390-9888; www.kisscomfortsuites.com**

**Rate per night** $100. **Pool** ★★★. **Fridge in room** Yes. **Shuttle to parks** Yes

(Disney, Universal, SeaWorld, Wet 'n Wild). **Maximum persons per room** 6. **Special comments** Complimentary continental breakfast daily.

**DESCRIPTION AND COMMENTS** This nice property has 150 spacious one-room suites with double sofa bed, microwave, fridge, coffeemaker, TV, hair dryer, and safe. The suites aren't lavish but are clean and contemporary with a muted deep-purple and beige color scheme. Extra counter space in the bathroom is especially convenient for larger families. The heated pool is large and amoeba-shaped with plenty of lounge chairs and moderate landscaping. A kiddie pool, whirlpool, and poolside bar complete the courtyard area. Other on-site amenities include an arcade and gift shop. But the big plus for this place is its location—right next door to a shopping center with just about everything a traveling family could possibly need. Here's what you'll find: seven dining options, including Outback Steakhouse, Dairy Queen, Subway, TGI Friday's, and Chinese, Japanese, and Italian eateries; a Goodings supermarket; one-hour film developing; a hair salon; a bank; a dry cleaner; a tourist information center with park passes for sale; and a Centra Care walk-in clinic, among other services. All this just a short walk from your room.

### Gaylord Palms Resort
**6000 West Osceola Parkway, Kissimmee; ☎ 407-586-0000; www.gaylordpalms.com**

**Rate per night** $200. **Pool** ★★★★. **Fridge in room** Yes. **Shuttle to parks** Yes (Disney). **Maximum persons per room** 4. **Special comments** Probably the closest thing to Disney-level extravagance off Disney grounds.

**DESCRIPTION AND COMMENTS** Originally meant to be an Opryland Resort, this place had its name changed before opening due to the owners' loss of confidence in the Opryland name as brand. Regardless of whether "Gaylord Palms" results in better name recognition, this is a decidedly upscale resort. Though it has a colossal convention facility and strongly caters to its business clientele, the Gaylord Palms is still a nice (if pricey) family resort. The hotel wings are defined by the three themed, glass-roofed atriums they overlook. Key West features design reminiscent of island life in the Florida Keys; the Everglades are an overgrown spectacle of shabby swamp chic, complete with piped-in cricket noise and a robotic alligator; and the immense, central St. Augustine hearkens back to old Spanish Colonial Florida. Lagoons, streams, and waterfalls cut through and connect all three, and little walkways and bridges abound.

The rooms themselves reflect the color schemes of their respective areas, though there's no particular connection in décor (the St. Augustine atrium-view rooms are the most opulent, but they're not in any way Spanish). The fourth wing of rooms, the Emerald Tower, overlooks the Emerald Bay shopping and dining area of the St. Augustine atrium; these rooms are the nicest and most expensive, and they're mostly used by convention-goers. Though rooms do have fridges and stereos with CD players (as well as other high-end perks, like high-speed Internet access), the rooms themselves really work better as retreats for adults than for kids. However, children will enjoy wandering the themed areas, playing in the family pool (complete with giant water-squirting octopus), or participating in the La Petite Academy Kids Station, which organizes a range of games and activities for wee ones.

## Holiday Inn Nikki Bird Resort
**7300 West US 192, Kissimmee; ☎ 407-396-7300 or 800-20-OASIS**

**Rate per night** $105. **Pools** ★★★★. **Fridge in room** Yes. **Shuttle to parks** Yes (Disney only). **Maximum persons per room** 5 (2 adults; 3 small children). **Special comments** Kids 12 and under eat free from special menus with a paying adult; room service includes Pizza Hut pizza.

**DESCRIPTION AND COMMENTS** In the Orlando hotel world, you're nobody unless you have a mascot. Here it's the Nikki Bird and Wacky the Wizard, who stroll the resort interacting with kids and posing for photos. This Holiday Inn offers standard guest rooms as well as Kidsuites. All rooms feature microwave, fridge, TV with PlayStation, coffeemaker, iron and board, hair dryer, and safe. Additionally, Kidsuites offer a themed kids area within the guest room with kid-size bunk beds and twin bed, TV/VCR, radio/CD player, and Playstation. Kidsuites are most suitable for families with children age 9 and under; children over age 9 will have a hard time fitting into the kids' beds. Parents beware: Kidsuites here also come with extremely bright décor. Sunglasses recommended. Standard rooms are spacious, but the Kidsuites are a bit cramped with the children's area. This sprawling resort offers three pools with whirlpools and two kiddie pools with squirt fountains and small playgrounds, so you won't have to walk far to cool off. On-site volleyball and tennis provide more outdoor recreation. Fitness equipment is also available. And a large arcade has air hockey, pool, and Sega games. Guest services include car rental and a tour desk with park passes for sale. The resort can also arrange a babysitter for $10 per hour, plus a $10 transportation fee; the minimum is four hours, so you'll drop at least $50. The full-service Angel's Diner has 1950s-style diner décor and a good buffet with American cuisine and some theme nights. After dinner, you'll find nightly family entertainment at "Nikki's Nest" with songs, puppet and magic shows, and games.

## Howard Johnson EnchantedLand
**4985 West US 192, Kissimmee; ☎ 407-396-4343 or 800-446-4656; www.hojo.com**

**Rate per night** $60. **Pool** ★★. **Fridge in room** Yes. **Shuttle to parks** Yes (Disney, Universal, SeaWorld). **Maximum persons per room** 4. **Special comments** Complimentary ice cream party; free video library.

**DESCRIPTION AND COMMENTS** Fairies, dragons, and superheroes have invaded the HoJo. If you stay here, be sure you book a Family Value Room: a standard room that has been transformed into a kids' suite. Approximately 300 square feet, these rooms feature a themed kids area (choose from a tree house, fairies, or action heroes) with a twin daybed that converts to two twins or one king, TV and VCR, microwave, fridge, coffeemaker, and safe. Note that the kids' area is separated from the double bed by a mere half-wall divider, so if you're looking for privacy and space from the kids, this probably isn't the place for you. While you're taking care of the real bill, kids can check in at their own desk in the form of a tree house. For $5 per child, the Adventure Club, based in a small playroom, offers supervised activities, games, and movies in the evenings Thursday–Saturday. There is a small market on site, and breakfast is served every morning from 7 to 11 a.m. (kids age 12 and under eat free with a paying adult). Other onsite amenities include a small arcade and a whirlpool. It may not offer the myriad amenities found in more deluxe properties, but EnchantedLand is a good value for your theme buck.

## Radisson Resort Parkway
**2900 Parkway Boulevard, Kissimmee; ☎ 407-396-7000 or 800-634-4774**

**Rate per night** $100. **Pool** ★★★★★. **Fridge in room** Minibar. **Shuttle to parks** Yes (Disney, Universal, SeaWorld). **Maximum persons per room** 4. **Special comments** Kids 10 and under eat free with a paying adult at any hotel restaurant.

**DESCRIPTION AND COMMENTS** Although the pool alone is worth a stay here, fortunately the Radisson Resort gets high marks in all areas. But first the pool: it's a huge free-form affair with a waterfall and water slide surrounded by lush palms and flowering plants, plus an additional smaller heated pool, two whirlpools, and a kiddie pool. Other outdoor amenities include two lighted tennis courts, volleyball, a playground, and jogging areas. Kids can also blow off steam at the arcade, while adults might visit the fitness center with a sauna. The guest rooms are elegant and feature Italian furnishings with clean lines and marble baths. Rooms are fairly large and include minibar, coffeemaker, color TV, iron and board, hair dryer, and safe. Dining options include The Court for breakfast and dinner buffets and a 1950s-style diner serving burgers, sandwiches, shakes, and Pizza Hut pizza, among other fare. A sports lounge with an 11-by-6-foot TV offers nighttime entertainment. Guest services can help with special tours, park passes, car rental, and babysitting. The only downside here is no organized children's programs. The good news is parents don't sacrifice their vacation for the kids—all will be equally happy here.

# HOTELS *and* MOTELS: RATED *and* RANKED

IN THIS SECTION, WE COMPARE HOTELS in three main areas outside Walt Disney World (pages 42–44) with those inside the World.

## What the Ratings Mean

| ★★★★★ | Superior Rooms | Tasteful and luxurious by any standard |
|---|---|---|
| ★★★★ | Extremely Nice Rooms | What you would expect at a Hyatt Regency or Marriott |
| ★★★ | Nice Rooms | Holiday Inn or comparable quality |
| ★★ | Adequate Rooms | Clean, comfortable, and functional without frills— like a Motel 6 |
| ★ | Super Budget | These exist but are not included in our coverage |

## ROOM RATINGS

TO EVALUATE PROPERTIES FOR THEIR QUALITY, tasteful-
ness, state of repair, cleanliness, and size of their *standard
rooms,* we have grouped the hotels and motels into classifi-
cations denoted by stars—the overall quality rating. Star
ratings in this guide apply to Orlando-area properties only
and don't necessarily correspond to ratings awarded by
Frommer's, Mobil, AAA, or other travel critics. Because
stars have little relevance when awarded in the absence of
recognized standards of comparison, we have tied our ratings to expected levels of quality established by specific
American hotel corporations.

Overall quality ratings apply *only to room quality* and
describe the property's standard accommodations. For most
hotels and motels, a standard accommodation is a room
with either one king bed or two queen beds. In an all-suite
property, the standard accommodation is either a one- or
two-room suite. In addition to standard accommodations,
many hotels offer luxury rooms and special suites, which
aren't rated in this guide. Star ratings for rooms are assigned
without regard to whether a property has restaurant(s),
recreational facilities, entertainment, or other extras.

In addition to stars (which delineate broad categories),
we use a numerical rating system—the room quality rating.
Our rating scale is 0–100, with 100 as the best possible rating and zero (0) as the worst. Numerical ratings are
presented to show the difference we perceive between one
property and another.

The location column identifies the area around Walt Disney World where you will find a particular property. The des-
ignation "WDW" means that the property is inside Walt
Disney World. A "1" means that the property is on or near International Drive. Properties on US 192 (a.k.a. Irlo Bronson
Memorial Highway, Vine Street, and Space Coast Parkway)
are indicated by a "3." All others are marked with "2" and for
the most part are along the I-4 corridor, though some are in
nearby locations that don't meet any other criteria.

| LODGING AREAS | |
|---|---|
| WDW | Walt Disney World |
| 1 | International Drive |
| 2 | I-4 Corridor |
| 3 | US 192 (Irlo Bronson Memorial Highway) |

Cost estimates are based on the hotel's published rack rates for standard rooms. Each "$" represents $50. Thus a cost symbol of "$$$" means a room (or suite) at that hotel will be about $150 a night.

## How the Hotels Compare

| HOTEL | LOCATION | OVERALL QUALITY RATING | ROOM QUALITY RATING | COST ($=$50) |
|---|---|---|---|---|
| Omni Orlando Resort at ChampionsGate | 3 | ★★★★★ | 96 | $$$– |
| Ritz-Carlton Orlando Grande Lakes | 1 | ★★★★½ | 94 | $$$$$$– |
| Contemporary Resort (renovated rooms) | WDW | ★★★★½ | 93 | $$$$$– |
| Grand Floridian Resort | WDW | ★★★★½ | 93 | $$$$$$$$– |
| Hard Rock Hotel | 1 | ★★★★½ | 93 | $$$$$+ |
| Westgate Resorts (Town Center) | 3 | ★★★★½ | 93 | $$$– |
| Marriott Orlando World Center | 2 | ★★★★½ | 92 | $$$$+ |
| Marriott Vista Grande Villas | 1 | ★★★★½ | 92 | $$$ |
| Polynesian Resort (2005 renovated suites) | WDW | ★★★★½ | 92 | $$$$$$+ |
| Portofino Bay Hotel | 1 | ★★★★½ | 92 | $$$$$$– |
| Westgate Lakes | 2 | ★★★★½ | 92 | $$– |
| Shades of Green | WDW | ★★★★½ | 91 | $$– |
| Swan | WDW | ★★★★½ | 91 | $$$$$– |
| Vacation Village Parkway | 3 | ★★★★½ | 91 | $$+ |
| Beach Club Resort | WDW | ★★★★½ | 90 | $$$$$$– |
| Beach Club Villas | WDW | ★★★★½ | 90 | $$$$$$$$ |
| BoardWalk Villas | WDW | ★★★★½ | 90 | $$$$$$$$ |
| Celebration Hotel | WDW | ★★★★½ | 90 | $$$$$– |
| Gaylord Palms Resort | 3 | ★★★★½ | 90 | $$$$ |
| Hyatt Regency Grand Cypress | 2 | ★★★★½ | 90 | $$$$+ |
| Old Key West Resort | WDW | ★★★★½ | 90 | $$$$$+ |
| Peabody Orlando | 1 | ★★★★½ | 90 | $$$$$$$$ |
| Rosen Plaza Hotel | 1 | ★★★★½ | 90 | $$$$$$– |
| Royal Pacific Resort | 1 | ★★★★½ | 90 | $$$$$– |
| Saratoga Springs | WDW | ★★★★½ | 90 | $$$$$+ |
| Westgate Resorts (villas) | 3 | ★★★★½ | 90 | $$$$ |
| Wilderness Lodge Villas | WDW | ★★★★½ | 90 | $$$$$$– |

## How the Hotels Compare (continued)

| HOTEL | LOCATION | OVERALL QUALITY RATING | ROOM QUALITY RATING | COST ($=$50) |
|---|---|---|---|---|
| Animal Kingdom Lodge | WDW | ★★★★ | 89 | $$$$$$– |
| BoardWalk Inn | WDW | ★★★★ | 89 | $$$$$– |
| Celebrity Resorts Orlando | 3 | ★★★★ | 89 | $$$ |
| DoubleTree Universal | 1 | ★★★★ | 89 | $$$+ |
| Hilton Grand Vacations Club SeaWorld | 1 | ★★★★ | 89 | $$$– |
| Yacht Club Resort | WDW | ★★★★ | 89 | $$$$$– |
| Contemporary Resort | WDW | ★★★★ | 88 | $$$$$– |
| Hilton Grand Vacations Club | 1 | ★★★★ | 88 | $$$– |
| Residence Inn Convention Center | 1 | ★★★★ | 88 | $$$$– |
| Caribe Royale Resort Suites | 3 | ★★★★ | 87 | $$$+ |
| Crowne Plaza Resort | 1 | ★★★★ | 87 | $$+ |
| Dolphin | WDW | ★★★★ | 87 | $$$$$– |
| Hawthorn Suites Lake Buena Vista | 2 | ★★★★ | 87 | $$$– |
| Hotel Royal Plaza (tower) | WDW | ★★★★ | 87 | $$$– |
| Wyndham Palms | 3 | ★★★★ | 87 | $$$$+ |
| Crowne Plaza Universal | 1 | ★★★★ | 86 | $$$+ |
| Fairfield Orlando Cypress Palms | 3 | ★★★★ | 86 | $$$ |
| Fort Wilderness Resort (cabins) | WDW | ★★★★ | 86 | $$$$$– |
| Marriott Cypress Harbour Villas | 1 | ★★★★ | 86 | $$$ |
| Marriott Imperial Palm Villas | 1 | ★★★★ | 86 | $$$$$$ |
| Polynesian Resort | WDW | ★★★★ | 86 | $$$$$$+ |
| Wilderness Lodge | WDW | ★★★★ | 86 | $$$$ |
| Wyndham Palace | WDW | ★★★★ | 86 | $$$ |
| Hilton Walt Disney World | WDW | ★★★★ | 85 | $$$$+ |
| Lake Buena Vista Resort | WDW | ★★★★ | 85 | $$+ |
| Orange Lake Country Club | 3 | ★★★★ | 85 | $$+ |
| Radisson Barcelo Inn I-Drive (tower) | 1 | ★★★★ | 85 | $$+ |
| Residence Inn SeaWorld | 1 | ★★★★ | 85 | $$$+ |
| DoubleTree Guest Suites | WDW | ★★★★ | 84 | $$ |
| Embassy Suites Orlando I-Drive | 1 | ★★★★ | 84 | $$$ |
| Port Orleans Resort (French Quarter) | WDW | ★★★★ | 84 | $$$ |
| Sheraton Vistana Resort | 2 | ★★★★ | 84 | $$$$– |

| HOTEL | LOCATION | OVERALL QUALITY RATING | ROOM QUALITY RATING | COST ($=$50) |
|---|---|---|---|---|
| Star Island Resort | 3 | ★★★★ | 84 | $$$$$– |
| Buena Vista Suites | 3 | ★★★★ | 83 | $$$– |
| Coronado Springs Resort | WDW | ★★★★ | 83 | $$$ |
| Cypress Pointe Resort | 2 | ★★★★ | 83 | $$$+ |
| Polynesian Isles Resort | 3 | ★★★★ | 83 | $$$– |
| Port Orleans Resort (Riverside) | WDW | ★★★★ | 83 | $$$+ |
| Extended Stay Deluxe Lake Buena Vista | 2 | ★★★★ | 83 | $$– |
| Radisson Resort Parkway | 3 | ★★★½ | 82 | $$ |
| AmeriSuites Lake Buena Vista South | 3 | ★★★½ | 82 | $$+ |
| Country Inn & Suites Calypso Cay | 3 | ★★★½ | 82 | $$+ |
| DoubleTree Castle Hotel | 1 | ★★★½ | 82 | $$$ |
| Hawthorn Suites Universal | 1 | ★★★½ | 82 | $$$– |
| Hilton Garden Inn Orlando | 3 | ★★★½ | 82 | $$– |
| Liki Tiki Village | 3 | ★★★½ | 82 | $$+ |
| Nickelodeon Family Suites by Holiday Inn | 1 | ★★★½ | 82 | $$$$– |
| Sheraton Royal Safari | 2 | ★★★½ | 82 | $$$ |
| Sheraton Studio City | 1 | ★★★½ | 82 | $$$– |
| Staybridge Suites Hotel | 1 | ★★★½ | 82 | $$$+ |
| Wyndham Orlando | 1 | ★★★½ | 82 | $$$+ |
| AmeriSuites Orlando Convention Ctenter | 1 | ★★★½ | 81 | $$$– |
| Club Hotel by DoubleTree | 2 | ★★★½ | 81 | $$+ |
| Embassy Suites Resort Lake Buena Vista | 2 | ★★★½ | 81 | $$$+ |
| Radisson Inn Lake Buena Vista | 2 | ★★★½ | 81 | $$– |
| Caribbean Beach Resort | WDW | ★★★½ | 80 | $$$ |
| DoubleTree Orlando Villas | 3 | ★★★½ | 80 | $$$+ |
| Embassy Suites Plaza I-Drive | 1 | ★★★½ | 80 | $$$– |
| Holiday Inn Nikki Bird Resort | 3 | ★★★½ | 80 | $$+ |
| Renaissance Orlando Resort | 1 | ★★★½ | 80 | $$$$ |
| Rosen Centre Hotel | 1 | ★★★½ | 80 | $$$$$$$ |
| Homewood Suites I-Drive | 1 | ★★★½ | 79 | $$$+ |
| Sheraton World Resort (tower) | 1 | ★★★½ | 79 | $$$ |

# How the Hotels Compare *(continued)*

| HOTEL | LOCATION | OVERALL QUALITY RATING | ROOM QUALITY RATING | COST ($=$50) |
|---|---|---|---|---|
| **Country Inn & Suites** (suites) | 2 | ★★★½ | 78 | $$+ |
| **Westgate Resorts** (tower) | 3 | ★★★½ | 78 | $$+ |
| **Hilton Garden Inn** | 1 | ★★★½ | 77 | $$+ |
| **Radisson Worldgate Resort** | 3 | ★★★½ | 77 | $$+ |
| **AmeriSuites Universal** | 1 | ★★★½ | 76 | $$− |
| **Celebrity Resorts** Lake Buena Vista | 2 | ★★★½ | 76 | $$$− |
| **Courtyard by Marriott I-Drive** | 1 | ★★★½ | 76 | $$+ |
| **Grand Lake Resort** | 3 | ★★★½ | 76 | $$+ |
| **Grosvenor Resort** | WDW | ★★★½ | 76 | $$ |
| **Radisson Barcelo Inn I-Drive** (garden) | 1 | ★★★½ | 76 | $$+ |
| **Residence Inn Lake Buena Vista** | 2 | ★★★½ | 76 | $$$− |
| **Residence Inn Orlando** | 1 | ★★★½ | 76 | $$$ |
| **Holiday Inn WDW Resort** | WDW | ★★★½ | 75 | $$$+ |
| **Parkway International Resort** | 3 | ★★★½ | 75 | $$+ |
| **Quality Suites Universal** | 1 | ★★★½ | 75 | $$+ |
| **Hawthorn Suites Orlando** at SeaWorld | 1 | ★★★ | 74 | $$− |
| **Holiday Inn Hotel & Suites** Convention Center | 1 | ★★★ | 74 | $$$− |
| **Holiday Inn Universal Studios** | 1 | ★★★ | 74 | $$− |
| **Homewood Suites Maingate** | 3 | ★★★ | 74 | $$ |
| **Marriott Village Spring Hill Suites** | 2 | ★★★ | 74 | $$$− |
| **RIU Orlando** | 2 | ★★★ | 74 | $$+ |
| **All-Star Resort** | WDW | ★★★ | 73 | $$− |
| **Comfort Suites Maingate** | 3 | ★★★ | 73 | $$ |
| **Fairfield Inn & Suites Universal** | 1 | ★★★ | 73 | $$+ |
| **Holiday Inn International Resort** | 1 | ★★★ | 73 | $$$− |
| **La Quinta Inn I-Drive** | 1 | ★★★ | 73 | $$− |
| **Quality Suites Maingate East** | 3 | ★★★ | 73 | $$$− |
| **Extended Stay Convention Center** | 1 | ★★★ | 73 | $+ |
| **Extended Stay Deluxe Universal** | 1 | ★★★ | 73 | $$− |
| **Staybridge Suites** Lake Buena Vista | 2 | ★★★ | 72 | $$$+ |
| **Country Inn & Suites** (rooms) | 2 | ★★★ | 72 | $$+ |

| HOTEL | LOCATION | OVERALL QUALITY RATING | ROOM QUALITY RATING | COST ($=$50) |
|---|---|---|---|---|
| Extended Stay Convention Center | 1 | ★★★ | 72 | $+ |
| Extended Stay Universal | 1 | ★★★ | 72 | $+ |
| Ramada Inn I-Drive Orlando | 1 | ★★★ | 72 | $$– |
| Spring Hill Suites by Marriott | 1 | ★★★ | 72 | $$$ |
| Clarion Maingate | 3 | ★★★ | 71 | $$ |
| Hotel Royal Plaza (garden) | WDW | ★★★ | 71 | $$+ |
| Marriott Village Lake Buena Vista | 2 | ★★★ | 71 | $$+ |
| Pop Century Resort | WDW | ★★★ | 71 | $$ |
| Ramada Plaza & Inn Gateway (tower) | 3 | ★★★ | 71 | $$– |
| Seralago Hotel | 3 | ★★★ | 71 | $$– |
| Comfort Suites Orlando | 2 | ★★★ | 69 | $$+ |
| Hampton Inn Maingate West | 3 | ★★★ | 69 | $$– |
| Holiday Inn Sun Spree Resort | 2 | ★★★ | 69 | $$+ |
| Homewood Suites Lake Buena Vista | 2 | ★★★ | 69 | $$+ |
| Best Western Movieland | 1 | ★★★ | 68 | $+ |
| Holiday Inn Maingate West | 3 | ★★★ | 68 | $$– |
| Sheraton World Resort (garden) | 1 | ★★★ | 68 | $$$– |
| Westgate Palace | 1 | ★★★ | 68 | $$$$– |
| Clarion Universal | 1 | ★★★ | 67 | $$+ |
| Courtyard by Marriott Lake Buena Vista | 2 | ★★★ | 67 | $$+ |
| Enclave Suites | 1 | ★★★ | 67 | $$$– |
| Hampton Inn Universal | 1 | ★★★ | 67 | $$– |
| La Quinta Inn Lakeside | 3 | ★★★ | 67 | $$ |
| Quality Inn & Suites Universal | 1 | ★★★ | 67 | $$– |
| Travelodge Suites Eastgate | 3 | ★★★ | 67 | $+ |
| Comfort Inn Sandlake | 1 | ★★★ | 66 | $$+ |
| Comfort Suites Universal | 1 | ★★★ | 66 | $$$– |
| Hampton Inn Maingate | 3 | ★★★ | 66 | $$ |
| Howard Johnson Enchanted Land Resort Hotel | 3 | ★★★ | 66 | $+ |
| Howard Johnson Inn Maingate West | 3 | ★★★ | 66 | $$– |
| Quality Inn & Suites Eastgate | 3 | ★★★ | 66 | $+ |

## How the Hotels Compare *(continued)*

| HOTEL | LOCATION | OVERALL QUALITY RATING | ROOM QUALITY RATING | COST ($=$50) |
|---|---|---|---|---|
| Ramada Eastgate Fountain Park | 3 | ★★★ | 66 | $$− |
| Days Inn Lake Buena Vista | 2 | ★★★ | 65 | $$ |
| Hampton Inn Convention Center | 1 | ★★★ | 65 | $$+ |
| Hampton Inn Lake Buena Vista | 2 | ★★★ | 65 | $$− |
| Quality Inn I-Drive | 1 | ★★★ | 65 | $$− |
| Suburban Lodge Universal | 1 | ★★★ | 65 | $+ |
| Travelodge Maingate East | 3 | ★★★ | 65 | $+ |
| AmeriHost Resort | 3 | ★★½ | 64 | $$$$+ |
| Comfort Inn Lake Buena Vista | 2 | ★★½ | 64 | $+ |
| Comfort Inn Maingate West | 3 | ★★½ | 64 | $+ |
| Days Inn Eastgate | 3 | ★★½ | 64 | $− |
| Hampton Inn Kirkman | 1 | ★★½ | 64 | $$ |
| Marriott Village Fairfield Inn | 2 | ★★½ | 64 | $$+ |
| Orlando Grand Plaza | 1 | ★★½ | 64 | $+ |
| Ramada Plaza & Inn Gateway (garden) | 3 | ★★½ | 64 | $+ |
| Silver Lake Resort | 3 | ★★½ | 64 | $$$$ |
| Best Western Universal Inn | 1 | ★★½ | 63 | $$− |
| Country Inn & Suites I-Drive | 1 | ★★½ | 63 | $$− |
| Howard Johnson Inn South I-Drive | 1 | ★★½ | 63 | $$− |
| I-Drive Inn | 1 | ★★½ | 63 | $$− |
| La Quinta Universal | 1 | ★★½ | 63 | $$ |
| Microtel Inn & Suites | 1 | ★★½ | 63 | $$− |
| Sleep Inn Maingate | 3 | ★★½ | 63 | $+ |
| Summer Bay Resort | 3 | ★★½ | 63 | $$− |
| Baymont Inn Kissimmee | 3 | ★★½ | 62 | $$ |
| Best Western Plaza I-Drive | 1 | ★★½ | 62 | $+ |
| Days Inn West Kissimmee | 3 | ★★½ | 62 | $$− |
| Econo Lodge Polynesian Resort | 3 | ★★½ | 62 | $− |
| Holiday Inn Express Summerbay Resort | 3 | ★★½ | 62 | $$− |
| Howard Johnson Express Inn and Suites (suites) | 3 | ★★½ | 62 | $$− |
| Quality Inn Plaza | 1 | ★★½ | 62 | $$− |
| Red Roof Inn Kissimmee | 3 | ★★½ | 62 | $− |

| HOTEL | LOCATION | OVERALL QUALITY RATING | ROOM QUALITY RATING | COST ($=$50) |
|---|---|---|---|---|
| Westgate Inn | 3 | ★★½ | 62 | $$− |
| Days Inn I-Drive | 1 | ★★½ | 61 | $$ |
| Days Inn Suites Maingate East | 3 | ★★½ | 61 | $+ |
| Howard Johnson Plaza Resort | 1 | ★★½ | 61 | $+ |
| Mainstay Suites | 3 | ★★½ | 61 | $$+ |
| Motel 6 I-Drive | 1 | ★★½ | 61 | $+ |
| Ramada Resort Maingate | 3 | ★★½ | 61 | $+ |
| Wellesley Inn Kissimmee/ Lake Cecile | 3 | ★★½ | 61 | $$− |
| Comfort Inn I-Drive | 1 | ★★½ | 60 | $$+ |
| Days Inn SeaWorld/ Convention Center | 1 | ★★½ | 60 | $+ |
| Days Inn Universal Studios | 1 | ★★½ | 60 | $+ |
| Super 8 Kissimmee | 3 | ★★½ | 60 | $ |
| Travelodge I-Drive | 1 | ★★½ | 60 | $+ |
| Econo Lodge Maingate Resort | 3 | ★★½ | 59 | $− |
| Howard Johnson Inn Orlando | 1 | ★★½ | 59 | $$− |
| Magic Castle Inn & Suites | 3 | ★★½ | 59 | $− |
| Rodeway Inn Maingate | 3 | ★★½ | 59 | $+ |
| Travelodge Convention Center | 1 | ★★½ | 59 | $+ |
| Park Inn & Suites Maingate East | 3 | ★★½ | 58 | $$− |
| Quality Inn Maingate West | 3 | ★★½ | 58 | $+ |
| Rodeway Inn Carrier | 1 | ★★½ | 58 | $+ |
| Red Roof Inn Convention Center | 1 | ★★½ | 58 | $$− |
| Extended Stay Deluxe Convention Center | 1 | ★★½ | 58 | $$− |
| Super 8 Lakeside | 3 | ★★½ | 58 | $ |
| Home Sweet Home | 3 | ★★½ | 57 | $$$$ |
| Howard Johnson Express Inn and Suites (rooms) | 3 | ★★½ | 57 | $ |
| Howard Johnson Inn Maingate East | 3 | ★★½ | 57 | $+ |
| Super 8 East | 3 | ★★½ | 57 | $ |
| Riande Continental Plaza | 1 | ★★½ | 56 | $− |
| Rodeway Inn I-Drive | 1 | ★★½ | 56 | $$− |
| Travelodge Suites Maingate | 3 | ★★½ | 56 | $+ |

## How the Hotels Compare (continued)

| HOTEL | LOCATION | OVERALL QUALITY RATING | ROOM QUALITY RATING | COST ($=$50) |
|---|---|---|---|---|
| Buena Vista Motel | 3 | ★★ | 55 | $– |
| Knights Inn Kissimmee | 3 | ★★ | 55 | $– |
| Masters Inn Kissimmee | 3 | ★★ | 55 | $– |
| Masters Inn Maingate | 3 | ★★ | 55 | $+ |
| Golden Link Motel | 3 | ★★ | 54 | $– |
| Inn of America | 1 | ★★ | 54 | $+ |
| Sleep Inn Convention Center | 1 | ★★ | 54 | $$– |
| Sun Inn & Suites | 3 | ★★ | 53 | $– |
| Knights Inn Maingate East | 3 | ★★ | 52 | $– |
| Motel 6 Maingate East | 3 | ★★ | 52 | $– |
| Motel 6 Maingate West | 3 | ★★ | 52 | $– |
| Super 8 Universal | 1 | ★★ | 52 | $$– |
| Central Motel | 3 | ★★ | 51 | $– |
| Key Motel | 3 | ★★ | 51 | $– |
| Master's Inn I-Drive | 1 | ★★ | 50 | $+ |
| Red Carpet Inn East | 3 | ★★ | 50 | $ |
| Red Horse Inn | 1 | ★★ | 50 | $+ |
| Monte Carlo | 3 | ★★ | 48 | $– |
| Condolodge | 3 | ★★ | 47 | $$– |
| Palm Lakefront Resort & Hostel | 3 | ★½ | 38 | $– |

## THE TOP 30 BEST DEALS

HAVING LISTED THE NICEST ROOMS IN TOWN, LET'S take
a look at the best combinations of quality and value in a
room. As before, the rankings are made without consideration
of location or the availability of restaurant(s), recreational facilities, entertainment, and/or amenities. Listed below are the
top 30 room buys for the money, regardless of location or star
classification, based on average rack rates.

## The Top 30 Best Deals

| HOTEL | LOCATION | OVERALL QUALITY RATING | ROOM QUALITY RATING | COST ($=$50) |
|---|---|---|---|---|
| 1. Westgate Lakes | 2 | ★★★★½ | 92 | $$− |
| 2. Shades of Green | WDW | ★★★★½ | 91 | $$− |
| 3. Hilton Garden Inn Orlando | 3 | ★★★½ | 82 | $$− |
| 4. Econo Lodge Polynesian Resort | 3 | ★★½ | 62 | $− |
| 5. Extended Stay Deluxe Lake Buena Vista | 2 | ★★★★ | 83 | $$− |
| 6. Red Roof Inn Kissimmee | 3 | ★★½ | 62 | $− |
| 7. Best Western Movieland | 1 | ★★★★ | 68 | $+ |
| 8. Days Inn Eastgate | 3 | ★★½ | 64 | $− |
| 9. DoubleTree Guest Suites | WDW | ★★★★ | 84 | $$ |
| 10. Extended Stay Convention Center | 1 | ★★★ | 72 | $+ |
| 11. Omni Orlando Resort at ChampionsGate | 3 | ★★★★★ | 96 | $$$− |
| 12. Radisson Inn Lake Buena Vista | 2 | ★★★½ | 81 | $$− |
| 13. Radisson Resort Parkway | 3 | ★★★½ | 84 | $$ |
| 14. Extended Stay Convention Center | 1 | ★★★ | 73 | $+ |
| 15. Vacation Village Parkway | 3 | ★★★★½ | 91 | $$+ |
| 16. Golden Link Motel | 3 | ★★ | 54 | $− |
| 17. Hawthorn Suites Orlando at SeaWorld | 1 | ★★★ | 74 | $$− |
| 18. Motel 6 Maingate East | 3 | ★★ | 52 | $− |
| 19. Motel 6 Maingate West | 3 | ★★ | 52 | $− |
| 20. Econo Lodge Maingate Resort | 3 | ★★★½ | 59 | $− |
| 21. Extended Stay Universal | 1 | ★★★ | 72 | $+ |
| 22. Howard Johnson Enchanted Land Resort Hotel | 3 | ★★★ | 66 | $+ |
| 23. Lake Buena Vista Resort | WDW | ★★★★ | 85 | $$+ |
| 24. Magic Castle Inn & Suites | 3 | ★★½ | 59 | $− |
| 25. Extended Stay Deluxe Universal | 1 | ★★★ | 73 | $$− |
| 26. Super 8 Kissimmee | 3 | ★★½ | 60 | $ |
| 27. Travelodge Suites Eastgate | 3 | ★★★ | 67 | $+ |
| 28. AmeriSuites Universal | 1 | ★★★½ | 76 | $$− |
| 29. Key Motel | 3 | ★★★ | 51 | $− |
| 30. Knights Inn Kissimmee | 3 | ★★ | 55 | $− |

# PART FOUR

# WALT DISNEY WORLD *with* KIDS

# RECOMMENDATIONS *for* MAKING *the* DREAM COME TRUE

WHEN PLANNING A DISNEY WORLD vacation with young children, consider:

**AGE** Although the color and festivity of Disney World excite all children and specific attractions delight toddlers and preschoolers, Disney entertainment is generally oriented to older children and adults. Children should be a fairly mature 7 years old to *appreciate* the Magic Kingdom and the Animal Kingdom, and a year or two older to get much out of Epcot or Disney-MGM Studios.

**TIME OF YEAR TO VISIT** Avoid the hot, crowded summer months, especially if you have preschoolers. Go in October, November (except Thanksgiving), early December, January, February, or May. If you have children of varied ages and they're good students, take the older ones out of school and visit during the cooler, less-congested off-season. Arrange special assignments relating to the educational aspects of Disney World. If your children can't afford to miss school, take your vacation as soon as the school year ends in late May or early June. Alternatively, try late August before school starts.

**BUILD NAPS AND REST INTO YOUR ITINERARY** The theme parks are huge; don't try to see everything in one day. Tour in early morning and return to your hotel around 11:30 a.m. for lunch, a swim, and a nap. Even during off-season when the crowds are smaller and the temperatures more pleasant, the size of the major theme parks will exhaust most children under age 8 by lunchtime. Return to the park in late afternoon or early evening and continue touring. If you plan to return to your hotel in midday and would like your room made up, let housekeeping know.

**WHERE TO STAY** The time and hassle involved in commuting to and from the theme parks will be lessened if you stay in a hotel close to the theme parks. We should point out that this doesn't necessarily mean you have to lodge at a hotel in Walt Disney World. Because Walt Disney World is so geographically dispersed, many off-property hotels are actually closer to the theme parks than some Disney resorts. Regardless of whether you stay in or out of the World, it's imperative that you take young children out of the parks each day for a few hours of rest. Neglecting to relax is the best way we know to get the whole family in a snit and ruin the day (or the vacation).

If you have young children, you must plan ahead. Make sure your hotel is within 20 minutes of the theme parks. It's true you can revive somewhat by retreating to a Disney hotel for lunch or by finding a quiet restaurant in the theme parks, but there's no substitute for returning to the familiarity and comfort of your own hotel. Regardless of what you have heard, children too large to sleep in a stroller won't relax unless you take them back to your hotel. If it takes renting a car to make returning to your hotel practicable, rent the car.

*unofficial* **TIP** Naps and relief from the frenetic pace of the theme parks, even during off-season, are indispensable.

If you are traveling with children ages 12 and younger and want to stay in the World, we recommend the Polynesian, Grand Floridian, or Wilderness Lodge and Villas Resorts (in that order) if they fit your budget. For less expensive rooms, try the Port Orleans Resort. Bargain accommodations are available at the All-Star and Pop Century resorts. Fully equipped log cabins at Fort Wilderness Campground are also good economy lodging. Outside Walt Disney World, check out our top hotels for families on pages 46–59.

**BE IN TOUCH WITH YOUR FEELINGS** When you or your children get tired and irritable, call time out and regroup. Trust your instincts. What would feel best? Another ride, an ice cream break, or going back to the room for a nap? *The way to protect your considerable investment in your Disney vacation is to stay happy and have a good time.* You don't have to meet a quota for experiencing attractions. Do what you want.

**LEAST COMMON DENOMINATORS** Somebody is going to run out of steam first, and when they do the whole family will be affected. Sometimes a snack break will revive the flagging member. Sometimes, however, it's better to just return to your hotel. Pushing the tired or discontented beyond their capacity will spoil the day for them—and you. Accept that energy levels vary and be prepared to respond to members of your group who poop out.

**BUILDING ENDURANCE** Though most children are active, their normal play usually doesn't condition them for the exertion required to tour a Disney theme park. We recommend starting a program of family walks four to six weeks before your trip to get in shape.

**SETTING LIMITS AND MAKING PLANS** Avoid arguments and disappointment by establishing guidelines for each day, and get everybody committed.

**BE FLEXIBLE** Any day at Walt Disney World includes some surprises; be prepared to adjust your plan. Listen to your intuition.

**OVERHEATING, SUNBURN, AND DEHYDRATION** These are the most common problems of younger children at Disney World. Carry and use sunscreen. Be sure to put some on children in strollers, even if the stroller has a canopy. To avoid overheating, rest regularly in the shade or in an air-conditioned restaurant or show. Plastic squeeze bottles with caps are sold in all major parks for about $3.

*unofficial* **TIP**
We recommend renting a stroller for children age 6 and younger and carrying plastic bottles of water.

**BLISTERS AND SORE FEET** Guests of all ages should wear comfortable, well-broken-in shoes and two pairs of thin socks (better than one pair of thick socks). If you or your children are susceptible to blisters, bring precut Moleskin bandages. When you feel a hot spot, stop, air out your foot, and place a Moleskin bandage over the area before a blister forms. Moleskin is available by name at all drug stores. Young children may not tell their parents about a developing blister until it's too late, so inspect the feet of preschoolers two or more times a day.

**FIRST AID** Each major theme park has a first-aid center. In the Magic Kingdom, it's behind the refreshment corner to the left after you enter. At Epcot, it's on the World Showcase side of the Odyssey Center. At Disney-MGM, it's in the Guest Relations Building just inside the main entrance. At Animal Kingdom, it's in Discovery Island. If you or your children have a medical problem, go to a first-aid center. Disney first-aid centers are warmer and friendlier than most doctor's offices and are accustomed to treating everything from paper cuts to allergies.

**CHILDREN ON MEDICATION** Some parents of hyperactive children on medication discontinue or decrease the child's dosage at the end of the school year. If you have such a child, be aware that Disney World might overly stimulate him/her. Consult your physician before altering your child's medication regimen.

**WALKIE-TALKIES** An increasing number of readers stay in touch while on vacation by using walkie-talkies. If you go the walkie-talkie route, get a set that operates on multiple channels, or opt for cellular phones.

**SUNGLASSES** If you want your younger children to wear sunglasses, put a strap or string on the frames so that the glasses will stay on during rides and can hang from the child's neck while indoors.

**THINGS YOU FORGOT OR THINGS YOU RAN OUT OF** Rain gear, diapers, formula, film, aspirin, topical sunburn treatments, and other sundries are sold at all major theme parks and at Typhoon Lagoon, Blizzard Beach, and Downtown Disney. Rain gear is a bargain, but most other items are high. A good place to find diapers is at the Baby Centers—two diapers plus ointment are $3.50. Ask for goods you don't see displayed.

**INFANTS AND TODDLERS AT THE THEME PARKS** The major theme parks have centralized facilities for infant and toddler care. Everything necessary for changing diapers, preparing formulas, and warming bottles and food is available. Baby supplies are for sale, and there are rockers and special chairs for nursing mothers. At the Magic Kingdom, the Baby Center is next to the Crystal Palace at the end of Main Street. At Epcot, Baby Services is near the Odyssey Center, right of the Test Track in Future World. At Disney-MGM Studios, Baby Care is in the Guest Relations Building left of the entrance. At the Animal Kingdom, Baby Changing/Nursing is in Discovery Island in the center of the park. Dads in charge of little ones are welcome at the centers and can use most services offered. In addition, many men's rooms in the major theme parks have changing tables.

Infants and toddlers are allowed to experience any attraction that doesn't have minimum height or age restrictions. If you think you might try nursing during a theater attraction, be advised that most shows run about 17–20 minutes. Exceptions are *The Hall of Presidents* at the Magic Kingdom and

*The American Adventure* at Epcot that run 23 and 29 minutes, respectively.

**STROLLERS** The good news is that strollers are available for a modest rental fee at all four theme parks. If you rent a stroller at the Magic Kingdom and decide to go to Epcot, the Animal Kingdom, or Disney-MGM Studios, turn in your Magic Kingdom stroller and present your receipt at the next park. You'll be issued another stroller without additional charge.

Strollers can be obtained to the right of the entrance at the Magic Kingdom, to the left of the Entrance Plaza at Epcot, and at Oscar's Super Service just inside the entrance of Disney-MGM Studios. Stroller rentals at the Animal Kingdom are just inside the entrance and to the right. Rental at all parks is fast and efficient, and returning the stroller is a breeze. If you don't mind forfeiting your dollar deposit, you can ditch your rental stroller anywhere in the park when you're ready to leave.

*unofficial* **TIP**
If you plan to rent a stroller for your infant or toddler, bring along some pillows, cushions, or rolled towels to buttress him.

When you enter a show or board a ride, you must park your stroller, usually in an open, unprotected area. If it rains before you return, you'll need a cloth, towel, or diaper to dry it. Strollers are a must for infants and toddlers, but we have observed many sharp parents renting strollers for somewhat older children (up to 5 or so years old). The stroller prevents parents from having to carry children when they sag and provides a convenient place to carry water and snacks.

If you go to your hotel for a break and intend to return to the park, leave your rental stroller by an attraction near the park entrance, marking it with something personal like a bandanna. When you return, you'll know in an instant which one is yours.

Be aware that rental strollers are too large for all infants and many toddlers.

It's permissible to bring your own stroller. Remember, however, that only collapsible strollers are permitted on monorails, parking-lot trams, and buses. Your stroller is unlikely to be stolen, but mark it with your name.

## DISNEY, KIDS, AND SCARY STUFF

MONSTERS AND SPECIAL EFFECTS AT Disney-MGM Studios are more real and sinister than those in the other parks. If your child has difficulty coping with the witch in Snow White's Adventures, think twice about exposing him to machine-gun battles, earthquakes, and the creature from *Alien* at the Studios.

Preschoolers should start with Dumbo and work up to the Jungle Cruise in late morning, after being revved up and before getting hungry, thirsty, or tired. Pirates of the Caribbean is out for preschoolers. You get the idea.

## SWITCHING OFF (A.K.A. THE BABY SWAP)

SEVERAL ATTRACTIONS HAVE MINIMUM HEIGHT and/or age requirements. Some couples with children too small or too young forgo these attractions, while others take turns to ride. Missing some of Disney's best rides is an unnecessary sacrifice, and waiting in line twice for the same ride is a tremendous waste of time.

Instead, take advantage of the "switching off" option, also called "The Baby Swap." To switch off, there must be at least two adults. Everybody waits in line together, adults and children. When you reach an attendant (called a "greeter"), say you want to switch off. The greeter will allow everyone, including the young children, to enter the attraction. When you reach the loading area, one adult rides while the other stays with the kids. Then the riding adult disembarks and takes charge of the children while the other adult rides. A third adult in the party can ride twice, once with each of the switching off adults, so that the switching off adults don't have to experience the attraction alone.

| ATTRACTIONS WHERE SWITCHING OFF IS COMMON | |
| --- | --- |
| **Magic Kingdom** | |
| Tomorrowland | Space Mountain |
| Frontierland | Splash Mountain |
| | Big Thunder Mountain Railroad |
| **Epcot** | |
| Future World | Body Wars |
| | Test Track |
| | Mission: Space |
| **Disney-MGM Studios** | |
| Star Tours | *The Twilight Zone* Tower of Terror |
| Rock 'n' Roller Coaster | |
| **Animal Kingdom** | |
| DinoLand U.S.A. | Dinosaur |
| Asia | Kali River Rapids |
| | Primeval Whirl |

# Small Child Fright-Potential Chart

Our "Fright-Potential Chart" is a quick reference to identify attractions to be wary of, and why. The chart represents a generalization, and all kids are different. It relates specifically to kids ages 3 to 7. On average, children at the younger end of the range are more likely to be frightened than children in their sixth or seventh year.

## Magic Kingdom

### MAIN STREET, U.S.A.

**Walt Disney World Railroad**  Not frightening in any respect.

**Main Street Vehicles**  Not frightening in any respect.

### ADVENTURELAND

**Swiss Family Treehouse**  Not frightening in any respect.

**Jungle Cruise**  Moderately intense, some macabre sights. A good test attraction for little ones.

***Enchanted Tiki Birds***  A thunderstorm, loud volume level, and simulated explosions frighten some preschoolers.

**Pirates of the Caribbean**  Slightly intimidating queuing area; intense boat ride with gruesome (though humorously presented) sights and a short, unexpected slide down a flume.

**Magic Carpets of Aladdin**  Much like Dumbo. A favorite of most younger children.

### FRONTIERLAND

**Splash Mountain**  Visually intimidating from outside, with moderately intense visual effects. The ride, culminating in a 52-foot plunge down a steep chute, is somewhat hair-raising for all ages. Switching-off option provided (page 75).

**Big Thunder Mountain Railroad**  Visually intimidating from outside, with moderately intense visual effects. The roller coaster is wild enough to frighten many adults, particularly seniors. Switching off provided (page 75).

**Tom Sawyer Island**  Some very young children are intimidated by dark, walk-through tunnels that can be easily avoided.

***Country Bear Jamboree***  Not frightening in any respect.

***Frontierland Shootin' Arcade***  Not frightening in any respect.

### LIBERTY SQUARE

***The Hall of Presidents***  Not frightening, but boring for young ones.

***Liberty Square* Riverboat**  Not frightening in any respect.

**The Haunted Mansion**  Name raises anxiety, as do sounds and sights of waiting area. Intense attraction with humorously presented macabre sights. The ride itself is gentle.

## FANTASYLAND

**Mad Tea Party**  Midway-type ride can induce motion sickness in all ages.

**The Many Adventures of Winnie the Pooh**  Frightens a small percentage of preschoolers.

**Snow White's Scary Adventures**  Moderately intense spook-house-genre attraction with some grim characters. Absolutely terrifies many preschoolers.

**Dumbo the Flying Elephant**  A tame midway ride; a great favorite of most young children.

**Cinderella's Golden Carousel**  Not frightening in any respect.

**It's a Small World**  Not frightening in any respect.

**Peter Pan's Flight**  Not frightening in any respect.

## MICKEY'S TOONTOWN FAIR

**All attractions except roller coaster**  Not frightening in any respect.

**The Barnstormer at Goofy's Wiseacres Farm**  (children's roller coaster)  May frighten some preschoolers.

## TOMORROWLAND

**Buzz Lightyear's Space Ranger Spin**  Dark ride with cartoonlike aliens may frighten some preschoolers.

**Tomorrowland Transit Authority**  Not frightening in any respect.

**Space Mountain**  Very intense roller coaster in the dark; the Magic Kingdom's wildest ride and a scary roller coaster by any standard. Switching off provided (page 75).

**Stitch's Great Escape**  Very intense. May frighten children ages 9 and younger. Switching off provided (page 75).

**Astro Orbiter**  Visually intimidating from the waiting area. The ride is relatively tame.

**Walt Disney's Carousel of Progress**  (open seasonally)  Not frightening in any respect.

**Tomorrowland Speedway**  Noise of waiting area slightly intimidates preschoolers; otherwise, not frightening.

**The Timekeeper**  (open seasonally)  Both loud and intense, with frightening film scenes. Audience must stand.

## Epcot

### FUTURE WORLD

**Spaceship Earth**  Dark and imposing presentation intimidates a few preschoolers.

**Innoventions East and West**  Not frightening in any respect.

## Small Child Fright-Potential Chart (cont'd.)

### Epcot (continued)

**FUTURE WORLD (continued)**

**Universe of Energy**  Dinosaur segment frightens some preschoolers; visually intense, with some intimidating effects.

**Wonders of Life—Body Wars** (open seasonally)  Very intense, with frightening visual effects. Ride causes motion sickness in riders of all ages. Switching off provided (page 75).

**Wonders of Life—Cranium Command** (open seasonally)  Not frightening in any respect.

**Wonders of Life—The Making of Me** (open seasonally)  Not frightening in any respect.

**Mission: Space**  Extremely intense space simulation ride frightens guests of all ages. Switching off provided (page 75).

**Test Track**  Intense thrill ride may frighten any age. Switching off provided (page 75).

**Journey into Imagination—Honey, I Shrunk the Audience**  Extremely intense visual effects and loudness frighten many young children.

**Journey into Imagination Ride**  Loud noises and unexpected flashing lights startle younger children.

**The Land—Living with the Land**  Not frightening in any respect.

**The Land—The Circle of Life**  Not frightening in any respect.

**The Land—Soarin'**  May frighten children age 7 and younger. Really a very sweet ride.

### WORLD SHOWCASE

**Mexico—El Río del Tiempo**  Not frightening in any respect.

**Norway—Maelstrom**  Visually intense in parts. Ride ends with a plunge down a 20-foot flume. A few preschoolers are frightened.

**China—Reflections of China**  Not frightening in any respect.

**Germany**  Not frightening in any respect.

**Italy**  Not frightening in any respect.

**The American Adventure**  Not frightening in any respect.

**Japan**  Not frightening in any respect.

**Morocco**  Not frightening in any respect.

**France—Impressions de France**  Not frightening in any respect.

**United Kingdom**  Not frightening in any respect.

**Canada—O Canada!**  Not frightening in any respect, but audience must stand.

## Disney-MGM Studios

**The Twilight Zone Tower of Terror**   Visually intimidating to young children; contains intense and realistic special effects. The plummeting elevator at the ride's end frightens many adults. Switching off provided (page 75).

**The Great Movie Ride**   Intense in parts, with very realistic special effects and some visually intimidating sights. Frightens many preschoolers.

**Who Wants to Be a Millionaire**   Not frightening in any respect.

**Sounds Dangerous**   Noises in the dark frighten some preschoolers.

**Indiana Jones Epic Stunt Spectacular!**   An intense show with powerful special effects, including explosions. Presented in an educational context that young children generally handle well.

**Rock 'n' Roller Coaster**   The wildest coaster at Walt Disney World. May frighten guests of any age. Switching off provided (page 75).

**Star Tours**   Extremely intense visually for all ages. Not as likely to cause motion sickness as Body Wars at Epcot. Switching off provided (page 75).

**Disney-MGM Studios Backlot Tour**   Sedate and nonintimidating except for "Catastrophe Canyon," where an earthquake and a flash flood are simulated. Prepare younger children for this part of the tour.

**Backstage Walking Tours**   Not frightening in any respect.

**Jim Henson's Muppet-Vision 3-D**   Intense and loud, but not frightening.

**Honey, I Shrunk the Kids Movie Set Adventure Playground**   Everything is oversized, but nothing is scary.

**Voyage of the Little Mermaid**   Not frightening in any respect.

**The Magic of Disney Animation**   Not frightening in any respect.

**Walt Disney: One Man's Dream**   Not frightening in any respect.

**Playhouse Disney: Live on Stage**   Not frightening in any respect.

**Fantasmic!**   Terrifies some preschoolers.

**Lights! Motors! Action! Extreme Stunt Show**   Intense with loud noises and explosions but not threatening in any way.

## Animal Kingdom

**The Boneyard**   Not frightening in any respect.

**Rafiki's Planet Watch**   Not frightening in any respect.

**Dinosaur**   High-tech thrill ride rattles riders of all ages. Switching off provided (page 75).

**TriceraTop Spin**   A midway-type ride that will frighten only a small percentage of younger children.

## Small Child Fright-Potential Chart (cont'd.)

### Animal Kingdom (continued)

**Primeval Whirl** A beginner roller coaster. Most children ages 7 and over will take it in stride.

**Festival of the Lion King** A bit loud, but otherwise not frightening in any respect.

**Flights of Wonder** Swooping birds alarm a few small children.

**Pangani Forest Exploration Trail** Not frightening in any respect.

**Pocahontas and Her Forest Friends** Not frightening in any respect.

**It's Tough to Be a Bug!** Very intense and loud with special effects that startle viewers of all ages and potentially terrify young children.

**Kilimanjaro Safaris** A "collapsing" bridge and the proximity of real animals make a few young children anxious.

**Maharaja Jungle Trek** Some children may balk at the bat exhibit.

**The Oasis** Not frightening in any respect.

**Kali River Rapids** Potentially frightening and certainly wet for guests of all ages. Switching off provided (page 75).

**Theater in the Wild** Not frightening in any respect, but loud.

**Wildlife Express Train** Not frightening in any respect.

**Expedition Everest** (opens 2006) Frightening to guests of all ages.

Most rides with age and height minimums load and unload in the same area, facilitating switching off. An exception is Space Mountain, where the first adult at the conclusion of the ride must also inform the unloading attendant that he or she is switching off. The attendant will admit the first adult to an internal stairway that goes back to the loading area.

# MEETING *the* DISNEY CHARACTERS

YOU CAN SEE DISNEY CHARACTERS IN live shows at all the theme parks and in parades at the Magic Kingdom and Disney-MGM Studios. Consult your daily entertainment schedule for times. If you want to meet the characters, get autographs, and take photos, consult the park map or the handout *Times Guide* sometimes provided to supplement the park map. If there is a particular character you're itching to meet, ask any cast member to call the character hotline for you. The hotline will tell you (via the cast member) if the character is out and about, and if so, where to find it.

*unofficial* **TIP**
If it's rainy at the Magic Kingdom, look for characters on the veranda of Tony's Town Square Restaurant or in the Town Square Exposition Hall next to Tony's.

**AT THE MAGIC KINGDOM** Characters are encountered more frequently here than anywhere else in Walt Disney World. There almost always will be a character next to City Hall on Main Street and usually one or more in Town Square or near the railroad station. Characters appear in all the lands but are more plentiful in Fantasyland and Mickey's Toontown Fair. At Mickey's Toontown Fair, you can meet Mickey privately in his "Judge's Tent." Characters actually work shifts at the Toontown Hall of Fame next to Mickey's Country House. Here, you can line up to meet different assortments of characters. Each assortment has its own greeting area and, of course, its own line. In Fantasyland, Cinderella regularly greets diners at Cinderella's Royal Table in the castle, and Ariel holds court in her own grotto. Nearby, check out the Fantasyland Character Festival by the lagoon opposite Dumbo. Also look for characters in the central hub and by Splash Mountain in Frontierland.

Characters are featured in afternoon and evening parades and also play a major role in Castle Forecourt shows (at the entrance to the castle on the moat side) and at the Galaxy Palace Theater in Tomorrowland. Find performance times for shows and parades in the park's daily entertainment schedule or *Times Guide*. Sometimes characters stay to greet the audience after shows.

**AT EPCOT** Although chance encounters with characters are less frequent at Epcot than at other parks, Epcot compensates by periodically bringing in characters by the busload (literally). Several times each day, a platoon of characters piles into a British double-decker bus and sets out for one of the countries in the World Showcase. When the bus stops, the characters hop off and mingle with the crowd, posing for pictures and signing autographs. The bus is dispatched about eight to ten times a day. Specific times and stops are listed in the Epcot handout park map. If you position yourself at a scheduled stop a few minutes before the bus arrives, you can score photos and autographs before everyone else arrives. In addition to the bus, character shows are performed daily at the

*unofficial* **TIP**
The Epcot character bus offers the easiest access to the most characters in one place in all of Walt Disney World.

American Gardens Theater World Showcase and at Guest Relations. Check the park's daily entertainment schedule or *Times Guide* for times.

**AT DISNEY-MGM STUDIOS** Characters are likely to turn up anywhere at the Studios but are most frequently found in front of the Animation Building, along Mickey Avenue (leading to the soundstages), at Al's Toy Barn, and at the end of the Streets of America backlot. Mickey and his "friends" pose for keepsake photos (about $14 each) on Hollywood Boulevard and Sunset Boulevard. Characters are also prominent in shows, with *Voyage of the Little Mermaid* running almost continuously and an abbreviated version of *Beauty and the Beast* performed several times daily at the Theater of the Stars. Check the daily entertainment schedule or *Times Guide* for show times at Crossroads of the World.

**AT THE ANIMAL KINGDOM** Camp Minnie-Mickey in the Animal Kingdom is a special location designed specifically for meeting characters. There are designated character greeting "trails" where you can meet Mickey, Minnie, and various characters from *The Jungle Book* and *The Lion King*. Also at Camp Minnie-Mickey are two stage shows featuring characters from *The Lion King* and *Pocahontas*.

## CHARACTER DINING

FRATERNIZING WITH CHARACTERS HAS become so popular that Disney offers character breakfasts, brunches, and dinners where families can dine in the presence of Mickey, Minnie, Goofy, and other costumed versions of animated celebrities. Besides grabbing customers from Denny's and Hardee's, character meals provide a familiar, controlled setting in which young children can warm gradually to characters. All meals are attended by several characters. Adult prices apply to persons ages 12 or older, children's prices to ages 3–11. Little ones under age 3 eat free. For additional information on character dining, call ☎ 407-939-3463 (WDW-DINE).

*unofficial* **TIP**
Many children particularly enjoy meals with "face characters" such as Snow White, Belle, Jasmine, Cinderella, and Aladdin, who speak and are thus able to engage children in a way not possible for the mute animal characters.

Because character dining is very popular, we recommend that you arrange advance reservation as far in advance as possible by calling ☎ 407-939-3463. Advance reservation is not a reservation, only a commitment to seat you ahead of walk-in patrons at the scheduled date and time. A reserved table won't await you, but you will be seated ahead of patrons who failed to call ahead. Even with advance reservation, expect to wait at least 10–30 minutes to be seated.

## How to Choose a Character Meal

We receive a lot of mail asking for advice about character meals. In fact, some *are* better than others, sometimes much better. Here's what we look for when we evaluate character meals:

**1. THE CHARACTERS** The various meals offer a diverse assortment of Disney characters. Selecting a meal that features your children's special favorites is a good first step. Check the Character Meal Hit Parade chart to see which characters are assigned to each meal.

**2. ATTENTION FROM THE CHARACTERS** In all character meals, the characters circulate among the guests hugging children, posing for pictures, and signing autographs. How much time a character spends with you and your children depends primarily on the ratio of characters to guests. The more characters and fewer guests the better. Because many character meals never fill to capacity, the Character-to-Guest Ratios found in our Character Meal Hit Parade chart have been adjusted to reflect an average attendance as opposed to a sell-out crowd. Even so, there's quite a range.

**3. THE SETTING** Some character meals are staged in exotic settings, while for others, moving the venue to an elementary school cafeteria would be an improvement. In our chart we rate the setting of each character meal with the familiar scale of 0–5 stars. Two restaurants, Cinderella's Royal Table in the Magic Kingdom and the Garden Grill in the Land pavilion at Epcot, deserve special mention. Cinderella's Royal Table is situated on the first and second floors of Cinderella Castle in Fantasyland, offering guests a look at the inside of the castle. The Garden Grill is a revolving restaurant that overlooks several scenes from the Living with the Land boat ride attraction.

**4. THE FOOD** Although some food served at character meals is quite good, most is average—in other words palatable but nothing to get excited about. In terms of variety, consistency, and quality, restaurants generally do a better job with breakfast than with lunch or dinner (if served). Some restaurants offer a buffet, while others opt for "one-skillet," family-style service where all the hot items on the bill of fare are served

# Character Meal Hit Parade

## 1. CINDERELLA'S ROYAL TABLE

RANK 1

**LOCATION**
Magic Kingdom

**MEALS SERVED**
Breakfast/Lunch

**CHARACTERS**
Cinderella, Snow White, Belle, Jasmine, Aladdin

**SERVED** Daily

**SETTING** ★★★★★

**SERVICE**
Buffet/Family style

**FOOD VARIETY AND QUALITY**
★★★

**NOISE LEVEL** Quiet

**CHARACTER TO GUEST RATIO**
1 to 26

## 2. AKERSHUS PRINCESS STORYBOOK BREAKFAST

RANK 2

**LOCATION**
Epcot

**MEALS SERVED**
Breakfast/Lunch/Dinner

**CHARACTERS**
4–6 characters chosen from Belle, Mulan, Snow White, Sleeping Beauty, Esmeralda, Mary Poppins, Jasmine, Pocahontas

**SERVED** Daily

**SETTING** ★★★★

**SERVICE** Family style

**FOOD VARIETY AND QUALITY**
★★★½

**NOISE LEVEL** Quiet

**CHARACTER TO GUEST RATIO**
1 to 54

## 3. CHEF MICKEY'S

RANK 3

**LOCATION**
Contemporary

**MEALS SERVED**
Breakfast/Dinner

**CHARACTERS**
*Breakfast:*
Minnie, Mickey, Chip, Pluto, Goofy
*Dinner:*
Mickey, Pluto, Chip, Dale, Goofy

**SERVED** Daily

**SETTING** ★★★

**SERVICE** Buffet

**FOOD VARIETY AND QUALITY**
★★★ (breakfast)
★★★½ (dinner)

**NOISE LEVEL** Loud

**CHARACTER TO GUEST RATIO**
1 to 56

## 7. LIBERTY TREE TAVERN

RANK 7

**LOCATION**
Magic Kingdom

**MEALS SERVED**
Dinner

**CHARACTERS**
Minnie, Pluto, Donald Duck, Meeko, Chip and/or Dale

**SERVED** Daily

**SETTING** ★★★½

**SERVICE** Family style

**FOOD VARIETY AND QUALITY**
★★★

**NOISE LEVEL** Moderate

**CHARACTER TO GUEST RATIO**
1 to 26

## 8. RESTURANTOSAURUS

RANK 8

**LOCATION**
Animal Kingdom

**MEALS SERVED**
Breakfast

**CHARACTERS**
Mickey, Donald, Pluto, Goofy

**SERVED** Daily

**SETTING** ★★★

**SERVICE** Buffet

**FOOD VARIETY AND QUALITY**
★★★

**NOISE LEVEL** Very loud

**CHARACTER TO GUEST RATIO**
1 to 112

## 9. CAPE MAY CAFE

RANK 9

**LOCATION**
Beach Club

**MEALS SERVED**
Breakfast

**CHARACTERS**
Goofy, Chip, Dale, Pluto

**SERVED** Daily

**SETTING** ★★★

**SERVICE** Buffet

**FOOD VARIETY AND QUALITY**
★★½

**NOISE LEVEL** Moderate

**CHARACTER TO GUEST RATIO**
1 to 67

## 4. CRYSTAL PALACE

**RANK** 4

**LOCATION**
Magic Kingdom

**MEALS SERVED**
Breakfast/Lunch/Dinner

**CHARACTERS**
*Breakfast:*
Pooh, Tigger, Eeyore, Piglet
*Dinner:*
Pooh, Tigger, Eeyore

**SERVED** Daily

**SETTING** ★★★

**SERVICE** Buffet

**FOOD VARIETY AND QUALITY**
★★½ (breakfast)
★★★ (dinner)

**NOISE LEVEL** Very loud

**CHARACTER TO GUEST RATIO**
1 to 67 (breakfast)
1 to 89 (dinner)

## 5. 1900 PARK FARE

**RANK** 5

**LOCATION**
Grand Floridian

**MEALS SERVED**
Breakfast/Dinner

**CHARACTERS**
*Breakfast:*
Mary Poppins and friends
*Dinner:*
Cinderella and friends

**SERVED** Daily

**SETTING** ★★★

**SERVICE** Buffet

**FOOD VARIETY AND QUALITY**
★★★ (breakfast)
★★★½ (dinner)

**NOISE LEVEL** Moderate

**CHARACTER TO GUEST RATIO**
1 to 54 (breakfast)
1 to 44 (dinner)

## 6. GARDEN GRILL

**RANK** 6

**LOCATION**
Epcot

**MEALS SERVED**
Lunch/Dinner

**CHARACTERS**
Chip, Dale,
Mickey, Pluto

**SERVED** Daily

**SETTING** ★★★★½

**SERVICE** Family style

**FOOD VARIETY AND QUALITY**
★★½

**NOISE LEVEL** Very quiet

**CHARACTER TO GUEST RATIO**
1 to 46

## 10. OHANA

**RANK** 10

**LOCATION**
Polynesian Resort

**MEALS SERVED**
Breakfast

**CHARACTERS**
Mickey, Goofy,
Chip, Dale

**SERVED** Daily

**SETTING** ★★

**SERVICE** Family style

**FOOD VARIETY AND QUALITY**
★★½

**NOISE LEVEL** Moderate

**CHARACTER TO GUEST RATIO**
1 to 57

## 11. GULLIVER'S GRILL

**RANK** 11

**LOCATION**
Swan

**MEALS SERVED**
Dinner

**CHARACTERS**
Goofy and
Pluto or Rafiki and
Timon

**SERVED** Daily

**SETTING** ★★★

**SERVICE** Buffet/Menu

**FOOD VARIETY AND QUALITY**
★★★½

**NOISE LEVEL** Moderate

**CHARACTER TO GUEST RATIO**
1 to 198

## 12. GARDEN GROVE CAFE

**RANK** 12

**LOCATION**
Swan

**MEALS SERVED**
Breakfast

**CHARACTERS**
Goofy and Pluto

**SERVED**
Saturday and Sunday

**SETTING** ★★★

**SERVICE** Buffet/Menu

**FOOD VARIETY AND QUALITY**
★★★½

**NOISE LEVEL** Moderate

**CHARACTER TO GUEST RATIO**
1 to 198

from the same pot or skillet. To help you sort it out, we rate the food at each character meal in our chart using the tried-and-true five-star scale.

**5. THE PROGRAM** Some larger restaurants stage modest performances where the characters dance, head up a parade, conga line around the room, or lead songs and cheers. For some guests, these productions lend a celebratory air to the proceedings; for others, they turn what was already mayhem into absolute chaos. In either event, the antics consume time that the characters could be spending with families at their table.

**6. NOISE** If you want to eat in peace, character meals are a bad choice. That having been said, some are much noisier than others. Once again, our chart gives you some idea of what to expect.

**7. WHICH MEAL?** Although character breakfasts seem to be the most popular, character lunches and dinners are usually more practical because they do not interfere with your early-morning touring. During hot weather especially, a character lunch at midday can be heavenly.

**8. COST** Dinners cost more than lunches, and lunches are more than breakfasts. Prices for any given meal vary only about $4 from the least expensive to the most expensive restaurant. Breakfasts run $15–$20 for adults and $8–$12 for children ages 3–9. For character lunches, expect to pay $18–$25 for adults and $10–$12 for kids. Dinners are $22–$25 for adults and $10–$12 for children. Little ones ages 2 and under eat free.

**9. ADVANCE RESERVATIONS** The Disney dining reservations system makes advanced reservations for character meals up to 90 days prior to the day you wish to dine. Advanced reservations for most character meals is easy to obtain even if you forget to call until a couple of weeks before you leave home. Breakfast and lunch at Cinderella's Royal Table are another story; it is without doubt the hottest ticket at Disney World.

**10. HOMELESS CHARACTERS** Because of decreased attendance at Walt Disney World through much of 2005, several character meals were eliminated. Our advice is reconfirm all character meal advance reservations three weeks or so before you leave home by calling ☎ 407-WDW-DINE.

**11. FRIENDS** For some venues, Disney has stopped specifying the characters scheduled for a particular character meal. Instead, they tell you that it's a certain character "and friends." For example, "Pooh and friends," meaning Eeyore, Piglet, and Tigger, or some combination thereof, or "Mickey and friends" with some assortment chosen from among Minnie, Goofy, Pluto, Donald, Daisy, Chip, and Dale. Most are pretty self-evident, but others such as "Mary Poppins and friends" are unclear.

# BABYSITTING

**CHILDCARE CENTERS** Childcare isn't available within the theme parks, but each Magic Kingdom resort connected by the monorail or boat, each Epcot resort (BoardWalk Inn and Villas, Yacht and Beach Club resorts), and the Animal Kingdom Lodge have a childcare center for potty-trained children older than age 3. Services vary, but children generally can be left between 4:30 p.m. and midnight. Milk and cookies and blankets and pillows are provided at all childcare centers, and dinner is provided at most. Play is supervised but not organized, and toys, videos, and games are plentiful. Guests at any Disney resort or campground may use the childcare services.

The most elaborate of the childcare centers (variously called "clubs" or "camps") is Neverland Club at the Polynesian Resort. The rates for children ages 4–12 are $10 per hour per child.

All clubs accept advance reservations (some six months in advance!) with a credit-card guarantee. Either call the club directly or reserve through Disney central reservations at ☎ 407-WDW-DINE. Most clubs require a 24-hour cancellation notice and levy a hefty penalty charge of $15 per child for no-shows. A limited number of walk-ins are usually available on a first-come, first-serve basis.

**IN-ROOM BABYSITTING** There are three companies that provide in-room sitting in Walt Disney World and surrounding tourists areas, including the International Drive/Orange County Convention Center area, the Universal Orlando area, and the Lake Buena Vista area. They are **Kid's Nite Out** (☎ 407-827-5444), **All About Kids** (☎ 407-812-9300) and the **Fairy Godmothers** (☎ 407-277-3724). Kid's Nite Out also serves hotels in the greater Orlando area, including downtown. All three provide sitters over 18 years of age who are insured, bonded, and trained in CPR. Some sitters have more advanced medical/first-aid training and/or education credentials. All sitters are screened, reference-checked, and police-checked. In addition to caring for your children in your guest room, the sitters will, if you direct (and pay), take your children to the theme parks or other venues of your choice. Many of the sitters arrive loaded with reading books, coloring books, and games. All three services offer bilingual sitters.

| CHILDCARE CLUBS* | | |
|---|---|---|
| HOTEL/PHONE | NAME OF PROGRAM | AGES |
| Animal Kingdom Lodge ☎ 407-938-4785 | Simba's Cubhouse | 4–12 |
| Dolphin ☎ 407-934-4241 | Camp Dolphin | 4–12 |
| Grand Floridian Beach Resort ☎ 407-824-1666 | Mouseketeer Club | 4–12 |
| The Hilton ☎ 407-812-9300 | All About Kids | 4–12 |
| Polynesian Resort ☎ 407-824-2000 | Neverland Club | 4–12 |
| Swan ☎ 407-934-1621 | Camp Dolphin | 4–12 |
| Yacht and Beach Club resorts ☎ 407-934-7000 | Sandcastle Club | 4–12 |
| Wilderness Lodge & Villas ☎ 407-824-1083 | Cub's Den | 4–12 |
| Wyndham Palace ☎ 407-812-9300 | All About Kids | All |

*Childcare clubs operate afternoons and evenings. Before 4 p.m., call the hotel rather than the number listed above. All programs require reservations.*

# PART FIVE

# SPECIAL TIPS *for* SPECIAL PEOPLE

# WALT DISNEY WORLD *for* SINGLES

WALT DISNEY WORLD IS GREAT FOR SINGLES. It is safe, clean, and low-pressure. If you're looking for a place to relax without being hit on, Disney World is perfect. Bars, lounges, and nightclubs are the most laid-back and friendly you're likely to find anywhere. In many, you can hang out and not even be asked to buy a drink (or asked to let someone buy a drink for you). Parking lots are well lit and constantly patrolled. For women alone, safety and comfort are unsurpassed.

*unofficial* **TIP**
Virtually every type of entertainment performed fully clothed is available at an amazingly reasonable price at a Disney nightspot.

There's also no need to while away the evening hours alone in your hotel room. Between the BoardWalk and Downtown Disney, nightlife options abound. If you drink more than you should and are a Disney resort guest, Disney buses will return you safely to your hotel.

# WALT DISNEY WORLD *for* COUPLES

### WEDDINGS AND HONEYMOONS

DISNEY'S FAIRY TALE WEDDINGS & HONEYMOONS department offers a range of wedding venues, services, and honeymoon packages (adaptations of the regular Walt Disney

Travel Company vacations). No special rooms or honeymoon suites are included unless you upgrade. In fact, the only honeymoon features are room service (in one package) and a photo session and keepsake album (in two others). Package rates range from $1,800–$4,200. Call the wedding coordinator at ☎ 407-939-4610 or 877-566-0969 or visit **www.disney wedding.com** for more information.

## ROMANTIC GETAWAYS

YOU DON'T HAVE TO BUY A HONEYMOON package to enjoy a romantic interlude, but not all Disney hotels are equally romantic. Some are too family oriented; others swarm with convention-goers. We recommend these Disney lodgings for romantics:

- Animal Kingdom Lodge
- Polynesian Resort
- Wilderness Lodge and Villas
- Grand Floridian Beach Resort
- BoardWalk Inn and Villas
- Yacht and Beach Club resorts

All of these properties are expensive. There are also secluded rooms in the Alligator Bayou section of Port Orleans Riverside.

## QUIET, ROMANTIC PLACES TO EAT

QUIET, ROMANTIC RESTAURANTS WITH good food are rare in the theme parks. Only the Coral Reef, the terrace at the Rose and Crown, and the San Angel Inn at Epcot satisfy both requirements. Waterfront dining is available at Portobello Yacht Club and Fulton's Crab House at Pleasure Island, and Narcoossee's at the Grand Floridian.

The California Grill atop the Contemporary Resort has the best view at Walt Disney World. If window tables aren't available, ask to be served in the adjoining lounge. Victoria & Albert's at the Grand Floridian is the World's showcase gourmet restaurant; expect to pay big bucks. Other good choices for couples include Shula's Steakhouse at the Dolphin, Jiko at the Animal Kingdom Lodge, and Spoodles and The Flying Fish Café at the BoardWalk.

Eating later in the evening and choosing among the restaurants we've mentioned will improve your chances for quiet, intimate dining, but children—well-behaved or otherwise—are everywhere at Walt Disney World, and you won't escape them.

# WALT DISNEY WORLD
# *for* SENIORS

MOST SENIORS WE INTERVIEW ENJOY Disney World much more when they tour with folks their own age. If, however, you're considering going to Disney World with your grand-children, we recommend an orientation visit without them first. If you know first-hand what to expect, it's much easier to establish limits, maintain control, and set a comfortable pace when you visit with the youngsters.

If you're determined to take the grandkids, read carefully those sections of this book that discuss family touring. Because seniors are a varied and willing lot, there aren't any attractions we would suggest they avoid. For seniors, as with other Disney visitors, personal taste is more important than age. We hate to see mature visitors pass an exceptional attraction like Splash Mountain because younger visitors call it a "thrill ride." A full-blown adventue, Splash Moun-tain gets its appeal more from music and visual effects than from the thrill of the ride. Because you must choose among attractions that might interest you, we provide facts to help you make informed decisions.

## GETTING AROUND

MANY SENIORS LIKE TO WALK, BUT A seven-hour visit to one of the theme parks normally includes four to eight miles on foot. If you aren't up for that much hiking, let a more ath-letic member of your party push you in a rented wheelchair. The theme parks also offer fun-to-drive electric carts (con-venience vehicles). You can rent a chair at the Magic Kingdom in the morning, return it, go to Epcot, present your deposit slip, and get another chair at no additional charge.

## LODGING

IF YOU CAN AFFORD IT, STAY IN Walt Disney World. If you're concerned about the quality of your accommodations or the availability of transportation, staying inside the Dis-ney complex will ease your mind. The rooms are some of the nicest in the Orlando area and are always clean and well maintained. Plus, transportation is always available to any destination in Disney World at no additional cost.

Disney hotels reserve rooms closer to restaurants and transportation for guests of any age who can't tolerate much walking. They also provide golf carts to pick up from and deliver guests to their rooms. Cart service can vary dramatically depending on the time of day and the number of guests requesting service. At check-in time (around 3 p.m.), for example, the wait for a ride can be as long as 40 minutes.

The Contemporary Resort is a good choice for seniors who want to be on the monorail system. So are the Grand Floridian and Polynesian resorts, though both sprawl over many acres, necessitating a lot of walking. For a restful, rustic feeling, choose the Wilderness Lodge and Villas. If you want a kitchen and all the comforts of home, book Old Key West Resort, the Beach Club Villas, or BoardWalk Villas. If you enjoy watching birds and animals, try Animal Kingdom Lodge.

RVers will find pleasant surroundings at Disney's Fort Wilderness Campground. There are also several KOA campgrounds within 20 minutes of Disney World. None offer the wilderness setting or amenities that Disney does, but they cost less.

## SENIOR DINING

EAT BREAKFAST AT YOUR HOTEL RESTAURANT or save money by having juice and rolls in your room. Although you aren't allowed to bring food into the parks, fruit, fruit juice, and soft drinks are sold throughout Disney World. Follow with an early dinner and be out of the restaurants, rested and ready for evening touring and fireworks, long before the main crowd begins to think about dinner. We recommend seniors fit dining and rest times into the day. Plan lunch as your break in the day. Sit back, relax, and enjoy. Then return to your hotel for a nap.

*unofficial* **TIP**
Make your advance reservations for before noon to avoid the lunch crowds.

# WALT DISNEY WORLD *for* DISABLED GUESTS

VALUABLE INFORMATION FOR TRIP PLANNING is available at the Web site **www.disneyworld.com.** At Walt Disney World, each of the major theme parks offers a free booklet describing disabled services and facilities at that park. The Disney people are somewhat resistant to mailing you the theme-park booklets in advance, but if you are polite and persistent, they can usually be persuaded. The same information can be found on the Web site. Type "Guest Disabilities FAQ" in the search tool and browse through the results.

For specific requests, including specialized accommodations at the resort hotels or on the Disney Transportation System, call ☎ 407-939-7807 (voice) or ☎ 407-939-7670 (TTY). When the recorded menu comes up, touch "1" on your Touch-Tone phone. Calls to this number should be strictly limited to questions and requests regarding disabled services and accommodations. Other questions should be addressed to ☎ 407-824-4321.

## VISITORS WITH SPECIAL NEEDS

**WHOLLY OR PARTIALLY NONAMBULATORY** Guests may easily rent wheelchairs. Most rides, shows, attractions, restrooms, and restaurants in the World accommodate the nonambulatory disabled. If you're in a theme park and need assistance, go to Guest Relations. A limited number of electric carts (motorized convenience vehicles) are available for rent. Easy and fun to drive, they give nonambulatory guests a tremendous degree of freedom and mobility.

Close-in parking is available for disabled visitors at all Disney lots. Request directions when you pay your parking fee. All monorails and most rides, shows, restrooms, and restaurants accommodate wheelchairs.

An information booklet for disabled guests is available at wheelchair rental locations in each park. Theme-park maps issued to each guest on admission are symbol-coded to show nonambulatory guests which attractions accommodate wheelchairs.

Even if an attraction doesn't accommodate wheelchairs, nonambulatory guests still may ride if they can transfer from their wheelchair to the ride's vehicle. Disney staff, however, aren't trained or permitted to assist in transfers. Guests must be able to board the ride unassisted or have a member of their party assist them. Either way, members of the nonambulatory guest's party will be permitted to go along on the ride.

Because waiting areas of most attractions won't accommodate wheelchairs, nonambulatory guests and their party should request boarding instructions from a Disney attendant as soon as they arrive at an attraction. Almost always, the entire group will be allowed to board without a lengthy wait.

**VISITORS WITH DIETARY RESTRICTIONS** can be assisted at Guest Relations in the theme parks. For Walt Disney World restaurants outside the theme parks, call the restaurant a day in advance for assistance.

**SIGHT- AND/OR HEARING-IMPAIRED GUESTS** Guest Relations at the theme parks provides complimentary tape cassettes and portable tape players to assist sight-impaired guests ($25 refundable deposit required). At the same locations, TDDs are available for hearing-impaired guests. In addition to TDDs, many pay phones in the major parks are equipped with amplifying headsets. See your Disney map for locations.

In addition, braille guide maps are available from Guest Relations at all theme parks. Closed captioning is provided on some rides, while many theater attractions provide reflective captioning. Walt Disney World will provide an interpreter for the live theater shows. To reserve an interpreter, call ☎ 407-824-4321 (voice) or 407-939-8255 (TTY).

**NON-APPARENT DISABILITIES** We receive many letters from readers whose traveling companion or child requires special assistance, but who, unlike a individual on crutches or in a wheelchair, is not visibly disabled. Some conditions, autism for example, make it very difficult or even impossible to wait in lines for more than a few minutes, or in queues surrounded by a large number of people.

One of the first things to do is obtain a letter from the disabled party's primary physician that explains the specific condition and any special needs the condition implies. The doctor's letter should be explicit enough to fully convey the nature of the condition to the Disney cast member reading the letter. Bring your doctor's note to the Guest Relations window at any Disney theme park and ask for a Guest Assistance Card. The Guest Assistance Card is a special pass designed to allow the disabled individual and his touring companions to wait in a separate, uncrowded holding area, apart from the regular queues at most attractions. One card is good for all four parks, so you do not need to obtain separate cards at each park. You should also pick up a copy of each park's *Guidebook for Guests with Disabilities* (also available online at **www.disneyworld.com**).

# PART SIX

# ARRIVING *and* GETTING AROUND

# GETTING THERE

## DIRECTIONS

MOTORISTS CAN REACH ANY WALT DISNEY World destination via World Drive off US 192, or via Epcot Drive off I-4
(see map, pages 6–7).

**WARNING!** I-4, connecting Daytona and Tampa, generally
runs east to west but takes a north/south slant through the
Orlando/Kissimmee area. This directional change compli-
cates getting oriented in and around Disney World. Logic
suggests that highways branching off I-4 should run north
and south, but most run east/west here. Until you're somewhat familiar with the area, have a good map at your side.

**FROM I-10** Take I-10 east across Florida to I-75 southbound.
Exit I-75 onto the Florida Turnpike. Exit onto I-4 westbound. Take Exit 67, marked Epcot/Downtown Disney, and
follow the signs to your Disney destination.

**FROM I-75 SOUTHBOUND** Follow I-75 south to the Florida
Turnpike. Exit onto I-4 westbound. Take Exit 67, marked
Epcot/Downtown Disney, and follow the signs to your Dis-
ney destination.

**FROM I-95 SOUTHBOUND** Follow I-95 south to I-4. Go west
on I-4, passing through Orlando. Take Exit 67, marked
Epcot/Downtown Disney, and follow signs to your Disney
destination.

**FROM DAYTONA OR ORLANDO** Go west on I-4 through
Orlando. Take Exit 67, marked Epcot/Downtown Disney,
and follow the signs.

## *Lake Buena Vista Resort Area and the I-4 Corridor*

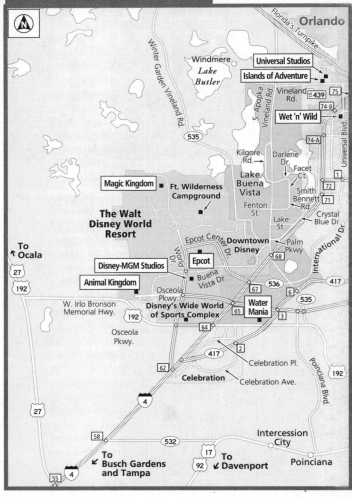

**FROM THE ORLANDO INTERNATIONAL AIRPORT** Leaving the airport, go southwest on the Central Florida Greenway (FL 417), a toll road. Take Exit 6 onto FL 536. FL 536 will cross over I-4 and become Epcot Drive. From here, follow the signs to your destination. An alternate route is to take FL 528 (Beeline Highway toll road) west for approximately 12 miles to the intersection with I-4. Go west on I-4 to Exit 67, marked Epcot/Downtown Disney, and follow the signs.

**FROM MIAMI, FORT LAUDERDALE, AND SOUTHEASTERN FLORIDA** Head north on the Florida Turnpike to I-4 westbound. Take Exit 67, marked as Epcot/Downtown Disney, and follow the signs.

**FROM TAMPA AND SOUTHWESTERN FLORIDA** Take I-75 northbound to I-4. Go east on I-4, take Exit 64 onto US 192 westbound, and then follow the signs.

## Walt Disney World Exits Off I-4

Going east to west (in the direction of Orlando to Tampa), four I-4 exits serve Walt Disney World. Note that exit numbers changed in 2002.

**EXIT 68** (marked FL 535/Lake Buena Vista) primarily serves the Downtown Disney Resort Area and Downtown Disney, including the Disney Village Marketplace, Pleasure Island, and Disney's West Side. This exit puts you on roads with lots of traffic signals. Avoid it unless you're headed to one of the above destinations.

**EXIT 67** (marked Epcot/Downtown Disney) delivers you to a four-lane expressway right into the heart of Disney World. It's the fastest and most convenient way for westbound travelers to access almost all Disney World destinations except the new Animal Kingdom and Disney's Wide World of Sports.

**EXIT 65** (marked Osceola Parkway) is the best exit for westbound travelers to access the Animal Kingdom, Animal Kingdom Ldoge, Pop Century Resort, All Star Resorts, and Wide World of Sports.

**EXIT 64** (marked US 192/Magic Kingdom) is the best route for eastbound travelers to all Disney World destinations. For westbound travelers, it's the best exit for accessing the Animal Kingdom and Disney's Wide World of Sports.

## GETTING TO WALT DISNEY WORLD FROM THE AIRPORT

IF YOU ARRIVE IN ORLANDO BY PLANE, there are three basic options for getting to Walt Disney World:

**1. TAXI** Taxis carry four to eight passengers (depending on the type of vehicle). Rates vary according to distance. If your hotel is in Walt Disney World, your fare will be about $35, not including tip. For the US 192 "Main Gate" area, your fare will be about $45. If you go to International Drive or downtown Orlando, expect to pay about $36.

**2. SHUTTLE SERVICE** Mears Motor Transportation Service (☎ 407-423-5566) operates from Orlando International Airport. Although this is the shuttle service that will provide your transportation if "airport transfers" are included in your vacation package, you do not have to be on a package to avail yourself of their services. In practice, the shuttles collect passengers until they fill a van (or sometimes a bus). Once the vehicle is full or close to full, it's dispatched. Mears charges *per-person* rates (children under age 4 ride free). Both one-way and round-trip service are available (**www.mearstransportation.com**).

| FROM THE AIRPORT TO: | ONE-WAY Adult/Child | ROUND TRIP Adult/Child |
|---|---|---|
| International Drive | $15/$11 | $25/$18 |
| Downtown Orlando | $15/$11 | $25/$18 |
| Walt Disney World/Lake Buena Vista | $17/$13 | $29/$21 |
| US 192 "Main Gate" Area | $17/$13 | $29/$21 |

**3. TOWN-CAR** Service Similar to taxi service, a town-car service will transport you directly from Orlando International Airport to your hotel. Instead of hailing a car outside the airport, however, the town-car driver will usually be waiting for you in the baggage claim area of your airline.

Tiffany Towncar Service (☎ 888-838-2161 or 407-251-5431 or check **www.tiffanytowncar.com**) provides a prompt, clean ride. They also received the best reviews from Disney bellhops. A round trip to a Disney resort will cost $85–$90, while the round-trip fee to a non-Disney resort is $80–$90, not including tip. Figure on about half as much for a one-way trip. What Tiffany offers that other taxi and town car services do not is a free stop at a local Publix supermarket on the way to your hotel.

*unofficial* **TIP**
Be sure to check Tiffany's Web site for a coupon worth $5 off a round trip.

Quicksilver Tours & Transportation (☎ 888-GO-TO-WDW or 407-299-1431; **www.quicksilver-tours.com**) offers 10-person limos and vans in addition to Town Cars. Rates for a round-trip range from $90 to $100 depending on location. Like Tiffany, Quicksilver throws in a stop at the supermarket en route.

**4. RENTAL CARS** Rental cars are readily available for both short- and long-term rentals. Most rental car companies allow you to drop a rental car at certain hotels or one of their subsidiary locations in the Walt Disney World general area if you do not want the car for your entire stay. Likewise, you can pick up a car at any time during your stay at the same hotels and locations without trekking back to the airport. A list of discount codes for rental cars also can be found at **www.mousesavers.com.** With a little effort, you can often get a great deal.

## DISNEY'S MAGICAL EXPRESS

DISNEY'S MAGICAL EXPRESS IS A FREE bus service running between the Orlando International Airport and most Walt Disney World hotels during Disney's "Happiest Celebration on Earth" promotion (ending November 2006). All guests staying at a Disney-owned and -operated resort are eligible, even if the stay was booked independent of the Disney Travel Company. (Guests staying at the Swan, Dolphin, and Shades of Green are not eligible, as these hotels are independently owned.) In addition to transportation, Magical Express provides free luggage service between your airline and Disney hotel.

You should receive special Magical Express luggage tags about two weeks prior to your departure date. Put a tag on any piece of luggage you plan to check with the airline. When you arrive at the airport, check the bags as you normally would. If you're traveling within the United States, you'll arrive in Orlando and follow the Magical Express signs to your bus; your luggage should be waiting in your hotel room when you check in. (International travelers must retrieve their bags to go through customs. After passing through customs, you'll also head for a bus. Your bags are returned to baggage claim and Disney takes over from there.) Behind the scenes, Disney baggage handlers work with your airline to retrieve suitcases marked with those special tags. All tagged luggage is sent to an airport warehouse, where it's sorted by destination then loaded onto a truck for delivery. At the resort, the luggage is matched to your reservation. If your room is ready, the luggage is brought up; otherwise it's held by the bellmen until you can check in.

In practice the logistical challenge of matching totes and tourists is proving to be a bit more than Disney bargained for, with lost and delayed baggage marring the service's rollout.

## RENTING A CAR

READERS PLANNING TO STAY IN THE WORLD frequently ask if they will need a car. If your plans don't include restaurants, attractions, or other destinations outside of Disney

World, the answer is a very qualified no. However, consider, the following:

**Plan to Rent a Car:**

1. If your hotel is outside Walt Disney World
2. If your hotel is in Walt Disney World and you want to dine someplace other than the theme parks and your own hotel
3. If you plan to return to your hotel for naps or swimming during the day
4. If you plan on going to other area theme parks or swimming parks (including Disney's)

# GETTING ORIENTED

## A GOOD MAP

READERS FREQUENTLY COMPLAIN ABOUT signs and maps provided by Disney. While it's easy to find the major theme parks, it can be quite an odyssey to locate other Walt Disney World destinations. Many Disney-supplied maps are stylized and hard to read, while others provide incomplete information. The most easily obtained map is the Walt Disney World Transportation Guide/Map. Available at any resort, theme-park bus information station, or theme-park guest relations office, the Guide/Map features a slightly reduced version of the Walt Disney World Property Map on one side and Disney Transportation System information on the other.

A very good map of the general Orlando/Kissimmee/Disney World area is available free at the **AAA Car Care Center,** operated by Goodyear and located in Walt Disney World near the Magic Kingdom parking lot (see map on pages 6–7). Just request the map at the counter.

# HOW *to* TRAVEL *around* *the* WORLD

## TRANSPORTATION TRADE-OFFS FOR GUESTS: LODGING OUTSIDE WALT DISNEY WORLD

DISNEY DAY-GUESTS (THOSE NOT STAYING inside Disney World) can use the monorail system, the bus system, and the boat system. If, for example, you go to Disney-MGM Studios in the morning, then decide to go to Epcot for lunch, you can take a bus directly there. The most important advice we can give day-guests is to park your car in the lot of the theme park (or other Disney destination) where you plan to finish your day. This is critical if you stay at a park until closing time.

## ALL YOU NEED TO KNOW ABOUT DRIVING TO THE THEME PARKS

**1. POSITIONING OF THE PARKING LOTS** The Animal Kingdom, Disney-MGM Studios, and Epcot parking lots are adjacent to the park entrance. The Magic Kingdom parking lot is adjacent to the Transportation and Ticket center (TTC). From the TTC you can take a ferry or monorail to the Magic Kingdom entrance.

**2. PAYING TO PARK** Disney resort guests and annual passholders park free. All others pay. If you pay to park, keep your receipt. If you move your car during the day to another theme park you will not have to pay again if you show your receipt.

**3. FINDING YOUR CAR WHEN IT'S TIME TO DEPART** The theme park parking lots are huge. Jot down the section and row where you park. If you are driving a rental car, jot down the license number (you wouldn't believe how many white rental cars there are).

**4. GETTING FROM YOUR CAR TO THE PARK ENTRANCE** Each parking lot provides trams to transport you to the park entrance, or in the case of the Magic Kingdom, to the TTC. If you arrive early in the morning, you may find that it is faster to walk to the entrance (or to the TTC) than to take the tram.

**5. A TIP FOR PARKING AT THE DISNEY-MGM STUDIOS** The Disney-MGM Studios has two parking entrances, one off World Drive and one off Buena Vista Drive. If you want to park within walking distance of the park entrance, access the Studios from World Drive (cars from the Buena Vista entrance are parked in the boonies no matter how early they arrive).

*unofficial* **TIP**
If you plan to park-hop, make sure your car is parked in the lot of the theme park where you plan to finish the day.

**6. HOW MUCH TIME TO ALLOT FOR PARKING AND GETTING TO THE PARK ENTRANCE** At Epcot and the Animal Kingdom, it will take about 10–15 minutes to pay, park, and walk or ride to the park entrance. At the Disney-MGM Studios, allow 10–15 minutes; at the Magic Kingdom, it's 15 minutes to get to the TTC and another 15–20 to reach the park entrance via the monorail (3½ minutes one way) or the ferry (6½ minutes one way).

**7. COMMUTING FROM PARK TO PARK** You can commute to the other theme parks via Disney bus, or to and from the

Magic Kingdom and Epcot by monorail. You can also, of course, commute via your own car. Using Disney transportation or your own car, allow 45–60 minutes entrance to entrance one way.

**8. LEAVING THE PARK AT THE END OF THE DAY** If you stay at a park until closing, expect the parking lot trams, the monorails, and the ferries to be mobbed. If the wait for the parking lot tram is unacceptable, you can either walk to your car, or walk to the first tram stop on the route and wait there until a tram arrives. When some people get off, you can get on and continue to your appropriate stop.

**9. DINNER AND A QUICK EXIT** One way to beat closing crowds at the Magic Kingdom is to arrange a advance reservation for dinner at one of the restaurants at the Contemporary Resort. When you leave the Magic kingdom to go to dinner, move your car from the TTC lot to the Contemporary Resort. After dinner, either walk (eight minutes) or take the monorail back to the Magic Kingdom. When the park closes and everyone else is fighting their way onto the monorail or ferry, you can stroll leisurely back to the Contemporary, pick up your car, and be on your way. You can pull the same trick at Epcot by arranging a advance reservation at one of the Epcot resorts. After *IllumiNations* when the park closes, simply exit the park by the International Gateway and walk back to the resort where your car is parked.

**10. CAR TROUBLE** All the parking lots have security patrols that circulate through the lots. If you have a dead battery or some other automotive problem, the security patrols will help get you going. If you have more serious trouble, the **AAA Car Care Center,** operated by Goodyear and located in Walt Disney World near the Magic Kingdom parking lot, will help you. Prices are comparable to what you'd pay at home for most services. The Car Center stays pretty busy, so expect to leave your car for a while unless the fix is simple. Phone: ☎ 407-824-0976.

**11. SCORING A GREAT PARKING PLACE** Anytime you arrive at a park after noon, there will some empty spots right up front vacated by early arriving guests who have already departed.

## Taking a Shuttle Bus from Your Out-of-the-World Hotel

MANY INDEPENDENT HOTELS AND MOTELS near Walt Disney World provide trams and buses. They're fairly carefree, depositing you near theme-park entrances and saving you parking fees. The rub is that they might not get you there as early as you desire (a critical point if you take our touring advice) or be available when you wish to return to your lodging. Also, some shuttles go directly to Disney World, while others stop at additional area lodgings. Each service is a bit different; check the particulars before you make reservations.

If you're depending on shuttles, leave the park at least 45 minutes before closing. If you stay until closing and lack the energy to hassle with the shuttle, take a cab. Cabstands are near the Bus Information buildings at the Animal Kingdom, Epcot, Disney-MGM Studios, and the Transportation and Ticket Center (TTC). If no cabs are on hand, staff at Bus Information will call one for you.

## THE DISNEY TRANSPORTATION SYSTEM

IN THE MOST BASIC TERMS, THE DISNEY Transportation System is a "hub and spoke" system. Hubs include the Transportation and Ticket Center, Downtown Disney, and all four major theme parks (from two hours before official opening time to two to three hours after closing). Although there are some exceptions, there is direct service from Disney resorts to the major theme parks and to Downtown Disney, and from park to park. If you want to go from resort to resort or most anywhere else, you will have to transfer at one of the hubs.

If a hotel offers boat or monorail service, its bus service will be limited, meaning you'll have to transfer at a hub for many Disney World destinations. If you're staying at a Magic Kingdom resort served by monorail (Polynesian, Contemporary, Grand Floridian), you'll be able to commute efficiently to the Magic Kingdom via monorail. If you want to visit Epcot, you must take the monorail to the TTC and transfer to the Epcot monorail. (Guests at the Polynesian can eliminate the transfer by walking five to ten minutes to the TTC and catching the direct monorail to Epcot.)

### Walt Disney World Bus Service

Buses in Disney World have an illuminated panel above the front windshield that flashes the bus's destination. Also, theme parks have designated waiting areas for each Disney World destination. To catch the bus to the Caribbean Beach Resort from Disney-MGM Studios, for example, go to the bus stop and wait in the area marked "To the Caribbean Beach Resort." At the resorts, go to any bus stop and wait for the bus with your destination displayed on the illuminated panel. Directions to Disney World destinations are available when you check in or at your hotel's guest relations desk. The clerk at guest relations can also answer your questions about the Disney Transportation System.

Buses begin service to the theme parks at about 7 a.m. on days when the parks' official opening time is 9 a.m. Generally, buses run every 20 minutes. Buses to Disney-MGM Studios, Epcot, or the Animal Kingdom deliver you to the park entrance. Until one hour before the park opens (before 8 a.m. in this example), buses to the Magic Kingdom deliver you to the TTC, where you transfer to the monorail or ferry to complete your commute. Buses take you directly to the Magic Kingdom starting one hour before the park's stated opening.

To be on-hand for the real opening time (when official opening is 9 a.m.), catch direct buses to Epcot, the Animal Kingdom, and Disney-MGM Studios between 7:30 and 8 a.m. Catch direct buses to the Magic Kingdom between 8 and 8:15 a.m. If you must transfer to reach your park, leave 15–20 minutes earlier. On days when official opening is 7 or 8 a.m., move up your departure time accordingly.

For your return bus trip in the evening, leave the park 40 minutes to an hour before closing to avoid the rush. If you're caught in the mass exodus, you may be inconvenienced, but you won't be stranded.

## Walt Disney World Monorail Service

Picture the monorail system as three loops. Loop A is an express route that runs counterclockwise connecting the Magic Kingdom with the Transportation and Ticket Center (TTC). Loop B runs clockwise alongside Loop A, making all stops, with service to (in this order) the TTC, Polynesian Resort, Grand Floridian Beach Resort, Magic Kingdom, Contemporary Resort, and back to the TTC. The long Loop C dips southeast like a tail, connecting the TTC with Epcot. The hub for all three loops is the TTC (where you usually park to visit the Magic Kingdom).

*unofficial* **TIP**
Buses, boats, and monorails continue to operate for two hours after the parks close.

The monorail system serving Magic Kingdom resorts usually starts an hour and a half before official opening on other days. If you're staying at a Magic Kingdom resort and wish to be among the first in the Magic Kingdom when official opening is 9 a.m., board the monorail at the times indicated below.

| | |
|---|---|
| From the Contemporary Resort | 7:45–8 a.m. |
| From the Polynesian Resort | 7:50–8:05 a.m. |
| From the Grand Floridian Beach Resort | 8–8:10 a.m. |

If you're a day-guest, you'll be allowed on the monorail at the TTC between 8:15 and 8:30 a.m. on a day when official opening is 9 a.m. If you want to board earlier, walk from the TTC to the Polynesian Resort and board there. The monorail loop connecting Epcot and the TTC begins operating at 7:30 a.m. on days when Epcot's official opening is 9 a.m. To be at Epcot when the park opens, catch the Epcot monorail at the TTC by 8:05 a.m. Monorails usually run for two hours after closing to ensure that everyone is served. If a train is too crowded or you need transportation after the monorails have stopped running, catch a bus.

# PART SEVEN

# BARE NECESSITIES

## CREDIT CARDS *and* MONEY

### CREDIT CARDS

- MasterCard, VISA, American Express, Discover, Diners Club, JCB, and the Disney Credit Card, as well as traveler's checks, are accepted throughout Walt Disney World.

### FINANCIAL MATTERS

**CASH** Bank service at the theme parks is limited to ATMs. Branches of Sun Bank are across the street from Downtown Disney Marketplace and at 1675 Buena Vista Drive. Both offices will:

- Provide cash advances on MasterCard and VISA (no minimum; maximum equals the patron's credit limit).
- Cash personal checks of $200 or less drawn on Sun Bank upon presentation of a driver's license and major credit card.
- Cash and sell traveler's checks. The bank cashes the first check up to $100 without charge but levies a $2 service fee for each additional check.
- Facilitate wiring of money from the visitor's bank to Sun Bank.
- Exchange foreign currency for dollars.

Most VISA and MasterCard cards are accepted at ATMs at Walt Disney World. To use an American Express card, however, you must sign an agreement with American Express before your trip. If your credit card doesn't work in the ATMs, a teller will be able to process your transaction at any Sun Bank full-service location.

# PROBLEMS *and* UNUSUAL SITUATIONS

## ATTRACTIONS CLOSED FOR REPAIRS

CHECK IN ADVANCE WITH DISNEY WORLD to see what rides and attractions may be closed for maintenance or repair during your visit. If you're interested in a specific attraction, the call could save you a lot of disappointment.

## CAR TROUBLE

SECURITY OR TOW-TRUCK PATROLS WILL help you if you lock the keys in your parked car or return to find the battery dead. For more serious problems, the closest repair facility is the Goodyear-operated **AAA Car Care Center** near the Magic Kingdom parking lot (☎ 407-824-0976).

The closest off-World repair center is **Maingate Exxon** (US 192 west of I-4; ☎ 407-396-2721); Disney security will help you contact the service station. Arrangements can be made to take you to your Disney World destination or the nearest phone.

## PAL MICKEY

THIS LITTLE BRAIN TULIP IS A wireless global-positioning communications device embedded in the chest cavity of a Mickey Mouse doll. As you carry Mickey around, he responds to wireless signals emanating from different places in the parks. When he receives a signal, he giggles and shakes. If you respond by squeezing one of his hands or pressing his belly, he commences yapping about whatever you happen to be standing near: He also volunteers park tips, and he tells you where to find Disney characters.

You can purchase Pal Mickey for $60, pal around with him in the parks, and then take him home (he'll still laugh and joke but he won't know where the hell he is). Although Pal Mickey is fun, he's kind of cumbersome to haul around all day. He comes with a belt clip, but we think he's a mite too heavy to hang from your belt. If you tuck him under your arm or toss him in a diaper bag, he can't receive signals.

## LOST AND FOUND

IF YOU LOSE (OR FIND) SOMETHING in the Magic King-dom, go to City Hall. At Epcot, Lost and Found is in the Entrance Plaza. At Disney-MGM Studios, it's at Hollywood Boulevard Guest Relations, and at the Animal Kingdom, it's at Guest Relations at the main entrance. If you discover your loss after you have left the park(s), call ☎ 407-824-4245 (for all parks). Ask to be transferred to the specific park's lost and found if you're still at the park(s) and discover something is missing.

## MEDICAL MATTERS

**RELIEF FOR A HEADACHE** Aspirin and other sundries are sold at the Emporium on Main Street in the Magic Kingdom (they're kept behind the counter; you must ask), at most retail shops in Epcot's Future World and World Showcase, and in Disney-MGM Studios and the Animal Kingdom.

**IF YOU NEED A DOCTOR** **Main Street Physicians** provides 24-hour service. Doctors are available for house calls to all area hotels and campgrounds (Disney and non-Disney). House calls are $165–$170 per visit. If your problem doesn't require a house call, visit the clinic on a walk-in basis (no appointments taken) at 2901 Parkway Boulevard, Suite 3-A, in Kissimmee. Minimum charge for a physician consultation at the clinic is $80. The clinic is open daily from 8 a.m. to 8 p.m., and its main phone is ☎ 407-396-1195.

**Centra Care** walk-in clinic operates one location at 12500 S. Apopka-Vineland Road and is open on weekdays from 8 a.m. to midnight and on weekends from 8 a.m. to 8 p.m. They operate a total of three locations in the Disney area. Call ☎ 407-239-7777 for fees and information. Centra Care also operates an "in-room," 24-hour physician (house call) service and runs a shuttle that will pick you up free of charge (☎ 407-238-2000).

**D.O.C.S.** (Docs on Call Service) offers 24-hour house-call service to your hotel room. All D.O.C.S. physicians are American-trained and Board-certified. Call ☎ 407-399-DOCS.

**PRESCRIPTION MEDICINE** The closest pharmacy is **Walgreens Lake Buena Vista** (☎ 407-238-0600). **Turner Drugs** (☎ 407-828-8125) charges $5 to deliver a filled prescription to your hotel's front desk. The service is available to Disney resort guests and guests at non-Disney hotels in the Turner Drugs area, and the fee is charged to your hotel account.

*unofficial* **TIP**
Rain gear is one of the few bargains at the parks. It isn't always displayed in shops; you have to ask for it.

## RAIN

WEATHER BAD? Go to the parks anyway. Crowds are lighter, and most attractions and waiting areas are under cover. Showers, especially during warmer months, are short. Ponchos are available for about $7; umbrellas go for about $13. Ponchos sold at Walt Disney World are all yellow; picking out somebody in your party on a rainy day is like trying to identify a particular bumblebee in a swarm.

# SERVICES

## MESSAGES

MESSAGES LEFT AT CITY HALL IN THE Magic Kingdom, Guest Relations at Epcot, Hollywood Boulevard Guest Relations at Disney-MGM Studios, or Guest Relations at the Animal Kingdom can be retrieved at any of the four.

## PET CARE

PETS AREN'T ALLOWED IN THE MAJOR or minor theme parks. But never leave an animal in a hot car while you tour; the pet will die. Kennels and holding facilities are provided for temporary care of your pets. They're located adjacent to the Transportation and Ticket Center, left of the Epcot entrance plaza, left of the Disney-MGM Studios entrance plaza, at the outer entrance of the Animal Kingdom, and at Fort Wilderness Campground.

## LOCKERS AND PACKAGE PICK-UP

LOCKERS ARE AVAILABLE ON THE GROUND floor of the Main Street railroad station in the Magic Kingdom, to the right of Spaceship Earth in Epcot, and on the east and west ends of the TTC. At Disney-MGM Studios, lockers are to the right of the entrance on Hollywood Boulevard at Oscar's Super Service. At the Animal Kingdom, lockers are inside the main entrance to the left. Lockers are $4 a day plus a $2 deposit.

Package Pick-up is available at each major theme park. Ask the salesperson to send your purchases to Package Pick-up. When you leave the park, they'll be waiting for you. Epcot has two exits, thus two Package Pick-ups, so specify whether you want your purchases sent to the main entrance or to the International Gateway.

*unofficial* **TIP**
Disney no longer offers a film developing service at the theme parks.

## CAMERAS AND FILM?

CAMERA CENTERS AT THE MAJOR PARKS sell disposable cameras for about $10 ($19 with flash). Film is sold throughout the World. Developing is available at most Disney hotel gift shops and at Camera Centers. Film processing is no longer available in any Disney theme park, but Disney will take your digital memory cards and convert them to a CD while you're in the parks. The cost is around $13 for 120 images, and around $6.50 for an additional 120 images. Prints are around $0.75 each. You'll need to leave your digital media with Disney while they create the CD, typically around two to five hours, so make sure you've got extra media on hand.

# PART EIGHT

# DINING *in* WALT DISNEY WORLD

 ## DISNEY DINING 101

### ADVANCE RESERVATIONS

DISNEY CEASELESSLY TINKERS WITH ITS restaurant reservations policy. In 2005, Disney abruptly decided to change the name from "advance reservation" to the somewhat redundant "Advance Reservation." The new system, however, is exactly the same as the old one except in name. When you call, your name and essential information are taken as if you were making a reservation. The Disney representative then says you have advance reservations for the restaurant on the date and time you requested and usually explains that advance reservation means you will be seated ahead of walk-ins, i.e., those without advance reservation.

### DRESS

DRESS IS INFORMAL AT ALL theme-park restaurants. While theme-park attire (shorts, T-shirts, sneakers, etc.) is tolerated at hotel restaurants, you probably would feel more comfortable if you dressed up a bit.

*unofficial* **TIP**
The only restaurant requiring jackets for men and dressy clothes for women is Victoria & Albert's at the Grand Floridian.

### SMOKING

WALT DISNEY WORLD RESTAURANTS adopted a nonsmoking policy several years ago, although smoking was allowed in the lounge areas of many restaurants. Florida voters recently passed an amendment to the state's constitution that also prohibits smoking in restaurant lounges. Free-standing bars—those that realize less than 10% of their revenues from food sales—are exempted. They're also hard to find on Disney property; Mizner's Lounge at Disney's Grand Floridian Resort is one possible exception. In most cases, however, diners may be required to go outside for a smoke—and in the theme parks, that might also mean going to one of the designated smoking areas.

## WALT DISNEY WORLD RESTAURANT CATEGORIES

IN GENERAL, FOOD AND BEVERAGE offerings at Walt Disney World are defined by service, price, and convenience:

**FULL-SERVICE RESTAURANTS** Full-service restaurants are in all Disney resorts except the All-Star and Pop Century, and all major theme parks, Downtown Disney Marketplace, Pleasure Island, and Disney's West Side. Disney operates the restaurants in the theme parks and its hotels. Contractors or franchisees operate the restaurants in hotels of the Downtown Disney Resort Area, the Swan and Dolphin resorts, Pleasure Island, Disney's West Side, and some in the Marketplace. Advance reservation (explained above) is recommended for all full-service restaurants except those in the DDRA. The restaurants accept VISA, MasterCard, American Express, Discover, Diners Club, and the Disney Credit Card.

**BUFFETS** There has been an explosion of buffets at Disney World during recent years. Many have Disney characters in attendance, and most have a separate children's menu featuring hot dogs, burgers, chicken nuggets, pizza, macaroni and cheese, and spaghetti and meatballs. In addition to the buffets, several restaurants serve a family-style, all-you-can-eat, fixed-price meal. Advance reservation arrangements are required for character buffets and recommended for all other buffets and family-style restaurants. Most major credit cards are accepted.

*unofficial* **TIP**
Food at Disney's family-style restaurants tends to be a little better than you'll find on a buffet line.

If you want to eat a lot but don't feel like standing in yet another line, consider one of the all-you-can-eat "family-style" restaurants. These feature platters of food brought to your table in courses by a server. You can sample everything on the menu and eat as much as you like. You can even go back to a favorite appetizer after you finish the main course.

Family-style all-you-can-eat service is available at the Liberty Tree Tavern in the Magic Kingdom and The Garden Grill Restaurant in the Land pavilion in Epcot (both with character dining); or at 'Ohana in the Polynesian Resort and Whispering Canyon Café in the Wilderness Lodge.

**CAFETERIAS AND FOOD COURTS** Cafeterias, found in all the major theme parks, offer a middle ground between full-service and counter-service dining. Food courts, featuring a collection of counter-service eateries under one roof, are found at the theme parks as well as at the moderate (Coronado Springs, Caribbean Beach, Port Orleans) and budget (All-Star and Pop Century) Disney resorts. No advance reservation is required or available at cafeterias or food courts.

**COUNTER SERVICE** Counter-service fast food is available in all theme parks and at Downtown Disney Marketplace, Pleasure Island, Disney's BoardWalk, and Disney's West Side. The food compares in quality with McDonald's, Captain D's, or Taco Bell, but is more expensive, though often served in larger portions.

## The Cost of Counter-Service Food

To help you develop your dining budget, here are prices of common counter-service items. Sales tax isn't included.

| FOOD ITEM | PRICE |
|---|---|
| Bagel/Muffin | $2.29–$2.50 |
| Brownie | $2.39–$2.79 |
| Cake or Pie | $2.79–$4.29 |
| Cereal with Milk | $2.59–$3.18 |
| Cheeseburger with Fries | $5.79–$6.19 |
| Chicken Breast Sandwich (grilled) | $5.19–$7.95 |
| Children's Meals | $3.99–$4.29 |
| Chips | $1.29–$2.50 |
| Cookies | $1.49–$2.79 |
| Sub/Deli Sandwich | $5.49–$7.25 |
| Fish Basket (fried) with Fries | $6.49–$6.89 |
| French Fries | $1.79–$3.09 (loaded) |
| Fried Chicken Strips with Fries | $5.49–$8.59 |
| Fruit (whole piece) | $0.99–$1.99 |
| Fruit Cup/Fruit Salad | $1.99–$3.95 |
| Hot Dogs | $3.69–$5.99 (foot-long) |
| Ice Cream Bars | $2.39–$3.75 |

## The Cost of Counter-Service Food (continued)

| FOOD ITEM | PRICE |
|---|---|
| Nachos with Cheese | $2.99–$4.59 |
| PBJ Sandwich | $2.29–$4.29 |
| Pizza | $5.49–$5.79 |
| Popcorn | $2.29–$4.00 |
| Pretzel | $2.79–$3.50 (with cheese) |
| Salad (entree) | $6.39–$7.59 |
| Salad (side) | $2.19–$4.39 |
| Smoked Turkey Leg | $5.19 |
| Soup/Chili | $2.49–$3.50 |
| Tacos (2) with Beans and Salsa | $4.79–$4.99 |
| Taco Salad | $4.79–$7.99 |
| Veggie Burger | $4.19–$6.19 |

| DRINKS | SMALL | LARGE |
|---|---|---|
| Beer (not available in the Magic Kingdom) | $5.00 | $7.25 |
| Bottled Water | $1.25 | $2.00 |
| Cappuccino/Espresso | $2.99 | $3.99 |
| Coffee | $1.69 | $1.89 |
| Fruit Juice | $1.49 | $2.39 |
| Milk | $1.29 | $1.99 |
| Milkshakes/Floats/Sundaes | $2.99 | $4.99 |
| Soft Drinks, Iced Tea, and Lemonade | $1.99 | $2.29–$4.99 |
| Refillable Souvenir Mug ($12 to buy) | $3.79 | $3.99 |
| Hot Tea and Cocoa | $1.69 | $1.99 |

**FAST CASUAL** Somewhere between burgers and formal dining are the establishments in Disney's new "fast casual" category. Initially launched with three restaurants (the Tomorrowland Noodle Station in the Magic Kingdom, Sunshine Seasons in Epcot, and Backlot Express at the Studios), fast-casual restaurants feature menu choices a cut above what you'd normally see at a typical counter-service location. The three initial locations all feature Asian or Mediterranean cuisine, something previously lacking inside the parks. Entrees cost about $2 more on average than traditional counter service, but the variety and food quality more than make up for the difference.

**VENDOR FOOD** Vendors abound at the theme parks, Downtown Disney Marketplace, Pleasure Island, Disney's West

Side, and Disney's BoardWalk. Offerings include popcorn, ice cream bars, churros (Mexican pastries), soft drinks, bottled water, and (in theme parks) fresh fruit. Prices include tax, and payment must be in cash.

# DISNEY DINING SUGGESTIONS

BELOW ARE SUGGESTIONS FOR DINING at each of the major theme parks. If you are interested in trying a theme-park full-service restaurant, be aware that the restaurants continue to serve after the park's official closing time. For example, we showed up at the Hollywood Brown Derby just as Disney-MGM Studios closed at 8 p.m. We were seated almost immediately and enjoyed a leisurely dinner while the crowds cleared out. Incidentally, don't worry if you are depending on Disney transportation: buses, boats, and monorails run two to three hours after the parks close.

## THE MAGIC KINGDOM

FOOD AT THE MAGIC KINGDOM HAS improved noticeably over the past several years. The Crystal Palace at the end of Main Street offers a good (albeit pricey) buffet chaperoned by Disney characters, while the Liberty Tree Tavern in Liberty Square features hearty family-style dining, also with Disney characters in attendance. Cinderella's Royal Table, a full-service restaurant on the second floor of the castle, delivers palatable meals in one of the World's most unique settings. Tony's Town Square Restaurant on Main Street also serves decent food. Because children love Cinderella and everyone's curious about the the castle, you need to make an advance reservation before you leave home if you want to eat breakfast at Cinderella's Royal Table. Advance reservations for lunch or dinner are easier to arrange.

## EPCOT

FOR THE MOST PART, Epcot's restaurants have always served decent food, though the World Showcase restaurants have occasionally been timid about delivering an honest representation of the host nation's cuisine. While these eateries have struggled with authenticity and have sometimes shied away from challenging the

*un*official **TIP**
Many Epcot restaurants are overpriced, most conspicuously Nine Dragons Restaurant (China) and the Coral Reef (The Living Seas).

meat-and-potatoes palate of the average tourist, they are bolder now, encouraged by America's exponentially expanding appreciation of ethnic dining. True, the less adventuresome can still find sanitized and homogenized meals, but the same kitchens will serve up the real thing for anyone with a spark of curiosity and daring. Representing relatively good value through the combination of ambience and well-prepared food are Chefs de France (France), Restaurant Akershus (Norway), Biergarten (Germany), and Restaurant Marrakesh (Morocco). The Biergarten and the Marrakesh also have entertainment.

## DISNEY-MGM STUDIOS

DISNEY-MGM HAS FIVE RESTAURANTS where advance reservation is recommended: The Hollywood Brown Derby, 50's Prime Time Café, Sci-Fi Dine-In Theater Restaurant, Mama Melrose's Ristorante Italiano, and the Hollywood and Vine Cafeteria. The upscale Brown Derby is by far the best restaurant at the Studios. For simple Italian food, including pizza, Mama Melrose's is fine. Just don't expect anything fancy. At the Sci-Fi Dine-In, you eat in little cars at a simulated drive-in movie of the 1950s. Though you won't find a more entertaining restaurant in Walt Disney World, the food is quite disappointing. Somewhat better is the 50's Prime Time Café, where you sit in Mom's kitchen of the 1950s and scarf down meat loaf while watching clips of vintage TV sitcoms.

## ANIMAL KINGDOM

THE ANIMAL KINGDOM MOSTLY OFFERS counter-service fast food. Although grilled meats are available, don't expect a broad choice of exotic dishes. Most Animal Kingdom eateries serve up traditional Disney theme-park fare: hot dogs, hamburgers, deli sandwiches, and the like. Even so, we found Animal Kingdom fast food to be a cut above the average Disney fare. For a quiet refuge away from the crowds, you can't beat Flame Tree Barbeque's waterfront dining pavilions. The only full-service restaurant is the Rainforest Café, with entrances both inside and outside the theme park (you don't have to purchase theme-park admission, in other words, to eat at the restaurant). Unlike the Rainforest Café at

*unofficial* **TIP**
Flame Tree Barbeque in Safari Village is our pick of the Animal Kingdom litter, both in terms of food quality and atmosphere.

the Downtown Disney Marketplace, the Animal Kingdom branch accepts advance reservation.

# WALT DISNEY WORLD RESTAURANTS: RATED *and* RANKED

**OVERALL RATING** The overall rating represents the entire dining experience: style, service, and ambience, in addition to taste, presentation, and quality of food. Five stars is the highest rating and indicates that the restaurant offers the best of everything. Four-star restaurants are above average, and three-star restaurants offer good, though not necessarily memorable meals. Two-star restaurants serve mediocre fare, and one-star restaurants are below average. Our star ratings don't correspond to ratings awarded by AAA, Mobil, Zagat's, or other restaurant reviewers.

**COST** The next rating tells how much a complete meal will cost. We include a main dish with vegetable or side dish, and a choice of soup or salad. Appetizers, desserts, drinks, and tips aren't included. We've rated the cost as inexpensive, moderate, or expensive.

| | |
|---|---|
| Inexpensive | $12 or less per person |
| Moderate | $13–$23 per person |
| Expensive | More than $23 per person |

**QUALITY RATING** The food quality is rated on a scale of one to five stars, five being the best rating attainable. The quality rating is based expressly on the taste, freshness of ingredients, preparation, presentation, and creativity of food served. There is no consideration of price. If you are a person who wants the best food available and cost is not an issue, you need look no further than the quality ratings.

**VALUE RATING** If, on the other hand, you are looking for both quality and value, then you should check the value rating, expressed as stars.

| | |
|---|---|
| ★★★★★ | Exceptional value, a real bargain |
| ★★★★ | Good value |
| ★★★ | Fair value, you get exactly what you pay for |
| ★★ | Somewhat overpriced |
| ★ | Significantly overpriced |

# WDW Restaurants by Cuisine

| CUISINE | LOCATION | OVERALL RATING | COST | QUALITY RATING | VALUE RATING |
|---|---|---|---|---|---|
| **AFRICAN** | | | | | |
| Jiko | Animal Kingdom Lodge | ★★★★ | Exp | ★★★★½ | ★★★½ |
| Boma | Animal Kingdom Lodge | ★★★★ | Mod | ★★★★ | ★★★★½ |
| **AMERICAN** | | | | | |
| California Grill | Contemporary | ★★★★ | Exp | ★★★★½ | ★★★½ |
| The Hollywood Brown Derby | Disney-MGM | ★★★★ | Exp | ★★★★ | ★★★ |
| Artist Point | Wilderness Lodge | ★★★½ | Mod | ★★★★ | ★★★ |
| Whispering Canyon Café | Wilderness Lodge | ★★★ | Mod | ★★★½ | ★★★★ |
| House of Blues | West Side | ★★★ | Mod | ★★★½ | ★★★ |
| Yacht Club Galley | Yacht Club | ★★★ | Mod | ★★★½ | ★★★ |
| The Garden Grill Restaurant | Epcot | ★★★ | Mod | ★★★ | ★★★ |
| Planet Hollywood | Pleasure Island | ★★★ | Mod | ★★★ | ★★★ |
| Grand Floridian Café | Grand Floridian | ★★★ | Mod | ★★★ | ★★ |
| All-Star Café | Wide World of Sports | ★★½ | Mod | ★★★ | ★★★ |
| ESPN Club | BoardWalk | ★★½ | Mod | ★★★ | ★★★ |
| Hollywood & Vine | Disney-MGM | ★★½ | Inexp | ★★★ | ★★★ |
| Liberty Tree Tavern | Magic Kingdom | ★★½ | Mod | ★★★ | ★★★ |
| Boatwright's Dining Hall | Port Orleans | ★★½ | Mod | ★★★ | ★★ |
| Cinderella's Royal Table | Magic Kingdom | ★★½ | Mod | ★★ | ★★ |
| Rainforest Café | Downtown Disney and Animal Kingdom | ★★½ | Mod | ★★ | ★★ |
| 50's Prime Time Cafe | Disney-MGM | ★★ | Mod | ★★★ | ★★★ |
| Gulliver's Grill | Swan | ★★ | Exp | ★★★ | ★★ |
| Olivia's Café | Old Key West | ★★ | Mod | ★★½ | ★★★ |
| Wolfgang Puck Café | West Side | ★★ | Exp | ★★½ | ★★½ |
| Sci-Fi Dine-In Theater Restaurant | Disney-MGM | ★★ | Mod | ★★½ | ★★ |
| Baskervilles | Grosvenor Resort | ★★ | Mod | ★★ | ★★★ |
| Big River Grille & Brewing Works | BoardWalk | ★★ | Mod | ★★ | ★★ |

| CUISINE | LOCATION | OVERALL RATING | COST | QUALITY RATING | VALUE RATING |
|---|---|---|---|---|---|
| **BUFFET** | | | | | |
| Boma | Animal Kingdom Lodge | ★★★★ | Mod | ★★★★ | ★★★★ ½ |
| Cape May Café | Beach Club | ★★★½ | Mod | ★★★½ | ★★★★ |
| Restaurant Akershus | Epcot | ★★★½ | Mod | ★★★ | ★★★★ |
| The Crystal Palace | Magic Kingdom | ★★★ | Mod | ★★★½ | ★★★★ |
| Biergarten | Epcot | ★★★ | Mod | ★★★ | ★★★★ |
| Chef Mickey's | Contemporary | ★★½ | Mod | ★★★ | ★★★ |
| Hollywood & Vine | Disney-MGM | ★★½ | Inexp | ★★★ | ★★★ |
| 1900 Park Fare | Grand Floridian | ★★½ | Mod | ★★★ | ★★★ |
| The Plaza Buffet | Magic Kingdom | ★★ | Mod | ★★ | ★★ |
| **CHINESE** | | | | | |
| Nine Dragons Restaurant | Epcot | ★★½ | Exp | ★★★ | ★★ |
| **CUBAN** | | | | | |
| Bongos Cuban Café | West Side | ★★ | Mod | ★★ | ★★ |
| **ENGLISH** | | | | | |
| Rose & Crown Dining Room | Epcot | ★★★ | Mod | ★★★½ | ★★ |
| **FRENCH** | | | | | |
| Bistro de Paris | Epcot | ★★★ | Exp | ★★★½ | ★★ |
| Les Chefs de France | Epcot | ★★★ | Mod | ★★★ | ★★★ |
| **GERMAN** | | | | | |
| Biergarten | Epcot | ★★★ | Mod | ★★★ | ★★★★ |
| **GOURMET** | | | | | |
| Victoria & Albert's | Grand Floridian | ★★★★ | Exp | ★★★★★ | ★★★★ |
| Arthur's 27 | Wyndham Palace | ★★★★ | Exp | ★★★★ | ★★★ |
| **ITALIAN** | | | | | |
| Palio | Swan | ★★★½ | Exp | ★★★½ | ★★★ |
| Portobello Yacht Club | Pleasure Island | ★★★ | Exp | ★★★ | ★★ |
| L'Originale Alfredo di Roma Ristorante | Epcot | ★★½ | Exp | ★★★ | ★★½ |
| Mama Melrose's Ristorante Italiano | Disney-MGM | ★★½ | Mod | ★★★ | ★★ |

## WDW Restaurants by Cuisine (continued)

| CUISINE | LOCATION | OVERALL RATING | COST | QUALITY RATING | VALUE RATING |
|---|---|---|---|---|---|
| **ITALIAN (CONTINUED)** | | | | | |
| Tony's Town Square Restaurant | Magic Kingdom | ★★½ | Mod | ★★★ | ★★ |
| **JAPANESE** | | | | | |
| Kimonos | Swan | ★★★★ | Mod | ★★★★½ | ★★★ |
| Teppanyaki Dining Room | Epcot | ★★★½ | Exp | ★★★★ | ★★★ |
| Tempura Kiku | Epcot | ★★★ | Mod | ★★★★ | ★★★ |
| Benihana— Steakhouse & Sushi | Hilton | ★★★ | Mod | ★★★½ | ★★★ |
| **MEDITERRANEAN** | | | | | |
| Cítricos | Grand Floridian | ★★★★ | Exp | ★★★★½ | ★★★ |
| Spoodles | BoardWalk | ★★★½ | Mod | ★★★★ | ★★★ |
| Fresh Mediterranean Market | Dolphin | ★★½ | Mod | ★★½ | ★★ |
| **MEXICAN** | | | | | |
| San Angel Inn Restaurante | Epcot | ★★★ | Exp | ★★★½ | ★★ |
| Maya Grill | Coronado Springs | ★ | Exp | ★ | ★ |
| **MOROCCAN** | | | | | |
| Restaurant Marrakesh | Epcot | ★★★ | Mod | ★★★½ | ★★★ |
| **NORWEGIAN** | | | | | |
| Restaurant Akershus | Epcot | ★★★½ | Mod | ★★★ | ★★★★ |
| **POLYNESIAN/PAN-ASIAN** | | | | | |
| 'Ohana | Polynesian | ★★★ | Mod | ★★★½ | ★★★ |
| Kona Café | Polynesian | ★★★ | Mod | ★★★ | ★★★★ |

| CUISINE | LOCATION | OVERALL RATING | COST | QUALITY RATING | VALUE RATING |
|---|---|---|---|---|---|
| **SEAFOOD** | | | | | |
| Flying Fish Café | BoardWalk | ★★★★½ | Exp | ★★★★½ | ★★★ |
| Artist Point | Wilderness Lodge | ★★★½ | Mod | ★★★★ | ★★★ |
| Narcoossee's | Grand Floridian | ★★★½ | Exp | ★★★½ | ★★ |
| Blue Zoo | Dolphin | ★★★ | Exp | ★★★ | ★★ |
| Fulton's Crab House | Pleasure Island | ★★½ | Exp | ★★★½ | ★★ |
| Cap'n Jack's Restaurant | Downtown Disney | ★★½ | Mod | ★★ | ★★ |
| Coral Reef | Epcot | ★★ | Exp | ★★★ | ★★ |
| Shutters at Old Port Royale | Caribbean Beach | ★★ | Mod | ★★½ | ★★ |
| Finn's Grill | Hilton | ★ | Mod | ★★ | ★★ |
| **STEAK** | | | | | |
| Shula's Steak House | Dolphin | ★★★★ | Exp | ★★★★ | ★★ |
| Le Cellier Steakhouse | Epcot | ★★★½ | Mod | ★★★½ | ★★★ |
| Yachtsman Steakhouse | Yacht Club | ★★★ | Exp | ★★★½ | ★★ |
| Concourse Steakhouse | Contemporary | ★★★ | Mod | ★★ | ★★ |
| The Outback | Wyndham Palace | ★★ | Exp | ★★★ | ★★ |
| Shutters at Old Port Royale | Caribbean Beach | ★★ | Mod | ★★½ | ★★ |

# PART NINE

# THE MAGIC KINGDOM

## ARRIVING

IF YOU DRIVE, THE MAGIC KINGDOM/Ticket and Transportation Center (TTC) parking lot opens about two hours before the park's official opening. After paying a fee, you are directed to a parking space, then transported by tram to the TTC, where you catch a monorail or ferry to the entrance.

If you're staying at the Contemporary, Polynesian, or Grand Floridian resorts, you can commute directly to the Magic Kingdom by monorail (guests at the Contemporary can walk there more quickly). If you stay at Wilderness Lodge and Villas or Fort Wilderness Campground, you will take a boat. Guests at other Disney resorts can reach the park by bus. All Disney lodging guests, whether they arrive by bus, monorail, or boat, are deposited at the park's entrance, bypassing the TTC.

*unofficial* **TIP**
If you don't already have a handout guidemap of the park, get one at City Hall.

## GETTING ORIENTED

AT THE MAGIC KINGDOM, STROLLER AND wheelchair rentals are to the right of the train station, and lockers are on the station's ground floor. On your left as you enter Main Street is City Hall, the center for information, lost and found, guided tours, and entertainment schedules.

The guidemap lists all attractions, shops, and eating places; provides helpful information about first aid, baby care, and assistance for the disabled; and gives tips for good photos.

It lists times for the day's special events, live entertainment, Disney character parades, and concerts, and it also tells when and where to find Disney characters. Often the guidemap is supplemented by a daily entertainment schedule known as a *Times Guide;* in addition to listing performance times, it also provides info on Disney character appearances.

Main Street ends at a central hub from which branch the entrances to five other sections of the Magic Kingdom: Adventureland, Frontierland, Liberty Square, Fantasyland, and Tomorrowland. Mickey's Toontown Fair is wedged like a dimple between the cheeks of Fantasyland and Tomorrowland and doesn't connect to the central hub.

 *unofficial* **TIP**
Minimize the time you spend on midway-type rides; you probably have something similar near your hometown.

Cinderella Castle is the entrance to Fantasyland and is the Magic Kingdom's visual center. If you start in Adventureland and go clockwise around the Magic Kingdom, the castle spires will always be roughly on your right; if you start in Tomorrowland and go counterclockwise through the park, the spires will always be roughly on your left. Cinderella Castle is an excellent meeting place if your group decides to split up during the day or is separated accidentally. Because the castle is large, designate a very specific meeting spot, like the entrance to Cinderella's Royal Table restaurant at the rear of the castle.

# STARTING THE TOUR

TAKE ADVANTAGE OF WHAT DISNEY does best: the fantasy adventures of Splash Mountain and The Haunted Mansion and the various audio-animatronic (talking robots) attractions, including *The Hall of Presidents* and Pirates of the Caribbean. Don't burn daylight browsing the shops unless you plan to spend a minimum of two and a half days at the Magic Kingdom, and even then wait until midday or later. Eat a good breakfast early, and avoid lines at eateries by snacking during the day on food from vendors. Fare at most Magic Kingdom eateries is on a par with Subway or McDonald's.

# FASTPASS *at the* MAGIC KINGDOM

THE MAGIC KINGDOM OFFERS EIGHT FASTPASS attractions, the most in any Disney park. Strategies for using

## Magic Kingdom

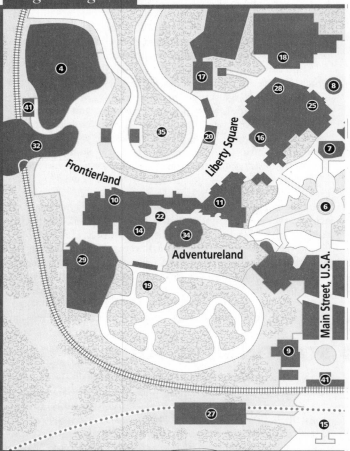

| | |
|---|---|
| **1.** Ariel's Grotto | **12.** Donald's Boat |
| **2.** Astro Orbiter | **13.** Dumbo the Flying Elephant |
| **3.** Barnstormer | **14.** Enchanted Tiki Birds |
| **4.** Big Thunder Mountain Railroad | **15.** Ferry dock |
| **5.** Buzz Lightyear's Space Ranger Spin | **16.** The Hall of Presidents |
| **6.** Central hub | **17.** The Haunted Mansion |
| **7.** Cinderella Castle 7 | **18.** It's a Small World |
| **8.** Cinderella's Golden Carrousel | **19.** Jungle Cruise |
| **9.** City Hall | **20.** Liberty Square Riverboat |
| **10.** *Country Bear Jamboree* | **21.** Mad Tea Party |
| **11.** The Diamond Horseshoe Saloon | **22.** Magic Carpets of Aladdin |

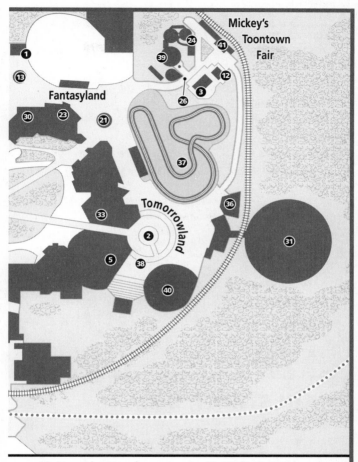

FASTPASS at the Magic Kingdom have been integrated into our touring plans.

| MAGIC KINGDOM FASTPASS ATTRACTIONS | |
| --- | --- |
| **Tomorrowland** | Space Mountain |
| | Buzz Lightyear's Space Ranger Spin |
| | *Stitch's Great Escape* |
| **Adventureland** | Jungle Cruise |
| **Frontierland** | Splash Mountain |
| | Big Thunder Mountain Railroad |
| **Liberty Square** | The Haunted Mansion |
| **Fantasyland** | The Many Adventures of Winnie the Pooh |
| | Peter Pan's Flight |

| NOT TO BE MISSED AT THE MAGIC KINGDOM | |
| --- | --- |
| **Fantasyland** | The Many Adventures of Winnie the Pooh |
| | *Mickey's PhilharMagic* |
| | Peter Pan's Flight |
| **Adventureland** | Pirates of the Caribbean |
| **Frontierland** | Big Thunder Mountain Railroad |
| | Splash Mountain |
| **Liberty Square** | The Haunted Mansion |
| **Tomorrowland** | Space Mountain |
| | *The Timekeeper* (open seasonally) |

# ▮ MAIN STREET, U.S.A.

YOU BEGIN AND END YOUR MAGIC KINGDOM visit on Main Street, which opens a half hour before, and closes a half hour to an hour after, the rest of the park. The Walt Disney World Railroad stops at the Main Street Station; board here for a grand tour of the park or a ride to Frontierland or Mickey's Toontown Fair.

Main Street is a sanitized Disney re-creation of a turn-of-the-19th-century, small-town American street. Its buildings are real, not elaborate props. Attention to detail is exceptional: all interiors, furnishings, and fixtures are true to period. Along the street are shops and eating places, City Hall, and a fire station. Horse-drawn trolleys, double-decker buses, fire engines, and horseless carriages transport visitors along Main Street to the central hub.

**MAIN STREET SERVICES**

Most park services are centered on Main Street, including:

**Wheelchair & Stroller Rental**   Right of the main entrance before passing under the railroad station

**Banking Services**   Automated tellers (ATMs) are underneath the Main Street railroad station

**Storage Lockers**   Ground floor of the railroad station at the end of Main Street; all lockers are cleaned out each night

**Lost & Found**   City Hall at the railroad station end of Main Street

**Live Entertainment & Parade info**   City Hall at the railroad station end of Main Street

**Lost Persons**   City Hall

**Walt Disney World & Local Attraction Information**   City Hall

**First Aid**   Next to The Crystal Palace, left around the central hub (toward Adventureland)

**Baby Center/Baby-Care Needs**   Next to The Crystal Palace, left around the central hub (toward Adventureland)

## Walt Disney World Railroad

| APPEAL BY AGE | PRESCHOOL ★★★★ | GRADE SCHOOL ★★½ | TEENS ★★★ |
|---|---|---|---|
| YOUNG ADULTS ★★★ | OVER 30 ★★ | | SENIORS ★★★ |

**What it is** Scenic railroad ride around perimeter of the Magic Kingdom, and transportation to Frontierland and Mickey's Toontown Fair. **Scope and scale** Minor attraction. **When to go** Anytime. **Special comments** Main Street is usually the least congested station. **Author's rating** Plenty to see; ★★½. **Duration of ride** About 20 minutes for a complete circuit. **Average wait in line per 100 people ahead of you** 8 minutes. **Assumes** 2 or more trains operating. **Loading speed** Moderate.

**DESCRIPTION AND COMMENTS** A transportation ride blending an unusual variety of sights and experiences with an energy-saving way to get around the park. The train provides a glimpse of all lands except Adventureland.

**TOURING TIPS** Save the train ride until after you have seen the featured attractions, or use it when you need transportation. On busy days, lines form at the Frontierland Station, but rarely at the Main Street Station. Strollers aren't allowed on the train. Wheelchair access is available only at the Frontierland and Mickey's Toontown Fair stations.

You cannot take your rental stroller on the train, but you can obtain a replacement stroller at your destination. Just take your personal belongings, your stroller name card, and your rental receipt with you on the train.

Finally, be advised that the railroad shuts down immediately preceding and during parades. Check your park guidemap or *Times Guide* for parade times. Needless to say, this is not the time to queue up for the train.

### Transportation Rides

**DESCRIPTION AND COMMENTS** Trolleys, buses, etc., which add color to Main Street.

**TOURING TIPS** Will save you a walk to the central hub. Not worth a wait.

# ADVENTURELAND

ADVENTURELAND IS THE FIRST LAND to the left of Main Street. It combines an African safari theme with an old New Orleans and Caribbean atmosphere.

## Swiss Family Treehouse

| APPEAL BY AGE | PRESCHOOL ★★★ | GRADE SCHOOL ★★★½ | TEENS ★★★ |
|---|---|---|---|
| YOUNG ADULTS ★★★ | | OVER 30 ★★★ | SENIORS ★★★ |

**What it is** Outdoor walk-through tree house. **Scope and scale** Minor attraction. **When to go** Before 11:30 a.m. or after 5 p.m. **Special comments** Requires climbing a lot of stairs. **Author's rating** A visual delight; ★★★. Duration of tour 10–15 minutes. **Average wait in line per 100 people ahead of you** 7 minutes. **Loading speed** Doesn't apply.

**DESCRIPTION AND COMMENTS** An immense replica of the ship-wrecked family's tree house will turn your children into arboreal architects. It's the king of all tree houses, with its multiple stories, clever jerry-rigging, and mechanical wizardry.

**TOURING TIPS** A self-guided walk-through tour involves a lot of stairs up and down, but no ropes, ladders, or anything fancy. People who stop for extra-long looks or to rest sometimes create bottlenecks that slow the crowd flow. Visit in late afternoon or early evening if you're on a one-day tour, or in the morning of your second day.

## Jungle Cruise (FASTPASS)

| APPEAL BY AGE | PRESCHOOL ★★★½ | GRADE SCHOOL ★★★½ | TEENS ★★½ |
|---|---|---|---|
| YOUNG ADULTS ★★★ | | OVER 30 ★★★ | SENIORS ★★★ |

**What it is** Outdoor safari-themed boat ride adventure. **Scope and scale** Major attraction. **When to go** Before 10 a.m. or 2 hours before closing. **Author's rating** A long-enduring Disney masterpiece; ★★★. **Duration of ride** 8–9 minutes. **Average wait in line per 100 people**

**ahead of you** 3½ minutes. **Assumes** 10 boats operating. **Loading speed** Moderate.

**DESCRIPTION AND COMMENTS** An outdoor cruise through jungle waterways. Passengers encounter animatronic elephants, lions, hostile natives, and a menacing hippo. Boatman's spiel adds to the fun. Once one of the most grand and elaborate attractions at the Magic Kingdom, the Jungle Cruise's technology now seems dated and worn. Since the advent of the Animal Kingdom, the attraction's appeal has diminished, but in its defense, you can always depend on the Jungle Cruise's robotic critters being present as you motor past.

**TOURING TIPS** Among the park's oldest attractions and one that occupies a good third of Adventureland. A convoluted queuing area makes it very difficult to estimate the length of the wait for the Jungle Cruise.

Fortunately, the Jungle Cruise is a FASTPASS attraction. Before you obtain a FASTPASS, however, ask a cast member what the estimated wait in the standby line is.

## Magic Carpets of Aladdin

| APPEAL BY AGE | PRESCHOOL ★★★★½ | GRADE SCHOOL ★★★★ |
| --- | --- | --- |
| TEENS ★½ | YOUNG ADULTS ★½ | OVER 30 ★½ | SENIORS ★½ |

**What it is** Elaborate midway ride. **Scope and scale** Minor attraction. **When to go** Before 10 a.m. or in the hour before park closing. **Author's rating** An eye-appealing children's ride; ★★★. **Duration of ride** 1½ minutes. **Average wait in line per 100 people ahead of you** 16 minutes. **Loading speed** Slow.

**DESCRIPTION AND COMMENTS** Magic Carpets of Aladdin is a midway ride like Dumbo, except with magic carpets instead of elephants. Copying the water innovation of the One Fish, Two Fish attraction at Universal's Islands of Adventure, Disney's Aladdin ride has a spitting camel positioned to spray jets of water on carpet riders. Riders can maneuver their carpets up and down to spit back and side to side to avoid getting wet.

**TOURING TIPS** Like Dumbo, this ride has great eye appeal but extremely limited capacity (that is, it's slow-loading). If your younger children see it, they'll probably want to ride. Try to get them on during the first 30 minutes the park is open or try just before park closing.

## Pirates of the Caribbean

| APPEAL BY AGE | PRESCHOOL ★★★ | GRADE SCHOOL ★★★★★ | TEENS |
| --- | --- | --- | --- |
| ★★★★ | YOUNG ADULTS ★★★★ | OVER 30 ★★★★½ | SENIORS ★★★★½ |

**What it is** Indoor pirate-themed adventure boat ride. **Scope and scale** Headliner. **When to go** Before noon or after 5 p.m. **Special comments**

Frightens some young children. **Author's rating** Disney audio-animatronics at its best; not to be missed; ★★★★★. **Duration of ride** About 7½ minutes. **Average wait in line per 100 people ahead of you** 1½ minutes. **Assumes** Both waiting lines operating. **Loading speed** Fast.

**DESCRIPTION AND COMMENTS** An indoor cruise through a series of sets depicting a pirate raid on an island settlement, from bombardment of the fortress to debauchery after the victory. Regarding debauchery, Pirates of the Caribbean is one of several Disney attractions that has been administered a strong dose of political correctness.

**TOURING TIPS** Undoubtedly one of the park's most elaborate and timeless attractions. Engineered to move large crowds in a hurry, Pirates is a good attraction to see during late afternoon. It has two covered waiting lines.

### Enchanted Tiki Birds

| APPEAL BY AGE | PRESCHOOL ★★★★ | GRADE SCHOOL ★★★½ | TEENS ★★★ |
|---|---|---|---|
| YOUNG ADULTS ★★★ | OVER 30 ★★★ | | SENIORS ★★★ |

**What it is** Audio-animatronic Pacific island musical theater show. **Scope and scale** Minor attraction. **When to go** Before 11 a.m. or after 3:30 p.m. **Special comments** Frightens some preschoolers. **Author's rating** Very, very unusual; ★★★½. **Duration of presentation** 15½ minutes. **Preshow entertainment** Talking birds. **Probable waiting time** 15 minutes.

**DESCRIPTION AND COMMENTS** Upgraded in 1998, this theater presentation features two of Disney's most beloved bird characters: Iago from *Aladdin* and Zazu from *The Lion King*. A new song, "Friend Like Me," and a revamped plotline add some much-needed zip, but the production remains (pardon the pun) a featherweight in the Disney galaxy of attractions. Even so, the Tiki Birds are a great favorite of the 8-and-under set and guests on drugs. It's also reported that the show has been known to induce labor. Although readers like the *Enchanted Tiki Birds* show, they caution that the new version is more frightening to younger children than was the old.

**TOURING TIPS** One of the more bizarre Magic Kingdom entertainments. It's usually not too crowded. We go in the late afternoon when we especially appreciate sitting briefly in an air-conditioned theater with our brains in park.

# ■ FRONTIERLAND

FRONTIERLAND ADJOINS ADVENTURELAND as you move clockwise around the Magic Kingdom. The focus is on the Old West, with stockade-type structures and pioneer trappings.

WARNING!

For Bouffants, Rug Wearers, and Elvis Impersonators

This Ride Will Muss Your 'Do

## Splash Mountain (FASTPASS)

| APPEAL BY AGE | PRESCHOOL † | GRADE SCHOOL ★★★★★ | TEENS ★★★★★ |
|---|---|---|---|
| YOUNG ADULTS ★★★★★ | | OVER 30 ★★★★★ | SENIORS ★★★★★ |

*† Many preschoolers are too short to meet the height requirement, and others are visually intimidated when they see the ride from the waiting line. Among preschoolers who actually ride, most give the attraction high marks (★★★–★★★★★).*

**What it is** Indoor/outdoor water-flume adventure ride. **Scope and scale** Super headliner. **When to go** As soon as the park opens, during afternoon or evening parades, just before closing, or use FASTPASS. **Special comments** Must be 40 inches tall to ride; children younger than 7 must ride with an adult. Switching-off option provided (page 75). **Author's rating** A wet winner; not to be missed; ★★★★★. **Duration of ride** About 10 minutes. **Average wait in line per 100 people ahead of you** 3½ minutes. **Assumes** Operating at full capacity. **Loading speed** Moderate.

**DESCRIPTION AND COMMENTS** Amusement park flume ride, Disney-style. Splash Mountain combines steep chutes and animatronics with at least one special effect for each of the senses. The ride covers over half a mile, splashing through swamps, caves, and backwood bayous before climaxing in a five-story plunge and Br'er Rabbit's triumphant return home. More than 100 audio-animatronic characters, including Br'er Rabbit (a.k.a. Br'er Hare), Br'er Bear, and Br'er Fox regale riders with songs, including "Zip-a-Dee-Doo-Dah."

**TOURING TIPS** This happy, exciting, adventuresome ride vies with Space Mountain in Tomorrowland as the park's most popular attraction. Crowds build fast in the morning, and waits of more than two hours can be expected once the park fills. Get in line first thing, certainly no later than 45 minutes after the park opens. Long lines will persist all day.

If you have only one day to see the Magic Kingdom, ride Space Mountain first, then Buzz Lightyear (also in Tomorrowland), then hot-foot it over to Splash Mountain. If the wait is less than 30 minutes, go ahead and ride. Otherwise, obtain a FAST-PASS and return later to enjoy Splash Mountain. FASTPASS strategies have been incorporated into the Magic Kingdom One-Day Touring Plans (see page 75). If you have two mornings to devote to the Magic Kingdom, experience Space Mountain one morning and Buzz Lightyear, Splash Mountain, and Big Thunder Mountain the next. Spreading your visit over two mornings will eliminate much crisscrossing of the park as well as the backtracking that is inevitable when you use FASTPASS.

As occurs with Space Mountain, when the park opens, hundreds are poised to dash to Splash Mountain. The best strategy is to go to the end of Main Street and turn left to The Crystal Palace restaurant. In front of the restaurant is a bridge that provides a shortcut to Adventureland. Stake out a position at the barrier rope. When the park opens and the rope drops, move as fast as you comfortably can and cross the bridge to Adventureland.

Here's another shortcut: Just past the first group of buildings on your right, roughly across from the Swiss Family Treehouse, is a small passageway containing restrooms and phones. Easy to overlook, it connects Adventureland to Frontierland. Go through the passageway into Frontierland and take a hard left. As you emerge along the waterfront, Splash Mountain is straight ahead. If you miss the passageway, don't fool around looking for it. Continue straight through Adventureland to Splash Mountain.

Less exhausting in the morning is to commute to Splash Mountain via the Walt Disney World Railroad. Board at Main Street Station and wait for the park to open. The train will pull out of the station a few minutes after the rope drops at the central hub end of Main Street. Ride to Frontierland Station (the first stop) and disembark. As you come down the stairs at the station, the entrance to Splash Mountain will be on your left. Because of the time required to unload at the station, train passengers will arrive at Splash Mountain about the same time as the lead element from the central hub.

At Splash Mountain, if you ride in the front seat, you almost certainly will get wet. Riders elsewhere get splashed, but usually not doused. Since you don't know which seat you'll be assigned, go prepared. On a cool day, carry a plastic garbage bag. Tear holes in the bottom and sides to make a water-resistant (not waterproof) sack dress. Be sure to tuck the bag under your bottom. Leave your camera with a nonriding member of your group or wrap it in plastic. An alternative to the garbage bag get-up is to store a change of clothes, including footwear, in one of the park's rental lockers. For any attraction where there's a distinct possibility of getting soaked, we recommend you wear Tevas or some other type of waterproof sandal. Change back to regular shoes after the ride.

The scariest part of this adventure ride is the steep chute you see when standing in line, but the drop looks worse than it is. Despite reassurances, however, many children wig out after watching it.

## Big Thunder Mountain Railroad (FASTPASS)

| APPEAL BY AGE | PRESCHOOL ★★★ | GRADE SCHOOL ★★★★ | TEENS ★★★★ |
|---|---|---|---|
| YOUNG ADULTS ★★★★ | | OVER 30 ★★★★ | SENIORS ★★★ |

**What it is** Tame, Western-mining-themed roller coaster. **Scope and scale** Headliner. **When to go** Before 10 a.m., in the hour before closing, or use FASTPASS. **Special comments** Must be 40 inches tall to ride; children younger than age 7 must ride with an adult. Switching-off option provided (page 75). **Author's rating** Great effects; relatively tame ride; not to be missed; ★★★★. **Duration of ride** Almost 3½ minutes. **Average wait in line per 100 people ahead of you** 2½ minutes. **Assumes** 5 trains operating. **Loading speed** Moderate to fast.

**DESCRIPTION AND COMMENTS** Roller coaster through and around a Disney "mountain." The idea is that you're on a runaway mine train during the Gold Rush. This roller coaster is about 5 on a "scary scale" of 10. First-rate examples of Disney creativity are showcased: realistic mining town, falling rocks, and an earthquake, all humorously animated with swinging possums, petulant buzzards, and the like.

**TOURING TIPS** A superb Disney experience, but not too wild a roller coaster. Emphasis is much more on the sights than on the thrill of the ride.

Nearby Splash Mountain affects the traffic flow to Big Thunder Mountain Railroad. Adventuresome guests ride Splash Mountain first, then go next door to ride Big Thunder. This means large crowds in Frontierland all day and long waits for Big Thunder Mountain. The best way to experience the Magic Kingdom's "mountains" is to ride Space Mountain one morning as soon as the park opens, and Splash Mountain and Big Thunder the next morning. If you only have one day, the order should be (1) Space Mountain (2) optional–Buzz Lightyear (3) Splash Mountain (4) Big Thunder Mountain. If the wait exceeds 30 minutes when you arrive, use FASTPASS.

## Country Bear Jamboree

| APPEAL BY AGE | PRESCHOOL ★★★ | GRADE SCHOOL ★★★ | TEENS ★★½ |
|---|---|---|---|
| YOUNG ADULTS ★★★ | | OVER 30 ★★★ | SENIORS ★★★ |

**What it is** Audio-animatronic country hoedown theater show. **Scope and scale** Major attraction. **When to go** Before 11:30 a.m., before a parade, or during the 2 hours before closing. **Special comments** Shows change at Christmas. **Author's rating** A Disney classic; ★★★.

**Duration of presentation** 15 minutes. **Preshow entertainment** None. **Probable waiting time** This attraction is moderately popular but has a comparatively small capacity. Waiting time between noon and 5:30 p.m. on a busy day will average 15–45 minutes.

**DESCRIPTION AND COMMENTS** A charming cast of audio-animatronic bears sing and stomp in a Western-style hoedown. Although one of the Magic Kingdom's most humorous and upbeat shows, *Country Bear Jamboree* geriatric bears have run for so long that the bears are a step away from assisted living.

**TOURING TIPS** The *Jamboree* remains popular and draws large crowds, from mid-morning on.

## Tom Sawyer Island and Fort Langhorn

| APPEAL BY AGE | PRESCHOOL ★★★★★ | | GRADE SCHOOL ★★★★★ |
|---|---|---|---|
| TEENS ★★ | YOUNG ADULTS ★★ | OVER 30 ★★ | SENIORS ★★ |

**What it is** Outdoor walk-through exhibit/rustic playground. **Scope and scale** Minor attraction. **When to go** Midmorning through late afternoon. **Special comments** Closes at dusk. **Author's rating** The place for rambunctious kids; ★★★.

**DESCRIPTION AND COMMENTS** Tom Sawyer Island is a getaway within the park. It has hills to climb, a cave and windmill to explore, a tipsy barrel bridge to cross, and paths to follow. You can watch riverboats chug past a toy rifle from the blockhouse of Fort Langhorn. It's a delight for adults and a godsend for children who have been in tow and closely supervised all day. They love the freedom to explore Fort Langhorn. There is even a "secret" escape tunnel.

**TOURING TIPS** Tom Sawyer Island isn't one of the Magic Kingdom's more celebrated attractions, but it's one of the park's better conceived ones. Attention to detail is excellent, and kids revel in its frontier atmosphere. It's a must for families with children ages 5–15. If your group is made up of adults, visit on your second day or on your first day after you've seen the attractions you most wanted to see.

Although children could spend a whole day on the island, plan on at least 20 minutes. Access is by raft from Frontierland; two operate simultaneously and the trip is pretty efficient, though you may have to stand in line to board both ways.

## Frontierland Shootin' Arcade

| APPEAL BY AGE | PRESCHOOL ★★★ | GRADE SCHOOL ★★★★ | TEENS ★★★ |
|---|---|---|---|
| YOUNG ADULTS ★★ | | OVER 30 ★★ | SENIORS ★★ |

**What it is** Electronic shooting gallery. **Scope and scale** Diversion. **When to go** Whenever convenient. **Special comments** Costs 50 cents per play. **Author's rating** Very nifty shooting gallery; ★½.

**DESCRIPTION AND COMMENTS**  Very elaborate. One of few attractions not included in Magic Kingdom admission.

**TOURING TIPS**  Not a place to blow your time if you're on a tight schedule. If time allows, go on your second day. The fun is entirely in the target practice—no prizes can be won.

### Walt Disney World Railroad

**DESCRIPTION AND COMMENTS**  Stops in Frontierland on its circle tour of the park. See the description under Main Street for additional details.

**TOURING TIPS**  Pleasant, feet-saving link to Main Street and Mickey's Toontown Fair, but the Frontierland Station is usually more congested than those stations. You cannot take your rental stroller on the train. If you don't want to make a round trip to pick up your stroller, take your personal belongings, your stroller name card, and your rental receipt with you on the train. You'll be issued a replacement stroller at your Walt Disney World Railroad destination.

# LIBERTY SQUARE

LIBERTY SQUARE RE-CREATES COLONIAL AMERICA at the time of the American Revolution. The architecture is Federal or Colonial. A real, 130-year-old live oak (dubbed the "Liberty Tree") lends dignity and grace to the setting.

### *The Hall of Presidents*

| APPEAL BY AGE | PRESCHOOL ★ | GRADE SCHOOL ★★½ | TEENS ★★★ |
|---|---|---|---|
| YOUNG ADULTS ★★★½ | | OVER 30 ★★★★ | SENIORS ★★★★ |

**What it is** Audio-animatronic historical theater presentation. **Scope and scale** Major attraction. **When to go** Anytime. **Author's rating** Impressive and moving; ★★★. **Duration of presentation** Almost 23 minutes. **Preshow entertainment** None. **Probable waiting time** Lines for this attraction look awesome but are usually swallowed up as the theater exchanges audiences. Your wait will probably be the remaining time of the show that's in progress when you arrive. Even during the busiest times, waits rarely exceed 40 minutes.

**DESCRIPTION AND COMMENTS**  President George W. Bush was added in 2001, but the content of the presentation remains largely the same. A 23-minute, strongly inspirational and patriotic program highlights milestones in American history. The performance climaxes with a roll call of presidents from Washington through the present, with a few words of encouragement from President Lincoln. A very moving show for Americans, coupled with one of Disney's best and most ambitious audio-animatronic efforts.

**TOURING TIPS** Detail and costumes are masterful. If your children fidget during the show, notice the Presidents do too. This attraction is one of the park's most popular among older visitors. Don't be put off by long lines. The theater holds more than 700 people, thus swallowing large lines at a single gulp when visitors are admitted.

## *Liberty Square* Riverboat

| APPEAL BY AGE | PRESCHOOL ★★★½ | GRADE SCHOOL ★★★ | TEENS ★★½ |
|---|---|---|---|
| YOUNG ADULTS ★★★ | | OVER 30 ★★★ | SENIORS ★★★ |

**What it is** Outdoor scenic boat ride. **Scope and scale** Major attraction. **When to go** Anytime. **Author's rating** Slow, relaxing, and scenic; ★★½. **Duration of ride** About 16 minutes. **Average wait to board** 10–14 minutes.

**DESCRIPTION AND COMMENTS** Large-capacity paddle-wheel riverboat navigates the waters around Tom Sawyer Island and Fort Langhorn. A beautiful craft, the riverboat provides a lofty perspective of Frontierland and Liberty Square.

**TOURING TIPS** The riverboat is a good attraction for the busy middle of the day. If you encounter huge crowds, chances are that the attraction has been inundated by a wave of guests coming from a just-concluded performance of *The Hall of Presidents*.

## The Haunted Mansion (FASTPASS)

| APPEAL BY AGE | PRESCHOOL [varies] | GRADE SCHOOL ★★★★★ | TEENS ★★★★ |
|---|---|---|---|
| YOUNG ADULTS ★★★★ | | OVER 30 ★★★★ | SENIORS ★★★★ |

**What it is** Haunted-house dark ride. **Scope and scale** Major attraction. **When to go** Before 11:30 a.m., or use FASTPASS after 8 p.m. **Special comments** Frightens some very young children. **Author's rating** Some of Walt Disney World's best special effects; not to be missed; ★★★★. **Duration of ride** 7-minute ride plus a 1½-minute preshow. **Average wait in line per 100 people ahead of you** 2½ minutes. **Assumes** Both "stretch rooms" operating. **Loading speed** Fast.

**DESCRIPTION AND COMMENTS** Only slightly more scary than a whoopee cushion, The Haunted Mansion serves up some of the Magic Kingdom's best visual effects. The Haunted Mansion is a masterpiece of detail. "Doom Buggies" on a conveyor belt transport you throughout the house from parlor to attic, and then through a graveyard. The story line is so thin and unemphasized you won't notice.

**TOURING TIPS** This attraction would be more at home in Fantasyland, but no matter. It's Disney at its best. Lines here ebb and flow more than those at most other Magic Kingdom hot spots because the Mansion is near *The Hall of Presidents* and the *Liberty Square* Riverboat. These two attractions disgorge 700 and

450 people respectively when each show or ride ends, and many of these folks head straight for the Mansion. If you can't go before 11:30 a.m. or after 8 p.m., try to slip in between crowds. Note that The Haunted Mansion is such a fast-loading attraction that FASTPASS really isn't warranted.

# FANTASYLAND

FANTASYLAND IS THE HEART OF THE MAGIC KINGDOM, a truly enchanting place spread gracefully like a miniature Alpine village beneath the steepled towers of Cinderella Castle.

## It's a Small World

| APPEAL BY AGE | PRESCHOOL ★★★½ | GRADE SCHOOL ★★★ | TEENS ★★½ |
|---|---|---|---|
| YOUNG ADULTS ★★½ | | OVER 30 ★★½ | SENIORS ★★★ |

**What it is** World brotherhood–themed indoor boat ride. **Scope and scale** Major attraction. **When to go** Anytime. **Author's rating** Exponentially cute; ★★★. **Duration of ride** Approximately 11 minutes. **Average wait in line per 100 people ahead of you** 11 minutes. **Assumes** Busy conditions with 30 or more boats operating. **Loading speed** Fast.

**DESCRIPTION AND COMMENTS** Totally rehabbed in 2005, Small World is a happy, upbeat indoor attraction with a mindnumbing tune that only a backhoe can remove from your brain. Small boats carry visitors on a tour around the world, with singing and dancing dolls showcasing the dress and culture of each nation. One of Disney's oldest entertainment offerings, It's a Small World first unleashed its brainwashing song and lethally cute ethnic dolls on the real world at the 1964 New York World's Fair. Though it bludgeons you with sappy redundancy, almost everyone enjoys It's a Small World (at least the first time). It stands, however, along with *Enchanted Tiki Birds,* in the What-Kind-of-Drugs-Were-They-On-When-They-Thought-This-Up? category.

**TOURING TIPS** Cool off here during the heat of the day. With two waiting lines, It's a Small World loads fast and usually is a good bet between 11 a.m. and 5 p.m. If you wear a hearing aid, turn it off.

## Peter Pan's Flight (FASTPASS)

| APPEAL BY AGE | PRESCHOOL ★★★½ | GRADE SCHOOL ★★★½ | TEENS |
|---|---|---|---|
| ★★★½ | YOUNG ADULTS ★★★½ | OVER 30 ★★★½ | SENIORS ★★★½ |

**What it is** Indoor track ride. **Scope and scale** Minor attraction. **When to go** Before 10 a.m., or use FASTPASS after 6 p.m. **Author's rating** Happy, mellow, and well done; ★★★★. **Duration of ride** A little over 3 minutes. **Average wait in line per 100 people ahead of you** 5½ minutes. **Loading speed** Moderate to slow.

**DESCRIPTION AND COMMENTS**  Though not considered a major attraction, Peter Pan's Flight is superbly designed and absolutely delightful, with a happy theme uniting some favorite Disney characters, beautiful effects, and charming music. An indoor attraction, Peter Pan's Flight offers a relaxing ride in a "flying pirate ship" over old London and thence to Never-Never Land. Unlike Snow White's Adventures, there's nothing here that will jump out at you or frighten young children.

**TOURING TIPS**  Because Peter Pan's Flight is very popular, count on long lines all day. Ride before 10 a.m., during a parade, just before the park closes, or use FASTPASS.

If you use FASTPASS, pick up your pass as early in the day as possible. Sometimes Peter Pan exhausts its whole day's supply of FASTPASSes by 2 p.m.

### Mickey's PhilharMagic (FASTPASS)

| APPEAL BY AGE | PRESCHOOL ★★★½ | GRADE SCHOOL ★★★★½ | TEENS ★★★★ |
| --- | --- | --- | --- |
| YOUNG ADULTS ★★★★ | OVER 30 ★★★★ | | SENIORS ★★★★ |

**What it is**  3-D movie. **Scope and scale**  Major attraction. **Special comments**  Not to be missed. **When to go**  Before 11 a.m., during parades, or use FASTPASS. **Author's rating**  ★★★★. A masterpiece **Duration of presentation**  About 20 minutes. **Probable waiting time** 12–30 minutes.

**DESCRIPTION AND COMMENTS**  With *Mickey's PhilharMagic* up and running, there is a 3-D movie attraction at each of the four Disney theme parks. The *PhilharMagic* features an odd collection of Disney characters, mixing Mickey and Donald with Simba, Ariel (from the *Little Mermaid*), as well as Jasmine and Aladdin. Presented in a theater large enough to accommodate a 150-foot-wide screen—huge by 3-D movie standards, the 3-D movie is augmented by an arsenal of special effects built into the theater. The plot involves Mickey as the conductor of the *PhilharMagic,* leaving the theater to solve a mystery. In his absence Donald appears and attempts to take charge, with disastrous results.

The attraction is one of Disney's best 3-D efforts. Brilliantly conceived, furiously paced, and laugh-out-loud funny, *PhilharMagic* incorporates a hit parade of Disney's most beloved characters in a production that will leave you grinning.

**TOURING TIPS**  Though the other 3-D movies are intense, loud, in-your-face productions, *Mickey's PhilharMagic* is much softer and cuddlier. Things still pop out of the screen in keeping with the time-tested 3-D model, but they're not scary things. Children for once are enthusiastic and astonished instead of quaking in their Nikes. You should still proceed cautiously if you have kids under age 5 in your group, but it's the rare child who is frightened. The show is very popular, but the theater is very large. Except on the busiest of days you shouldn't wait more than 35 minutes (usually less) in the standby line.

## Cinderella's Golden Carousel

| APPEAL BY AGE | PRESCHOOL ★★★★ | GRADE SCHOOL ★★½ | TEENS — |
|---|---|---|---|
| YOUNG ADULTS — | | OVER 30 — | SENIORS — |

**What it is** Merry-go-round. **Scope and scale** Minor attraction. **When to go** Before 11 a.m. or after 8 p.m. **Special comments** Adults enjoy the beauty and nostalgia of this ride. **Author's rating** A beautiful children's ride; ★★★. **Duration of ride** About 2 minutes. **Average wait in line per 100 people ahead of you** 5 minutes. **Loading speed** Slow.

DESCRIPTION AND COMMENTS One of the most elaborate and beautiful merry-go-rounds you'll ever see, especially when its lights are on.

TOURING TIPS Unless young children in your party insist on riding, appreciate this attraction from the sidelines. While lovely to look at, the carousel loads and unloads very slowly.

## The Many Adventures of Winnie the Pooh (FASTPASS)

| APPEAL BY AGE | PRESCHOOL ★★★★½ | GRADE SCHOOL ★★★★ | TEENS |
|---|---|---|---|
| ★★★ | YOUNG ADULTS ★★★ | OVER 30 ★★★ | SENIORS ★★★ |

**What it is** Indoor track ride. **Scope and scale** Minor attraction. **When to go** Before 10 a.m., in the 2 hours before closing, or use FASTPASS. **Author's rating** Cute as the Pooh-bear himself: ★★★½. **Duration of ride** About 4 minutes. **Average wait in line per 100 people ahead of you** 4 minutes. **Loading speed** Moderate.

DESCRIPTION AND COMMENTS Opened in the summer of 1998, this addition to Fantasyland replaced the alternately praised and maligned Mr. Toad's Wild Ride (Toadsters are still pissed). Pooh is sunny, upbeat, and fun—more in the image of Peter Pan's Flight or Splash Mountain. You ride a "Hunny Pot" through the pages of a huge picture book into the Hundred Acre Wood, where you encounter Pooh, Piglet, Eeyore, Owl, Rabbit, Tigger, Kanga, and Roo as they contend with a blustery day. There's even a dream sequence with Heffalumps and Woozles.

TOURING TIPS Because of its relatively small capacity, the daily allocation of FASTPASSes for Winnie the Pooh is often distributed by noon or 1 p.m. For this same reason, your scheduled return time to enjoy the ride might be hours away. It's not unusual to pick up a FASTPASS for Winnie the Pooh at 12:30 p.m. with a scheduled return time of 5 p.m. or later.

## Snow White's Scary Adventures

| APPEAL BY AGE | PRESCHOOL ★ | GRADE SCHOOL ★★½ | TEENS ★★ |
|---|---|---|---|
| YOUNG ADULTS ★★½ | | OVER 30 ★★½ | SENIORS ★★½ |

**What it is** Indoor track ride. **Scope and scale** Minor attraction. **When to go** Before 11 a.m. or after 6 p.m. **Special comments** Terrifying to many young children. **Author's rating** Worth seeing if the wait isn't long; ★★½. **Duration of ride** Almost 2½ minutes. **Average wait in line per 100 people ahead of you** 6¼ minutes. **Loading speed** Moderate to slow.

DESCRIPTION AND COMMENTS Mine cars travel through a spook house showing Snow White as she narrowly escapes harm at the hands of the wicked witch. Action and effects are not as good as Peter Pan's Flight or Winnie the Pooh.

TOURING TIPS We get more mail about this ride than any other Disney attraction. It terrifies many children ages 6 and younger. Though a 1994 upgrade gave Snow White a larger role, the witch (who is relentless and ubiquitous) continues to be the focal character. Many readers tell us their children have refused to ride any attraction that operates in the dark after having experienced Snow White's Scary Adventures.

## Ariel's Grotto

| APPEAL BY AGE | PRESCHOOL ★★★★★ | GRADE SCHOOL ★★★★★ |
|---|---|---|
| TEENS ★★ | YOUNG ADULTS ★ | OVER 30 ★ | SENIORS ★ |

**What it is** Interactive fountain and character-greeting area. **Scope and scale** Minor attraction. **When to go** Before 10 a.m. or after 9 p.m. **Author's rating** One of the most elaborate of the character-greeting venues; ★★★. **Average wait in line per 100 people ahead of you** 30 minutes.

DESCRIPTION AND COMMENTS On the lagoon side of Dumbo, Ariel's Grotto consists of a small children's play area with an interactive fountain and a rock grotto where Ariel, the Little Mermaid, poses for photos and signs autographs. If "interactive fountain" is new to you, it means an opportunity for your children to get ten times wetter than a trout. Can you say "hy-po-ther-mi-a"?

TOURING TIPS The Grotto is small, and the wait to meet Ariel is usually long. Because kids in line are fresh from the fountain, it's very difficult for adults to remain dry.

A mother from Hagerstown, Maryland, said the experience was "like being packed in a pen with wet cocker spaniels."

If your children spot the Grotto before you do, there's no turning back. Count on a long queue and a 20–40-minute wait to see Ariel except the first 15 minutes she's open for business (usually 10 a.m.). Then there's the fountain. Allow your children to disrobe to the legal limit. (Don't bother with umbrellas or ponchos, because water squirts up from below.) When you're finished meeting Ariel, you will have to navigate an armada of variously aged males plowing upstream through the exit to admire the Little Mermaid's cleavage.

## Dumbo the Flying Elephant

| APPEAL BY AGE | PRESCHOOL ★★★★★ | GRADE SCHOOL ★★★★ | TEENS ★½ |
|---|---|---|---|
| YOUNG ADULTS ★½ | OVER 30 ★½ | | SENIORS ★½ |

**What it is** Disneyfied midway ride. **Scope and scale** Minor attraction. **When to go** Before 10 a.m. or after 9 p.m. **Author's rating** An attractive children's ride; ★★★. **Duration of ride** 1½ minutes. **Average wait in line per 100 people ahead of you** 20 minutes. **Loading speed** Slow.

**DESCRIPTION AND COMMENTS** A tame, happy children's ride based on the lovable flying elephant, Dumbo. Despite being little different from rides at state fairs and amusement parks, Dumbo is the favorite Magic Kingdom attraction of many younger children.

**TOURING TIPS** If Dumbo is essential to your child's happiness, make it your first stop, preferably within 15 minutes of park opening.

## Mad Tea Party

| APPEAL BY AGE | PRESCHOOL ★★★★ | GRADE SCHOOL ★★★★ | TEENS ★★★★ |
|---|---|---|---|
| YOUNG ADULTS ★★★★ | OVER 30 ★★ | | SENIORS ★★ |

**What it is** Midway-type spinning ride. **Scope and scale** Minor attraction. **When to go** Before 11 a.m. or after 5 p.m. **Special comments** You can make the teacups spin faster by turning the wheel in the center of the cup. **Author's rating** Fun, but not worth the wait; ★★. **Duration of ride** 1½ minutes. **Average wait in line per 100 people ahead of you** 7½ minutes. **Loading speed** Slow.

**DESCRIPTION AND COMMENTS** Riders whirl feverishly in big teacups. Alice in Wonderland's Mad Hatter provides the theme. A version of this ride without Disney characters can be found at every local carnival. Teenagers like to lure adults onto the teacups, then turn the wheel in the middle (making the cup spin faster), until the adults are plastered against the sides and on the verge of throwing up. Unless your life's ambition is to be the test subject in a human

Motion Sickness

WARNING!

centrifuge, don't even consider getting on this ride with anyone younger than 21.

**TOURING TIPS** This ride, well done but not unique, is notoriously slow-loading. Skip it on a busy schedule—if the kids will let you. Ride the morning of your second day if your schedule is more relaxed.

# ■ MICKEY'S TOONTOWN FAIR

MICKEY'S TOONTOWN FAIR IS SANDWICHED between Fantasyland and Tomorrowland, like an afterthought, on about three acres formerly part of the Tomorrowland Speedway. It's the smallest of the lands and more like an attraction than a section of the park. Though you can wander in on a somewhat obscure path from Fantasyland or on a totally obscure path from Tomorrowland, Mickey's Toontown Fair generally receives guests arriving by the Walt Disney World Railroad.

Mickey's Toontown Fair serves as the Magic Kingdom's character-greeting headquarters. The Fair provides a place where Disney characters are available to guests on a continuing and reliable schedule. Mickey, in the role of the Fair's chief judge, meets guests for photos and autographs in the Judge's Tent. Other characters appear in the Toontown Hall of Fame. Characters are available throughout the day except during parades.

In general, Mickey's Toontown Fair doesn't handle crowds very well. If your children are into collecting character autographs and want to enjoy the various Toontown attractions without extraordinary waits, we recommend touring first thing in the morning. If you only have one day to visit the Magic Kingdom and hitting the child-oriented attractions is a priority, head first to Fantasyland and ride Dumbo, Pooh, and Peter Pan, then split for Toontown. In Toontown, ride Goofy's Barnstormer first and then tour Mickey's and Minnie's houses. Go next to the Toontown Hall of Fame for character pics and autographs. For adults without children, Toontown is visually interesting but otherwise expendable.

## Mickey's Country House and Judge's Tent

| APPEAL BY AGE | PRESCHOOL ★★★½ | GRADE SCHOOL ★★★ | TEENS ★★½ |
|---|---|---|---|
| YOUNG ADULTS ★★½ | OVER 30 ★★½ | | SENIORS ★★½ |

**What it is** Walk-through tour of Mickey's house and meeting with Mickey. **Scope and scale** Minor attraction. **When to go** Before 11:30

a.m. or after 4:30 p.m. **Author's rating** Well done; ★★★. Duration of tour 15–30 minutes (depending on the crowd). **Average wait in line per 100 people ahead of you** 20 minutes. **Touring speed** Slow.

**DESCRIPTION AND COMMENTS** Mickey's Country House is the starting point of a self-guided tour through the famous Mouse's house, into his backyard, and past Pluto's doghouse. If you want to tour Mickey's house, but skip meeting Mickey, you'll find an exit just before entering his tent.

**TOURING TIPS** Discerning observers will see immediately that Mickey's Country House is a cleverly devised queuing area for delivering guests to Mickey's Judge's Tent for the Mouse Encounter. It also heightens anticipation by revealing the corporate symbol on a more personal level. Mickey's Country House is well conceived and contains a lot of Disney memorabilia. Children touch *everything* as they proceed through the house, hoping to find some artifact not welded into the set. (An especially tenacious child actually ripped a couple of books from a bookcase.)

Meeting Mickey and touring his house are best done during the first hour Mickey's Toontown Fair is open, or in the evening. If meeting the great Mouse is your child's priority, you can be certain of finding Mickey here. Some children are so obsessed with seeing Mickey that they can't enjoy anything else until they have him in the rearview mirror.

## Minnie's Country House

| APPEAL BY AGE | PRESCHOOL ★★★ | GRADE SCHOOL ★★★★ | TEENS ★★½ |
|---|---|---|---|
| YOUNG ADULTS ★★½ | OVER 30 ★★½ | | SENIORS ★★½ |

**What it is** Walk-through exhibit. **Scope and scale** Minor attraction. **When to go** Before 11:30 a.m. or after 4:30 p.m. **Author's rating** Great detail; ★★. **Duration of tour** About 10 minutes. **Average wait in line per 100 people ahead of you** 12 minutes. **Touring speed** Slow.

**DESCRIPTION AND COMMENTS** Minnie's Country House offers a self-guided tour through the rooms and backyard of Mickey's main squeeze. Similar to Mickey's Country House, only predictably more feminine, Minnie's also showcases fun Disney memorabilia. Among highlights of the short tour are the fanciful appliances in Minnie's kitchen.

**TOURING TIPS** The main difference between Mickey's and Minnie's houses is that Mickey is home to receive guests. Minnie was never home during our visits. We did, however, bump into her on the street and in the Toontown Hall of Fame. Minnie's Country House is one of the more accessible attractions in the Fair, but we nonetheless recommend touring early or late in the day.

## Toontown Hall of Fame

| APPEAL BY AGE | PRESCHOOL ★★★★ | GRADE SCHOOL ★★★★★ |
| --- | --- | --- |
| TEENS ★★ | YOUNG ADULTS ★★ OVER 30 ★★ | SENIORS ★★ |

**What it is** Character-greeting venue. **Scope and scale** Minor attraction. **When to go** Before 10:30 a.m. or after 5:30 p.m. **Author's rating** You want characters? We got 'em! ★★. Duration of greeting About 7–10 minutes. **Average wait in line per 100 people ahead of you** 35 minutes. **Touring speed** Slow.

**DESCRIPTION AND COMMENTS** The Toontown Hall of Fame is at the end of a small plaza between Mickey's and Minnie's houses. It offers one of the largest and most dependably available collection of characters in Walt Disney World. Just inside to the right are entrances to three queuing areas. Signs over each suggest, somewhat ambiguously, which characters you will meet. Character assortments in each greeting area change, as do the names of the assortments themselves. Thus, on a given day you will find two or three groupings available: Famous Friends (also called Toon Pals and sometimes Minnie's Famous Pals) include Minnie, Goofy, Donald, Pluto, and sometimes Uncle Scrooge, Chip 'n' Dale, Roger Rabbit, and Daisy. The 100-Acre-Wood Pals are mostly Winnie the Pooh characters but may include any character that fits the forest theme. Storybook Friends are Snow White, various dwarfs, Belle, the Beast, Sleeping Beauty, Prince Charming, etc. Other categories include Mickey's Pals, Disney chicks (a.k.a. Princesses), Disney Villains, Characters on Weight Watchers, Corporate Symbols, and so on.

Each category of characters occupies a greeting room where 15–20 guests are admitted at a time. They're allowed to stay 7–10 minutes, long enough for a photo, autograph, and hug with each character.

**TOURING TIPS** If your children want to visit each category, you'll have to queue up three times. Each line is long and slow-moving, and during busier hours you can lose a lot of time here. While Famous Friends (a.k.a. Toon Pals and Minnie's Famous Pals) are slightly more popular than other categories, the longest wait is for groupings that include "face characters." Face characters are actors who strongly resemble the character they portray and don't wear any head-covering costume. They are allowed to speak and thus engage children in conversation, prolonging the visit. All characters work in 25-minute shifts, with breaks on the hour and half hour. Because characters in each category change frequently during the day, it's possible to see quite an assortment if you keep recirculating.

If the cast member can't tell you, walk over to the exit and ask departing guests which characters are on duty. Remember that there is some switching of characters on the hour and half hour.

On many days, during the first hour the park is open, a multitude of characters roam the Magic Kingdom Streets. It's just like the old days: spontaneous contact and no lines.

**WARNING!**

For Bouffants, Rug Wearers, and Elvis Impersonators

This Ride Will Muss Your 'Do

## The Barnstormer at Goofy's Wiseacres Farm

**APPEAL BY AGE   PRESCHOOL ★★★★   GRADE SCHOOL ★★★   TEENS ★★½**
**YOUNG   ADULTS   ★★½         OVER   30   ★★½         SENIORS   ★★**

**What it is** Small roller coaster. **Scope and scale** Minor attraction. **When to go** Before 10:30 a.m., during parades, or in the evening just before the park closes. **Special comments** Must be 35 inches or taller to ride. **Author's rating** Great for little ones, but not worth the wait for adults; ★★. **Duration of ride** About 53 seconds. **Average wait in line per 100 people ahead of you** 7 minutes. **Loading speed** Slow.

**DESCRIPTION AND COMMENTS** The Barnstormer is a very small roller coaster. The ride is zippy but super short. In fact, of the 53 seconds the ride is in motion, 32 seconds are consumed in leaving the loading area, being racheted up the first hill, and braking into the off-loading area. The actual time you spend careening around the track is 21 seconds.

Barnstormer is a fairly benign introduction to the roller-coaster genre and a predictably positive way to help your child step up to more adventuresome rides. Simply put, a few circuits on the Barnstormer will increase your little one's confidence and improve his chances for enjoying Disney's more-adult attractions. As always, be sensitive and encouraging, but respect your child's decision whether or not to ride.

**TOURING TIPS** The cars of this dinky coaster are too small for most adults and tend to whiplash taller people. This, plus the limited capacity, equals an engineering marvel along the lines of Dumbo. Parties without children should skip the Barnstormer. If you're touring with children, you have a problem. Like Dumbo, the ride is visually appealing. All kids want to ride, subjecting the whole family to slow-moving lines. If the Barn-stormer is high on your children's hit parade, try to ride as soon as Mickey's Toontown Fair opens.

### Donald's Boat

| APPEAL BY AGE | PRESCHOOL ★★★★ | | GRADE SCHOOL ★★½ |
|---|---|---|---|
| TEENS ★ | YOUNG ADULTS ★½ | OVER 30 ★½ | SENIORS ★½ |

**What it is** Playground and (when the water is running) interactive fountain. **Scope and scale** Diversion. **When to go** Anytime. **Author's rating** A favorite of the 5-and-under set. ★★½.

**DESCRIPTIONS AND COMMENTS** Donald's Boat is an interactive playground themed as a fat, cartoon-style tugboat.

**TOURING TIPS** A great opportunity for easing regimentation and allowing small children to expend pent-up energy.

# ▌ TOMORROWLAND

TOMORROWLAND IS A MIX OF RIDES and experiences relating to the technological development of man and what life will be like in the future. If this sounds like Epcot's theme, it's because Tomorrowland was a breeding ground for ideas that spawned Epcot. Yet, Tomorrowland and Epcot are very different in more than scale. Epcot is mostly educational. Tomorrowland is more for fun, depicting the future as envisioned in science fiction.

### Space Mountain (FASTPASS)

| APPEAL BY AGE | PRESCHOOL † | GRADE SCHOOL ★★★★★ | TEENS ★★★★★ |
|---|---|---|---|
| YOUNG ADULTS ★★★★½ | | OVER 30 ★★★★ | SENIORS † |

† Some preschoolers loved Space Mountain; others were frightened. The sample size of senior citizens who experienced this ride was too small to develop an accurate rating.

**What it is** Roller coaster in the dark. **Scope and scale** Super headliner. **When to go** When the park opens, between 6 and 7 p.m., during the hour before closing, or use FASTPASS. **Special comments** Great fun and action; much wilder than Big Thunder Mountain Railroad. Must be 44 inches tall to ride; children younger than age 7 must be accompanied by an adult. Switching-off option provided (page 75). **Author's rating** An unusual roller coaster with excellent special effects; not to be missed; ★★★★. **Duration of ride** Almost 3 minutes. **Average wait in line per 100 people ahead of you** 3 minutes. **Assumes** Two tracks, one dedicated to FASTPASS riders, dispatching at 21-second intervals. **Loading speed** Moderate to fast.

**DESCRIPTION AND COMMENTS** Totally enclosed in a mammoth futuristic structure, Space Mountain has always been the Magic Kingdom's most popular attraction. The theme is a space flight through dark recesses of the galaxy. Effects are superb, and the ride is the fastest and wildest in the Magic Kingdom. As a roller coaster, Space Mountain is much zippier than Big Thunder Mountain Railroad, but much tamer than the Rock 'n' Roller Coaster at the Studios.

Roller-coaster aficionados will tell you (correctly) that Space Mountain is a designer version of The Wild Mouse, a midway ride that's been around for at least 50 years. There are no long drops or swooping hills like on a traditional roller coaster, only quick, unexpected turns and small drops. Disney's contribution essentially was to add a space theme to The Wild Mouse and put it in the dark. And indeed, this does make the Mouse seem wilder.

**TOURING TIPS** People who can handle a fairly wild roller-coaster ride will take Space Mountain in stride. What sets Space Mountain apart is that cars plummet through darkness, with only occasional lighting. Half the fun of Space Mountain is not knowing where the car will go next.

Space Mountain is the favorite attraction of many Magic Kingdom visitors ages 7–60. Each morning before opening, particularly during summer and holiday periods, several hundred S.M. junkies crowd the rope barriers at the central hub, awaiting the signal to head to the ride's entrance. To get ahead of the competition, be one of the first in the park. Proceed to the end of Main Street and wait at the entrance to Tomorrowland.

Couples touring with children too small to ride Space Mountain can both ride without waiting in line twice by taking advantage of "switching off." Here's how it works: When you enter the Space Mountain line, tell the first Disney attendant (Greeter One) that you want to switch off. The attendant will allow you, your spouse, and your small child (or children) to continue together, phoning ahead to tell Greeter Two to expect you. When you reach Greeter Two (at the turnstile near the boarding area), you'll be given specific directions. One of you will proceed to ride, while the other stays with the kids. Whoever rides will be admitted by the unloading attendant to stairs leading back up to the boarding area. Here you switch off. The second parent rides, and the first parent takes the kids down the stairs to the unloading area where everybody is reunited and exits together. Switching off is also available at Big Thunder Mountain Railroad and Splash Mountain.

Seats are one behind another, as opposed to side-by-side. Parents whose children meet the height and age requirements for Space Mountain can't sit next to their kids.

If you don't catch Space Mountain early in the morning, use FASTPASS or try again during the hour before closing. Often, would-be riders are held in line outside the entrance until all those previously in line have ridden, thus emptying the attraction. The appearance from the outside is that the line is enormous when, in fact, the only people waiting are those visible. This crowd-control technique, known as "stacking," discourages visitors from getting in line. Stacking is used in several Disney rides and attractions during the hour before closing to ensure that the ride will be able to close on schedule. It is also used to keep the number of people waiting inside from overwhelming the air-conditioning. Despite the apparently long line, the wait is usually no longer than if you had been allowed to queue inside.

Splash Mountain siphons off some guests who would have made Space Mountain their first stop. Even so, a mob rushes to Space Mountain as soon as the park opens. If you especially like the thrill attractions and have only one day, see Space Mountain first in the morning, followed by Splash Mountain and Big Thunder Mountain.

## Tomorrowland Indy Speedway

| APPEAL BY AGE | PRESCHOOL ★★★★ | | GRADE SCHOOL ★★★ |
|---|---|---|---|
| TEENS ★ | YOUNG ADULTS ½ | OVER 30 ½ | SENIORS ½ |

**What it is** Drive-'em-yourself miniature cars. **Scope and scale** Major attraction. **When to go** Before 11 a.m. or after 5 p.m. **Special comments** Must be 52 inches tall to drive unassisted. **Author's rating** Boring for adults (★); great for preschoolers. **Duration of ride** About 4¼ minutes. **Average wait in line per 100 people ahead of you** 4½ minutes. **Assumes** 285-car turnover every 20 minutes. **Loading speed** Slow.

DESCRIPTION AND COMMENTS An elaborate miniature raceway with gasoline-powered cars that travel up to seven miles per hour. The raceway, with sleek cars and racing noises, is quite alluring. Unfortunately, the cars poke along on a guide rail, leaving the driver little to do. Pretty ho-hum for most adults and teenagers. The height requirement excludes small children who would enjoy the ride.

TOURING TIPS This ride is visually appealing but definitely one adults can skip. Preschoolers, however, love it. If your child is too short to drive, ride along and allow the child to steer the car while you work the foot pedal.

The line for the Tomorrowland Indy Speedway snakes across a pedestrian bridge to the loading areas. For a shorter wait, turn right off the bridge to the first loading area (rather than continuing to the second).

## Astro Orbiter

| APPEAL BY AGE | PRESCHOOL ★★★★ | | GRADE SCHOOL ★★★ |
|---|---|---|---|
| TEENS ★★½ | YOUNG ADULTS ★★½ | OVER 30 ★★ | SENIORS ★ |

**What it is** Buck Rogers–style rockets revolving around a central axis. **Scope and scale** Minor attraction. **When to go** Before 11 a.m. or after 5 p.m. **Special comments** This attraction, formerly StarJets, is not as innocuous as it appears. **Author's rating** Not worth the wait; ★★. **Duration of ride** 1½ minutes. **Average wait in line per 100 people ahead of you** 13½ minutes. **Loading speed** Slow.

**DESCRIPTION AND COMMENTS** Though visually appealing, the Astro Orbiter is still a slow-loading carnival ride. The fat little rocket ships simply fly in circles. The best thing about the Astro Orbiter is the nice view when you're aloft.

**TOURING TIPS** Expendable on any schedule. If you ride with preschoolers, seat them first, then board. The Astro Orbiter flies higher and faster than Dumbo and frightens some young children. It also apparently messes with some adults.

## Tomorrowland Transit Authority

| APPEAL BY AGE | PRESCHOOL ★★★½ | GRADE SCHOOL ★★★ | TEENS ★★½ |
|---|---|---|---|
| YOUNG ADULTS ★★½ | | OVER 30 ★★½ | SENIORS ★★★ |

**What it is** Scenic tour of Tomorrowland. **Scope and scale** Minor attraction. **When to go** During hot, crowded times of day (11:30 a.m.–4:30 p.m.). **Special comments** A good way to check out the FASTPASS line at Space Mountain. **Author's rating** Scenic, relaxing, informative; ★★★. **Duration of ride** 10 minutes. **Average wait in line per 100 people ahead of you** 1½ minutes. **Assumes** 39 trains operating. **Loading speed** Fast.

**DESCRIPTION AND COMMENTS** A once-unique prototype of a linear induction–powered mass-transit system, the Authority's tramlike cars carry riders on a leisurely tour of Tomorrowland, including a peek inside Space Mountain. In ancient times the attraction was formerly called the WEDway PeopleMover.

**TOURING TIPS** A relaxing ride, where lines move quickly, and you seldom have to wait. It's a good choice during busier times of day, and it can double as a nursery.

## *Walt Disney's Carousel of Progress* *(open seasonally)*

| APPEAL BY AGE | PRESCHOOL ★★ | GRADE SCHOOL ★★½ | TEENS ★★½ |
|---|---|---|---|
| YOUNG ADULTS ★★★ | | OVER 30 ★★★ | SENIORS ★★★½ |

**What it is** Audio-animatronic theater production. **Scope and scale** Major attraction. **When to go** Anytime. **Author's rating** Nostalgic, warm, and happy; ★★★. **Duration of presentation** 18 minutes. **Preshow entertainment** Documentary on the attraction's long history. **Probable waiting time** Less than 10 minutes.

**DESCRIPTION AND COMMENTS** Updated and improved during the Tomorrowland renovation, *Walt Disney's Carousel of Progress* offers a nostalgic look at how technology and electricity have changed the lives of an audio-animatronic family over several generations. The family is easy to identify with, and a cheerful, sentimental tune bridges the generations.

**TOURING TIPS** This attraction is a great favorite among repeat visitors and is included on all of our one-day touring plans. *The Carousel* handles big crowds effectively and is a good choice during busier times of day.

### The Timekeeper (open seasonally)

| APPEAL BY AGE | PRESCHOOL ★★ | GRADE SCHOOL ★★★½ | TEENS ★★★★ |
| --- | --- | --- | --- |
| YOUNG ADULTS ★★★★ | | OVER 30 ★★★★ | SENIORS ★★★★ |

**What it is** Time-travel movie adventure. **Scope and scale** Major attraction. **When to go** Anytime. **Special comments** Audience must stand throughout entire presentation. **Author's rating** Outstanding; not to be missed; ★★★★. **Duration of presentation** About 20 minutes. **Preshow entertainment** Robots, lasers, and movies. **Probable waiting time** 8–15 minutes.

Motion Sickness

WARNING!

**DESCRIPTION AND COMMENTS** Developed as *Le Visionarium* for Disneyland Paris, *The Timekeeper* adds audio-animatronic characters and a story line to the long-successful Circle-Vision 360 technology. The preshow introduces Timekeeper (a humanoid) and 9-Eye (a time-traveling robot so-named because she has nine cameras that serve as eyes). Afterward, the audience enters the main theater, where Timekeeper places 9-Eye into a time machine and dispatches her on a crazed journey into the past and future. What 9-Eye sees on her odyssey is projected onto huge screens that surround the audience with action. The robot travels to prehistoric Europe and then forward to meet French author Jules Verne, who hitches a ride into the future. Audio-animatronics, Circle-Vision 360 technology, and high-tech special effects combine to make *The Timekeeper* one of Tomorrowland's premier attractions.

**TOURING TIPS** Operating seasonally on days of expected high attendance, and occasionally when other Tomorrowland attractions are closed for maintenance, *The Timekeeper* draws crowds from mid-morning on. Because the theater accommodates more than 1,000 guests per show, there is never much of a wait. Go during early afternoon when the park is hot and crowded.

## Buzz Lightyear's Space Ranger Spin (FASTPASS)

| APPEAL BY AGE | PRESCHOOL ★★★★ | GRADE SCHOOL ★★★★★ | TEENS ★★★★½ |
| YOUNG ADULTS ★★★★ | | OVER 30 ★★★★ | SENIORS ★★★★ |

**What it is** Whimsical space travel–themed indoor ride. **Scope and scale** Minor attraction. **When to go** Before 10:30 a.m., after 6 p.m., or use FASTPASS. **Author's rating** A real winner! ★★★★. **Duration of ride** About 4½ minutes. **Average wait in line per 100 people ahead of you** 3 minutes. **Loading speed** Fast.

DESCRIPTION AND COMMENTS This attraction is based on the space-commando character of Buzz Lightyear from the film *Toy Story*. The marginal story line has you and Buzz Lightyear trying to save the universe from the evil Emperor Zurg. The indoor ride is interactive to the extent that you can spin your car and shoot simulated "laser cannons" at Zurg and his minions.

TOURING TIPS Each car is equipped with two laser cannons and a scorekeeping display. Each scorekeeping display is independent, so you can compete with your riding partner. A joystick allows you to spin the car to line up the various targets. Each time you pull the trigger you'll release a red laser beam that you can see hitting or missing the target. Most folks' first ride is occupied with learning how to use the equipment (fire off individual shots as opposed to keeping the trigger depressed) and figuring out how the targets work. The next ride (like certain potato chips, one is not enough), you'll surprise yourself by how much better you do. *Unofficial* readers are unanimous in their praise of Buzz Lightyear. Some, in fact, spend several hours on it, riding again and again.

See Buzz Lightyear after riding Space Mountain first thing in the morning or use FASTPASS.

## Stitch's Great Escape

| APPEAL BY AGE | PRESCHOOL N/A | GRADE SCHOOL ★★½ | TEENS ★★★ |
| YOUNG ADULTS ★★½ | | OVER 30 ★★ | SENIORS ★★ |

**What it is** Theater-in-the-round sci-fi adventure show. **Scope and scale** Major attraction. **When to go** Before 11 a.m. or after 6 p.m.; try during parades. **Special comments** Frightens children of all ages; 40-inch minimum height requirement. **Author's rating** A cheap coat of paint on a broken car; ★★. **Duration of presentation** About 12 minutes. **Preshow entertainment** About 6 minutes. **Probable waiting time** 12–35 minutes.

**DESCRIPTION AND COMMENTS** *Stitch's Great Escape* is a virtual clone of the oft-maligned *Alien Encounter* attraction. Same theater, same teleportation theme, but this time starring the havoc-wreaking little alien from the feature film *Lilo & Stitch*. In *Great Escape*, Stitch is a prisoner of the galactic authorities and is being transferred to a processing facility en route to his final place of incarceration. He manages to escape by employing an efficient though gross trick, knocking out power to the facility in the process. At this juncture Stitch lumbers around in the dark in much the same way as the theater's previous resident Alien. One wonders why an alien civilization smart enough to master teleportation hasn't yet invented a backup power source.

Since its opening, this attraction has received more cosmetic surgery than Joan Rivers' forehead. The pitch-black darkness in the ride was changed to dim lighting, and several scenes were reworked in an attempt to make it less frightening. Even these measures may not have been enough, as Disney has raised the height requirement from 35 inches to 38 inches, and finally to 40 inches (the same as Big Thunder Mountain Railroad) in an attempt to keep out smaller children. The fact that Big Thunder is a roller coaster and this ride doesn't move should be a warning to parents about its fright potential. In our opinion, tinkering at the margins will be futile when it comes to resuscitating this puppy. We think Disney will keep *Stitch* around only long enough to save face.

**TOURING TIPS** Disney's press release touting *Stitch* as a child-friendly attraction was about as accurate as Enron's bookkeeping. As in the *Alien Encounter,* you're held in your seat by overhead restraints and subjected to something weird clambering around you and whispering to you in a theater darker than a stack of black cats. The *Stitch* version is perhaps slightly less frightening to small children than *Alien Encounter,* but more than enough to scare the pants off many kids ages 6 and younger. Parents note: The overhead restraints will prevent you from leaving your seat to comfort your child if the need arises.

#  LIVE ENTERTAINMENT *in the* MAGIC KINGDOM

BANDS, DISNEY CHARACTER APPEARANCES, parades, ceremonies, and singing and dancing further enliven the Magic Kingdom. For specific events the day you visit, check the live entertainment schedule in your Disney guidemap (free as you enter the park or at City Hall); or alternatively in the *Times Guide* available along with the guidemap.

Our one-day touring plans exclude live performances in favor of seeing as much of the park as time permits. This tactical decision is based on the fact that some parades and performances siphon crowds away from the more popular rides, thus shortening lines.

Nonetheless, the color and pageantry of live events are integral to the Magic Kingdom and a persuasive argument for a second day of touring. Here's a list and description of some performances and events presented with regularity that don't require reservations.

**FANTASYLAND PAVILION** Site of various concerts in Fantasyland.

**FRONTIERLAND HOEDOWN** Characters join square dancers and guests for a hoedown in front of the *Country Bear Jamboree;* check the daily entertainment schedule (*Times Guide*).

**CASTLE FORECOURT STAGE** The forecourt show called *Cinderellabration* was launched in 2005 as part of the Disneyland 50th Anniversary observances. The show begins with Cinderella being crowned royalty and features 18 minutes of almost nonstop music with the major princesses (Sleeping Beauty, Snow White, Belle, Jasmine), their male hangers-on, and their celebrity-sized entourages. Small children will love the singing and the whirlwind of activity, which even manages to incorporate the castle itself. For many adults it's more like Celine Dion on Xanax.

**STORYTIME WITH BELLE AT THE FAIRYTALE GARDEN** Belle and several helpers select children from the small amphitheater audience and dress them up as characters from *Beauty and the Beast.* As Belle tells the story, the children act out the roles. There is a three- to five-minute meet-and-greet with photo and autograph opportunities afterward. Storytime is staged six to eight times each day according to the daily entertainment schedule. To find the Fairytale Garden, follow the path on the Fantasyland side of the castle moat toward Tomorrowland.

**FLAG RETREAT** At 5 p.m. daily at Town Square (railroad station end of Main Street). Sometimes performed with great fanfare and college marching bands, sometimes with a smaller Disney band.

**SWORD IN THE STONE CEREMONY** A ceremony based on the Disney animated feature of the same name. Merlin the Magician selects youngsters from the audience to test their courage and strength by removing the sword, Excalibur, from the stone. Staged several times each day behind Cinderella Castle; check the daily entertainment schedule.

**BAY LAKE AND SEVEN SEAS LAGOON FLOATING ELECTRICAL PAGEANT** This is one of our favorites among the Disney extras, but it's necessary to leave the Magic Kingdom to view it. The pageant is a stunning electric light show afloat on small barges and set to nifty electronic music. It's performed at nightfall (about 9 p.m. most of the year) on Seven Seas Lagoon and Bay Lake. Leave the Magic Kingdom and take the monorail to the Polynesian Resort. Get yourself a drink and walk to the end of the pier to watch the show.

***WISHES* FIREWORKS** Memorable vignettes and music from beloved Disney films combine with a stellar fireworks display while Jiminy Cricket narrates a lump-in-your-throat story about making wishes come true. For an uncluttered view and lighter crowds, watch from the terrace of the Plaza Pavilion restaurant in Tomorrowland. Another good fireworks viewing area is between Dumbo and the carousel.

***WISHES* FIREWORKS CRUISE** For a different view, you can watch the fireworks from the Seven Seas Lagoon aboard a chartered pontoon boat. The charter costs $120 and accommodates up to 12 persons. Your Disney cast member captain will take you for a little cruise and then position the boat in a perfect place to watch the fireworks. For an additional $80 per four persons, the captain will provide deli sandwiches, snacks, and beverages. A major indirect benefit of the charter is that you can enjoy the fireworks without fighting the mob afterwards. Because this is a private charter rather than a tour, only your group will be aboard. Life jackets are provided, but you can wear them at your discretion. Because the Disney reservations system counts days in a somewhat atypical manner, we recommend phoning at about 95 days out to have a Disney agent specify the exact morning to call for reservations. Similar charters are available to watch *IllumiNations* at Epcot.

> *unofficial* **TIP**
> Because there are few boats, charters sell out fast. To reserve, call ☎ 407-WDW-PLAY at exactly 7 a.m. 90 days before the day you want to charter.

**DISNEY CHARACTER SHOWS AND APPEARANCES** Usually, a number of characters are on hand to greet guests when the park opens. Because they snarl pedestrian traffic and stop most children dead in their tracks, this is sort of a mixed blessing. Most days, a character is on duty for photos and autographs from 9 a.m. to 10 p.m. next to City Hall. Mickey and two or three assortments of other characters are available most of the day at Mickey's Toontown Fair. Shows at the Castle Forecourt Stage and Tomorrowland's Galaxy Palace Theater feature Disney characters several times daily (check the entertainment schedule). In Fantasyland, Ariel can be found in her Grotto daily, while a host of others can be seen at the Character Festival next to Dumbo. Characters also roam the park.

**MAGIC KINGDOM BANDS** Banjo, Dixieland, steel drum, marching, and fife-and-drum bands roam the park daily.

**TINKER BELL'S FLIGHT** This nice special effect in the sky above Cinderella Castle heralds the beginning of *Wishes* fireworks (when the park is open late).

# PARADES

PARADES AT THE MAGIC KINGDOM ARE full-fledged spectaculars with dozens of Disney characters and amazing special effects. We rate the afternoon parade as outstanding and the evening parade as "not to be missed."

In addition to providing great entertainment, parades lure guests away from the attractions. If getting on rides appeals to you more than watching a parade, you'll find substantially shorter lines just before and during parades. Because the parade route doesn't pass through Adventureland, Tomorrowland, or Fantasyland, attractions in these lands are particularly good bets. Be forewarned: Parades disrupt traffic in the Magic Kingdom. It's nearly impossible, for example, to get to Adventureland from Tomorrowland, or vice versa, during one.

## AFTERNOON PARADE

USUALLY STAGED AT 3 P.M., THE PARADE features bands, floats, and marching Disney characters. A new afternoon parade is introduced every year or two. While some elements, such as Disney characters, remain constant, the theme, music, and float design change. Seasonal parades during major holidays round out the mix.

## EVENING PARADE(S)

THE EVENING PARADE IS A HIGH-TECH AFFAIR employing electroluminescent and fiber-optic technologies, light-spreading thermoplastics (do not try this at home!), and clouds of underlit liquid-nitrogen smoke. Don't worry, you won't need a gas mask or lead underwear to watch. For those who flunked chemistry and physics, the parade also offers music, Mickey Mouse, twinkling lights, and snapshots of classic animated features inside giant snow globes. Disney says the snow globes are just part of the show, but we think maybe the characters are worried about anthrax. The evening parade is staged once or twice each evening, depending on the time of year.

During less busy times of year, the evening parade is held only on weekends, and sometimes not even then.

## PARADE ROUTE AND VANTAGE POINTS

MAGIC KINGDOM PARADES CIRCLE Town Square, head down Main Street, go around the central hub, and cross the bridge to Liberty Square. In Liberty Square, they follow the waterfront and end in Frontierland. Sometimes they begin in Frontierland and run the route in the opposite direction.

Most guests watch from the central hub, or from Main Street. One of the best and most popular vantage points is the upper platform of the Walt Disney World Railroad station at the Town Square end of Main Street. This is also a good place for watching the *Wishes* fireworks, as well as for ducking out of the park ahead of the crowd when the fireworks end. Problem is, you have to stake out your position 30–45 minutes before the events.

*unofficial* **TIP**
Be advised that the Walt Disney World Railroad shuts down during parades, thus making it impossible to access other lands by train.

Because most spectators pack Main Street and the central hub, we recommend watching the parade from Liberty Square or Frontierland. Great vantage points, frequently overlooked, are:

1. Sleepy Hollow snack and beverage shop, immediately to your right as you cross the bridge into Liberty Square. If you arrive early, buy refreshments and claim a table by the rail. You'll have a perfect view of the parade as it crosses the Liberty Square bridge, but only when the parade begins on Main Street.

2. The pathway on the Liberty Square side of the moat from Sleepy Hollow snack and beverage shop to Cinderella Castle. Any point along this path offers a clear and unobstructed view as the parade crosses the Liberty Square bridge. Once again, this spot works only for parades coming from Main Street.

3. The covered walkway between Liberty Tree Tavern and the Diamond Horseshoe Saloon. This elevated vantage point is perfect (particularly on rainy days) and usually goes unnoticed until just before the parade starts.

4. Elevated wooden platforms in front of the Frontierland Shootin' Arcade, Frontier Trading Post, and the building with the sign reading "frontier merchandise." These spots usually get picked off 10–12 minutes before parade time.

5. Benches on the perimeter of the central hub, between the entrances to Liberty Square and Adventureland. Usually unoccupied until after the parade begins, they offer a comfortable resting place and unobstructed (though somewhat distant) view of the parade as it crosses Liberty Square bridge. What you lose in proximity, you gain in comfort.

6. Liberty Square and Frontierland dockside areas. These spots usually go early.

7. The elevated porch of Tony's Town Square Restaurant on Main Street provides an elevated viewing platform and an easy path to the park exit when the fireworks are over.

Assuming it starts on Main Street (evening parades normally do), the parade takes 16–20 minutes to reach Liberty Square or Frontierland.

# MAGIC KINGDOM TOURING PLANS

OUR STEP-BY-STEP TOURING PLANS ARE field-tested for seeing *as much as possible* in one day with a minimum of time wasted in lines. They're designed to help you avoid crowds and bottlenecks on days of moderate to heavy attendance. Understand, however, that there's more to see in the Magic Kingdom than can be experienced in one day. Since we began covering the Magic Kingdom, four headliner attractions and a new land have been added.

On days of lighter attendance (see "Selecting the Time of Year for Your Visit," pages 14–15), our plans will save you time but won't be as critical to successful touring as on busier days. Don't worry that other people will be following the plans and render them useless. Fewer than 1 in every 350 people in the park will have been exposed to this information.

### CHOOSING THE APPROPRIATE TOURING PLAN

WE PRESENT FIVE Magic Kingdom touring plans:

- Magic Kingdom One-Day Touring Plan for Adults
- Author's Selective Magic Kingdom One-Day Touring Plan for Adults
- Magic Kingdom One-Day Touring Plan for Parents with Young Children
- Magic Kingdom Dumbo-or-Die-in-a-Day Touring Plan for Parents with Young Children
- Magic Kingdom Two-Day Touring Plan

If you have two days (or two mornings) at the Magic Kingdom, the Two-Day Touring Plan is *by far* the most relaxed and efficient. The two-day plan takes advantage of early morning, when lines are short and the park hasn't filled with guests. This plan works well year-round and eliminates much of the extra walking required by the one-day plans. The plan is perfect for guests who wish to sample both the attractions and the atmosphere of the Magic Kingdom.

If you only have one day but wish to see as much as possible, use the One-Day Touring Plan for Adults. It's exhausting, but it packs in the maximum. If you prefer a more relaxed visit, use the Author's Selective One-Day Touring Plan. It includes the best the park has to offer (in the author's opinion), eliminating some less impressive attractions.

If you have children younger than age 8, adopt the One-Day Touring Plan for Parents with Young Children. It's a compromise, blending the preferences of younger children with those of older siblings and adults. The plan includes many children's rides in Fantasyland but omits roller coaster rides and other attractions that frighten young children or are off-limits because of height requirements. Or, use the One-Day Touring Plan for Adults or the Author's Selective One-Day Touring Plan and take advantage of switching off, a technique where children accompany adults to the loading area of a ride with age and height requirements but don't board (page 75). Switching off allows adults to enjoy the more adventuresome attractions while keeping the group together.

The Dumbo-or-Die-in-a-Day Touring Plan for Parents with Young Children is designed for parents who will withhold no sacrifice for the children. On the Dumbo-or-Die plan, adults generally stand around, sweat, wipe noses, pay for stuff, and watch the children enjoy themselves. It's great.

## Two-Day Touring Plan for Families with Young Children

If you have young children and are looking for a two-day itinerary, combine the Magic Kingdom One-Day Touring Plan for Parents with Young Children with the second day of the Magic Kingdom Two-Day Touring Plan.

## Two-Day Touring Plan for Early Morning Touring on Day One and Afternoon-Evening Touring on Day Two

Many of you enjoy an early start at the Magic Kingdom on one day, followed by a second day with a lazy, sleep-in morning, resuming your touring in the afternoon and/or evening. If this appeals to you, use the Magic Kingdom One-Day

Touring Plan for Adults or the Magic Kingdom One-Day Touring Plan for Parents with Young Children on your early day. Adhere to the touring plan for as long as feels comfortable (many folks leave after the afternoon parade). On the second day, pick up where you left off. If you intend to use FASTPASS on your second day, try to arrive at the park by 1 p.m. or the FASTPASSes may be gone. Customize the remaining part of the touring plan to incorporate parades, fireworks, and other live performances according to your preferences.

> *unofficial* **TIP**
> No matter when the park closes, our two-day plan guarantees the most efficient touring and the least time in lines.

## THE SINGLE-DAY TOURING CONUNDRUM

TOURING THE MAGIC KINGDOM IN A DAY is complicated by the fact that the premier attractions are at almost opposite ends of the park: Splash Mountain and Big Thunder Mountain Railroad in Frontierland and Space Mountain and Buzz Lightyear in Tomorrowland. It's virtually impossible to ride all four without encountering lines at one or another. If you ride Space Mountain and see Buzz Lightyear immediately after the park opens, you won't have much wait, if any. By the time you leave Tomorrowland and hurry to Frontierland, however, the line for Splash Mountain will be substantial. The same situation prevails if you ride the Frontierland duo first: Splash Mountain and Big Thunder Mountain Railroad, no problem; Space Mountain and Buzz Lightyear, fair-sized lines. From ten minutes after opening until just before closing, lines are long at these headliners.

The best way to ride all four without long waits is to tour the Magic Kingdom over two mornings: Ride Space Mountain and Buzz Lightyear first thing one morning, then ride Splash Mountain and Big Thunder Mountain first thing on the other. If you only have one day, be present at opening time. Speed immediately to Space Mountain, then take in Buzz Lightyear. After Buzz Lightyear, rush to Frontierland and scope out the situation at Splash Mountain. If the posted wait time is 30 minutes or less, go ahead and hop in line. If the wait exceeds 30 minutes, get a FASTPASS for Splash Mountain, then ride Big Thunder Mountain.

## PRELIMINARY INSTRUCTIONS FOR ALL MAGIC KINGDOM TOURING PLANS

ON DAYS OF MODERATE TO HEAVY ATTENDANCE, follow your chosen touring plan exactly, deviating only:

1. When you aren't interested in an attraction it lists. For example, the plan may tell you to go to Tomorrowland and ride Space Mountain, a roller coaster. If you don't enjoy roller coasters, skip this step and proceed to the next.

2. When you encounter a very long line at an attraction the touring plan calls for. Crowds ebb and flow at the park, and an unusually long line may have gathered at an attraction to which you're directed. For example, you arrive at The Haunted Mansion and find extremely long lines. It's possible that this is a temporary situation caused by several hundred people arriving en masse from a recently concluded performance of *The Hall of Presidents* nearby. If this is the case, skip The Haunted Mansion and go to the next step, returning later to retry The Haunted Mansion.

## PARK OPENING PROCEDURES

YOUR SUCCESS DURING YOUR FIRST HOUR of touring will be affected somewhat by the opening procedure Disney uses that day:

A. All guests are held at the turnstiles until the entire park opens (which may or may not be at the official opening time). If this happens on the day you visit, blow past Main Street and head for the first attraction on the touring plan you're following.

B. Guests are admitted to Main Street a half hour to an hour before the remaining lands open. Access to other lands will be blocked by a rope barrier at the central hub end of Main Street. Once admitted, stake out a position at the rope barrier as follows:

If you're going to Frontierland first (Splash Mountain and Big Thunder Mountain Railroad), stand in front of The Crystal Palace restaurant, on the left at the central hub end of Main Street. Wait next to the rope barrier blocking the walkway to Adventureland. When the rope is dropped, move quickly to Frontierland by way of Adventureland. This is also the place to line up if your first stop is Adventureland.

If you're going to Buzz Lightyear and Space Mountain first, wait at the entrance of the bridge to Tomorrowland. When the rope drops, dash across into Tomorrowland.

Between Fantasyland and Tomorrowland is Toontown, which opens at 10 a.m. If you're going to Fantasyland or Liberty Square first, go to the end of Main Street and line up left of center at the rope.

## BEFORE YOU GO

1. Call ☎ 407-824-4321 the day before you go to check the official opening time.

2. Purchase admission before you arrive.
3. Familiarize yourself with park opening procedures (above) and reread the touring plan you've chosen so that you know what you're likely to encounter.

## MAGIC KINGDOM TOURING PLANS

### Magic Kingdom One-Day Touring Plan for Adults

**FOR**  Adults without young children
**ASSUMES**  Willingness to experience all major rides (including roller coasters) and shows

THIS PLAN REQUIRES CONSIDERABLE WALKING and some backtracking; this is necessary to avoid long lines. Extra walking plus some morning hustle will spare you two to three hours of standing in line. You might not complete the tour. How far you get depends on how quickly you move from ride to ride, how many times you rest or eat, how quickly the park fills, and what time the park closes.

1. If you're a Disney hotel guest, use Disney transportation to commute to the park, arriving 30 minutes before official opening time.

   If you're a day guest, arrive at the Magic Kingdom's parking lot 50 minutes before official opening time. Arrive 70 minutes before official opening time if it's a holiday period. Add 15 minutes to the above if you have to buy your admission. These arrivals give you time to park and catch the tram to the Transportation and Ticket Center. At the TTC, transfer to the monorail or ferry to reach the park's entrance. If the line for the monorail is short, take the monorail; otherwise, catch the ferry.

2. At the park, proceed through the turnstiles and have one person go to City Hall for guidemaps and the daily entertainment schedule (*Times Guide*).

3. Regroup and move quickly down Main Street to the central hub. Because the Magic Kingdom has two opening procedures, you probably will encounter one of the following:
   a. The entire park will be open. In this case, proceed quickly to Space Mountain in Tomorrowland.
   b. Only Main Street will be open. In this case, go to the central hub and position yourself at the entrance to Tomorrowland. When the rope barrier is dropped at opening time, walk as fast as possible to Space Mountain. Ride.

4. Backtrack toward the entrance to Tomorrowland, bearing left to Buzz Lightyear's Space Ranger Spin. Ride.

5. After Buzz, proceed to Fantasyland via Tomorrowland passing the Tomorrowland Speedway en route. In Fantasyland, experience The Many Adventures of Winnie the Pooh.

6. Exit left from Winnie the Pooh and ride Snow White's Scary Adventures next door.

7. Cross Fantasyland Plaza in the direction of Liberty Square and ride Peter Pan's Flight.

8. Across from Peter Pan, ride It's a Small World.

9. Exit Small World and bear right to Liberty Square. Experience The Haunted Mansion.

10. Proceed right after departing The Haunted Mansion and follow the Liberty Square waterfront into Frontierland and on to Splash Mountain. At Splash Mountain, obtain a FASTPASS.

11. Next door to Splash Mountain, ride Big Thunder Mountain Railroad.

12. Proceed to Adventureland via the bridge in front of Splash Mountain. In Adventureland, experience Pirates of the Caribbean.

13. By now it should be time to return and ride Splash Mountain using your FASTPASS. If you still have some time to kill, try the Swiss Family Treehouse in Adventureland.

14. At this point you will have most of the Magic Kingdom bottlenecks in the rearview mirror. Feel free to stop for lunch, a break, or scheduled live entertainment.

15. Catch the Walt Disney Railroad at the Frontierland station next to Splash Mountain. Ride the train to Mickey's Toontown Fair.

16. Tour Mickey's Toontown Fair.

17. Reboard the train at Mickey's Toontown Fair and complete your round trip, disembarking at the Frontierland Station.

18. Return to Adventureland. Obtain a FASTPASS for the Jungle Cruise.

19. In Adventureland, drop in on the *Enchanted Tiki Birds*.

20. Cross the plaza passing the Aladdin ride and cut through the passage into Frontierland. "Bear" left and see the *Country Bear Jamboree*.

21. Return to Adventureland through the same passage. Ride the Jungle Cruise using your FASTPASS. Skip to Step 22 if you still have some time to kill before your FASTPASS return window starts.

22. Explore the Swiss Family Treehouse if you didn't see it earlier.

23. Return to Liberty Square via the passage opposite Aladdin. Experience the *Liberty Square* Riverboat and *The Hall of Presidents* in whichever order is most convenient.

24. Return to Fantasyland and see *Mickey's PhilharMagic*.

25. Return to Tomorrowland via the central hub and experience *Stitch's Great Escape.*

26. Also in Tomorrowland, ride the Tomorrowland Transit Authority.

27. Also in Tomorrowland, see *The Timekeeper* and the *Carousel of Progress* if they are operating (both open only occasionally according to attendance levels).

28. Experience any attractions you might have missed. View any parades, fireworks, or live performances that interest you. Grab a bite. Save Main Street for last because it remains open after the rest of the park closes.

29. Browse Main Street.

## Author's Selective Magic Kingdom One-Day Touring Plan for Adults

**FOR** Adults touring without young children

**ASSUMES** Willingness to experience all major rides (including roller coasters) and shows

THIS PLAN INCLUDES ONLY THOSE ATTRACTIONS the author believes are the best in the Magic Kingdom. It requires a lot of walking and some backtracking to avoid long lines. Extra walking and morning hustle will spare you three or more hours of standing in line. You might not complete the tour. How far you get depends on how quickly you move from ride to ride, how many times you rest or eat, how quickly the park fills, and what time the park closes.

1. If you're a Disney hotel guest, use Disney transportation to commute to the park, arriving 30 minutes before official opening time.

    If you're a day guest, arrive at the parking lot 50 minutes before the Magic Kingdom's official opening time. Arrive 70 minutes earlier than official opening if it's a holiday period. Add 15 minutes to the above if you must buy your admission. These arrivals will give you time to park and catch the tram to the Transportation and Ticket Center. At the TTC, transfer to the monorail or ferry to reach the park's entrance. If the line for the monorail is short, take the monorail; otherwise, catch the ferry.

2. At the park, proceed through the turnstiles and have one person go to City Hall for guidemaps and the daily entertainment schedule.

3. Regroup and move quickly down Main Street to the central hub. Because the Magic Kingdom has two opening procedures, you probably will encounter one of the following:

    a. The entire park will be open. In this case, proceed quickly to Space Mountain in Tomorrowland.

b. Only Main Street will be open. In this case, proceed to the central hub and position yourself at the entrance to Tomorrowland. When the rope drops, head to Space Mountain.

4. Backtrack toward the entrance to Tomorrowland, bearing left to Buzz Lightyear's Space Ranger Spin. Ride.

5. After Buzz, proceed to Fantasyland via Tomorrowland, passing the Tomorrowland Speedway en route. In Fantasyland, experience The Many Adventures of Winnie the Pooh.

6. Exit left from Winnie the Pooh, cross Fantasyland Plaza in the direction of Liberty Square, and ride Peter Pan's Flight.

7. Across from Peter Pan, ride It's a Small World.

8. Exit Small World and bear right to Liberty Square. Experience The Haunted Mansion.

9. Proceed right after departing The Haunted Mansion and follow the Liberty Square waterfront into Frontierland and on to Splash Mountain. At Splash Mountain, obtain a FASTPASS.

10. Next door to Splash Mountain, ride Big Thunder Mountain Railroad.

11. Proceed to Adventureland via the bridge in front of Splash Mountain. In Adventureland, experience Pirates of the Caribbean.

12. By now it should be time to return and ride Splash Mountain using your FASTPASS. If you still have some time to kill, try the Swiss Family Treehouse in Adventureland.

13. At this point, you will have most of the Magic Kingdom bottlenecks in the rearview mirror. Feel free to stop for lunch, a break, or scheduled live entertainment.

14. Catch the Walt Disney Railroad at the Frontierland station next to Splash Mountain. Ride the train to Mickey's Toontown Fair. Toontown doesn't hold much appeal for adults. If you think you can live without it, stay on the train for a round trip all the way back to Frontierland and skip to Step 17.

15. Tour Mickey's Toontown Fair.

16. Reboard the train at Mickey's Toontown Fair and complete your round trip, disembarking at the Frontierland Station.

17. Return to Adventureland. Obtain a FASTPASS for the Jungle Cruise.

18. In Adventureland, drop in on the *Enchanted Tiki Birds*.

19. Cross the plaza passing the Aladdin ride and cut through the passage into Frontierland. Bear left and see the *Country Bear Jamboree*.

20. Return to Adventureland through the same passage. Ride the Jungle Cruise using your FASTPASS. Skip to Step 21 if you still

have some time to kill before your FASTPASS return window starts.

21. Explore the Swiss Family Treehouse if you didn't see it earlier.

22. Return to Liberty Square via the passage opposite Aladdin. Experience the *Liberty Square* Riverboat and *The Hall of Presidents* in whichever order is most convenient.

23. Return to Fantasyland and see *Mickey's PhilharMagic.*

24. Return to Tomorrowland via the central hub and experience *Stitch's Great Escape*

25. Also in Tomorrowland, see *The Timekeeper* and the *Carousel of Progress* if they are operating (both open only occasionally according to attendance levels).

26. Experience any attractions you might have missed. View any parades, fireworks, or live performances that interest you. Grab a bite. Save Main Street for last because it remains open after the rest of the park closes.

27. Browse Main Street.

## Magic Kingdom One-Day Touring Plan for Parents with Young Children

**FOR** Parents with children younger than age 8
**ASSUMES** Periodic stops for rest, restrooms, and refreshments

THIS PLAN REPRESENTS A COMPROMISE between the observed tastes of adults and those of younger children. Included are many amusement park rides that children may have the opportunity to experience at fairs and amusement parks back home. Although these rides are included in the plan, omit them if possible. These cycle-loading rides often have long lines, consuming valuable touring time:

Mad Tea Party                    Dumbo the Flying Elephant

Cinderella's Golden Carousel      Magic Carpets of Aladdin

This time could be better spent experiencing the many attractions that better demonstrate the Disney creative genius and are found only in the Magic Kingdom. Instead of this plan, try either of the one-day plans for adults and take advantage of "switching off." This allows parents and young children to enter the ride together. At the boarding area, one parent watches the children while the other rides.

Before entering the park, decide whether you will return to your hotel for a midday rest. You won't see as much, but everyone will be more relaxed and happy.

This touring plan requires a lot of walking and some backtracking to avoid long lines. A little extra walking and some morning hustle will spare you two to three hours of standing in line. You probably won't complete the tour. How far you get depends on how quickly you move from ride to ride, how many times you rest or eat, how quickly the park fills, and what time the park closes.

1. If you're a Disney hotel guest, use Disney transportation to commute to the park, arriving 30 minutes before official opening time

    If you're a day guest, arrive at the parking lot 50 minutes before the Magic Kingdom's official opening time. Arrive 70 minutes earlier than official opening if it's a holiday period. Add 15 minutes to the above if you must purchase your admission. These arrivals will give you time to park and catch the tram to the Transportation and Ticket Center. At the TTC, transfer to the monorail or ferry to reach the park's entrance. If the line for the monorail is short, take the monorail; otherwise, catch the ferry.

2. At the Magic Kingdom, proceed through the turnstiles and have one person go to City Hall for guidemaps and the daily entertainment schedule.

3. Rent strollers (if necessary). This can be accomplished most days before you pass through the turnstiles.

4. Move briskly to the end of Main Street. If the entire park is open, go quickly to Fantasyland. Otherwise, position your group by the rope barrier at the central hub. When the park opens and the barrier drops, go through the main door of the castle and ride Dumbo the Flying Elephant in Fantasyland.

5. Enjoy The Many Adventures of Winnie the Pooh. Use the standby line—not FASTPASS.

6. Ride Peter Pan's Flight. Use the standby line—not FASTPASS.

7. Across the walkway, ride It's a Small World.

8. Head toward the castle. See *Mickey's PhilharMagic* on your right.

9. Exit *Mickey's PhilharMagic* and bear left, passing Peter Pan, and cross into Liberty Square. In Liberty Square, experience The Haunted Mansion, directly on your right.

10. On exiting The Haunted Mansion, head towards Frontierland, keeping the waterfront on your right. To the left of the Frontierland Shootin' Arcade is a passageway the leads directly to Adventureland. Continue to Adventureland and ride the Jungle Cruise. If the wait exceeds 30 minutes, use FASTPASS.

11. Turn left on exiting the Jungle Cruise and head for Frontierland. In Frontierland, take the rafts to Tom Sawyer Island. Allocate at least 30 minutes for your kids to explore the island.

12. Return via raft to the mainland. If you have a FASTPASS for the Jungle Cruise, go ahead and ride. If you need to kill some time before your FASTPASS time slot, explore the Swiss Family Treehouse, next door to the Jungle Cruise. If you've already experienced the Jungle Cruise, skip to Step 13.

13. Proceed to the Frontierland railroad station, situated on the far right side of Splash Mountain. Take the Walt Disney World Railroad from Frontierland to Main Street USA. Depart the Magic Kingdom for lunch and a nap. If you insist on forgoing the nap, skip the train ride and proceed to Step 15.

14. After your afternoon break, return refreshed to the Magic Kingdom and head for Splash Mountain in Frontierland on foot or via the railroad from the Main Street Station. Be advised that the train is suggested solely to save some walking. There's virtually nothing to see between Main Street and the Frontierland station.

15. In Frontierland, obtain FASTPASSes for Splash Mountain.

16. In Frontierland, see the *Country Bear Jamboree.*

17. Return to Adventureland and ride Pirates of the Caribbean.

18. In Adventureland, explore the Swiss Family Treehouse if you didn't see it earlier.

19. Return to Splash Mountain and ride using your FASTPASSes. If your kids aren't up for Splash Mountain, take advantage of switching off. If you still have some time remaining before your FASTPASS window, ride the *Liberty Square* Riverboat.

20. After Splash Mountain, cross the park to Tomorrowland via the central hub. On entering Tomorrowland, obtain FAST-PASSes for Buzz Lightyear if the return time is acceptable to you. Be aware that on exceedingly busy days, all of the FAST-PASSes may have been distributed.

21. In Tomorrowland, ride the Tomorrowland Transit Authority.

22. Keeping the Tomorrowland Indy Speedway on your right, proceed to Mickey's Toontown Fair and explore.

23. If you have FASTPASSes for Buzz Lightyear, return to Tomorrowland and ride. If not, this ends the touring plan. If you have any energy left, check the daily entertainment schedule for live shows, fireworks, and parades.

## To Convert This One-Day Touring Plan into a Two-Day Touring Plan

Skip steps 14–23 on the first day. On the second day, arrive 30 minutes prior to opening, take the Walt Disney World Railroad from Main Street to Frontierland, and

> *un**official** **TIP**
> We strongly recommend that you break from touring and return to your hotel for a swim and a nap (even if you aren't lodging in Walt Disney World).

pick up the plan with step 15, but do not use FASTPASS unless the wait exceeds 35 minutes.

## Magic Kingdom Dumbo-or-Die-in-a-Day Touring Plan for Parents with Young Children

**FOR** Adults compelled to devote every waking moment to the pleasure and entertainment of their young children, or rich people who are paying someone else to take their children to the theme park

**PREREQUISITE** This plan is designed for days when the Magic Kingdom doesn't close until 9 p.m. or later

**ASSUMES** Frequent stops for rest, restrooms, and refreshment

*Note:* Name aside, this touring plan is not a joke. Regardless of whether you're loving, guilty, masochistic, selfless, insane, or saintly, this itinerary will provide a young child with about as perfect a day as is possible at the Magic Kingdom.

THIS PLAN IS A CONCESSION to adults determined to give their young children the ultimate Magic Kingdom experience. It addresses the preferences, needs, and desires of young children to the virtual exclusion of those of adults or older siblings. If you left the kids with a sitter yesterday or wouldn't let little Marvin eat barbecue for breakfast, this plan will expiate your guilt. It is also a wonderful itinerary if you're paying a sitter, nanny, or chauffeur to take your children to the Magic Kingdom.

1. If you're a Disney hotel guest, use Disney transportation to commute to the park, arriving 30 minutes before official opening time.

   If you're a day guest, arrive at the parking lot 50 minutes before the Magic Kingdom's official opening time. Arrive 70 minutes earlier than official opening if it's a holiday period. Add 15 minutes to the above if you must purchase your admission. These arrivals will give you time to park and catch the tram to the Transportation and Ticket Center. At the TTC, transfer to the monorail or ferry to reach the park's entrance. If the line for the monorail is short, take the monorail; otherwise, catch the ferry.

2. At the Magic Kingdom, proceed through the turnstiles and have one person go to City Hall for guidemaps and the daily entertainment schedule.

3. Rent a stroller (if needed).

4. Move briskly to the end of Main Street. If the entire park is open, go quickly to Fantasyland. Otherwise, position your group by the rope barrier at the central hub. When the park

opens and the barrier is dropped, go through the main door of the castle to Cinderella's Royal Table, on your right as you enter Cinderella Castle.

5. Make a dinner advance reservation at the Royal Table for 7 p.m. Eating there will let your kids see the inside of the castle and possibly meet Cinderella. To make your advance reservation before you leave home, call ☎ 407-939-3463.

6. Enter Fantasyland. Ride Dumbo the Flying Elephant.

7. Hey, you're on vacation! Ride Dumbo again.

8. Experience The Many Adventures of Winnie the Pooh, near Dumbo. Use the standby line, not FASTPASS.

9. Ride Peter Pan's Flight. Use the standby line—not FASTPASS.

10. Ride Cinderella's Golden Carousel.

11. In Tomorrowland, ride the Tomorrowland Speedway. Let your child steer (cars run on a guide rail) while you work the foot pedal.

12. Ride the Astro Orbiter. Safety note: Seat your children in the vehicle before you get in. Also, the Astro Orbiter goes higher and faster than Dumbo and may frighten some children.

13. Ride Buzz Lightyear's Space Ranger Spin (near Astro Orbiter). Do not use FASTPASS.

14. Return to Main Street via the central hub and leave the park for your hotel. Eat lunch and rest. (Have your hand stamped for re-entry when you leave the park. Keep your parking receipt to show upon return so you won't have to pay again for parking.) If you elect not to take a break out of the park, skip to Step 17.

15. Return to the Magic Kingdom refreshed about 4 or 4:30 p.m. Take the Walt Disney World Railroad to Frontierland.

16. Take the raft to Tom Sawyer Island. Stay as long as the kids want. If you're hungry, Aunt Polly's Dockside Inn on Tom Sawyer Island is a winner for both kids and adults.

17. After you return from the island, see the *Country Bear Jamboree.*

18. Return to the Frontierland Station. Ride the train to Mickey's Toontown Fair.

19. Walk through Mickey's Country House and Minnie's Country House and play on Donald's Boat. Meet Disney characters at the Toontown Hall of Fame and pose for photos.

20. You should be within an hour of your dinner advance reservation at Cinderella's Royal Table. Take the direct path from Mickey's Toontown Fair to Fantasyland. In Fantasyland, if you have 20 minutes or more before your advance reservation, ride It's a Small World. Don't forget to sing.

21. After dinner, see *Mickey's PhilharMagic,* also in Fantasyland.

22. Leave Fantasyland and go to Liberty Square. If your children are up to it, see The Haunted Mansion. If not, skip to Step 23.

23. Evening parades are quite worthwhile. If you're interested, adjust the remainder of the touring plan to allow you to take a viewing position about 10 minutes before the early parade starts (usually 8 or 9 p.m.). See our recommendations for good vantage points (page 156). If you aren't interested in the parade, enjoy attractions in Adventureland while the parade is in progress. Lines will be vastly diminished.

24. Go to Adventureland by way of Liberty Square, Frontierland, or the central hub. Take the Jungle Cruise if the lines aren't long. If they're prohibitive, obtain FASTPASSes and experience *Enchanted Tiki Birds,* Magic Carpets of Aladdin, and Swiss Family Treehouse. If your children can stand a few skeletons, also see Pirates of the Caribbean.

25. After the birds, carpets, tree house, and pirates, return with your FASTPASSes to ride the Jungle Cruise.

26. If you have time or energy left, repeat any attractions the kids especially liked, or try ones on the plan you might have bypassed because of long lines. Buy Goofy hats if that cranks your tractor.

27. If you're parked at the Transportation and Ticket Center, catch the ferry or express monorail. If the express monorail line is long, catch the resort monorail and disembark at the TTC.

## To Convert This One-Day Touring Plan into a Two-Day Touring Plan

Skip steps 19 and 20 on the first day. On the second day, arrive 30 minutes prior to opening and take the Walt Disney World Railroad from Main Street to Mickey's Toontown Fair. See Mickey's Toontown Fair in its entirety.

## Magic Kingdom Two-Day Touring Plan

**FOR** Parties wishing to spread their Magic Kingdom visit over two days

**ASSUMES** Willingness to experience all major rides (including roller coasters) and shows

**TIMING** This two-day touring plan takes advantage of early-morning touring. Each day, you should complete the structured part of the plan by about 4 p.m. This leaves plenty of time for live entertainment. If the park is open late (after 8 p.m.), consider returning to your hotel at midday for a swim and a nap. Eat an early dinner outside Walt Disney World and return refreshed to enjoy the park's nighttime festivities.

**DAY ONE**

1. If you're a Disney hotel guest, use Disney transportation to commute to the park, arriving 30 minutes before official opening time.

   If you're a day guest, arrive at the parking lot 50 minutes before the Magic Kingdom's official opening time. Arrive 70 minutes earlier than official opening if it's a holiday period. Add 15 minutes to the above if you must purchase your admission. These arrivals will give you time to park and catch the tram to the Transportation and Ticket Center. At the TTC, transfer to the monorail or ferry to reach the park's entrance. If the line for the monorail is short, take the monorail; otherwise, catch the ferry.

2. At the park, proceed through the turnstiles and have one person go to City Hall for guidemaps and the daily entertainment schedule.

3. Move as fast as you can down Main Street to the central hub. Because the Magic Kingdom uses two procedures for opening, you probably will encounter one of the following:

   a. The entire park will be open. In this case, proceed quickly to Space Mountain in Tomorrowland.

   b. Only Main Street will be open. In this case, position yourself in the central hub at the entrance to Tomorrowland. When the park opens and the rope barrier drops, walk as fast as possible to Space Mountain.

4. After exiting Space Mountain, proceed to Fantasyland via the central hub. Bear left after passing through the castle. Experience the Many Adventures of Winnie the Pooh.

5. Exit Pooh and bear left past the carousel to Peter Pan's Flight. Ride.

6. Exit Peter Pan to the right and see *Mickey's PhilharMagic*.

7. Also in Fantasyland, ride It's a Small World.

8. Exit Small World to the right and proceed to Liberty Square. Immediately on entering, turn right to The Haunted Mansion. Enjoy.

9. Also in Liberty Square, ride the riverboat.

10. Feel free to stop for lunch from this point on. Fast food eateries that are generally less crowded include the Columbia Harbour House in Liberty Square and Aunt Polly's Dockside Inn on Tom Sawyer Island.

11. Also in Liberty Square, see *The Hall of Presidents.*

12. Continue along the waterfront into Frontierland. See the *Country Bear Jamboree*. At this point, check the daily

entertainment schedule for parades and other live performances that might interest you. Because you already have seen all the attractions that cause bottlenecks and have long lines, interrupting the touring plan here won't cause any problems. Simply pick up where you left off before the parade or show.

13. At the Frontierland waterfront, take a raft to Tom Sawyer Island. Explore.

14. After returning from Tom Sawyer Island, head for Tomorrowland via the central hub.

15. In Tomorrowland, see *Stitch's Great Escape*.

16. Also in Tomorrowland, ride the Tomorrowland Transit Authority.

17. This concludes the touring plan for the day. Enjoy the shops, see some of the live entertainment, or revisit favorite attractions until you're ready to leave.

### DAY TWO

1. If you're a Disney hotel guest, use Disney transportation to commute to the park, arriving 30 minutes before official opening time.

   If you're a day guest, arrive at the parking lot 50 minutes before the Magic Kingdom's official opening time. Arrive 70 minutes earlier than official opening if it's a holiday period. Add 15 minutes to the above if you must purchase your admission. These arrivals will give you time to park and catch the tram to the Transportation and Ticket Center. At the TTC, transfer to the monorail or ferry to reach the park's entrance. If the line for the monorail is short, take the monorail; otherwise, catch the ferry.

2. At the park, proceed through the turnstiles. Stop at City Hall for guidemaps containing the day's entertainment schedule.

3. Proceed to the end of Main Street. If the entire park is open, go immediately to Buzz Lightyear in Tomorrowland and ride. Otherwise, position yourself along the rope at the entrance to Tomorrowland and wait to be admitted. When the rope drops, go directly to Buzz Lightyear.

4. After Buzz Lightyear, head for Frontierland via the central hub. In Frontierland, ride Splash Mountain. Do not use FASTPASS.

5. Ride Big Thunder Mountain Railroad, next to Splash Mountain.

6. Proceed to Adventureland. Ride the Jungle Cruise. If the wait seems prohibitive, use FASTPASS.

7. Across the street, see *Enchanted Tiki Birds*.

8. Walk through the Swiss Family Treehouse.

9. Exit the Treehouse to the left. Enjoy Pirates of the Caribbean. *Note:* At this point, check the daily entertainment schedule to see if any parades or live performances interest you. Note the times, and alter the touring plan accordingly. Since you already have seen all the attractions that cause bottlenecks and have big lines, interrupting the touring plan here won't cause any problems. Simply pick up where you left off before the parade or show.

10. If you're hungry, eat.

11. Exit Adventureland and go to the Frontierland train station between Splash and Big Thunder Mountains. Catch the Walt Disney World Railroad. Disembark at Mickey's Toontown Fair (first stop).

12. Tour the Fair and meet the Disney characters.

13. Exit the Fair via the path to Tomorrowland.

14. In Tomorrowland, if you haven't eaten, try Cosmic Ray's Starlight Cafe or The Plaza Pavilion.

15. See *Walt Disney's Carousel of Progress* (open seasonally).

16. See *The Timekeeper* (open seasonally).

17. This concludes the touring plan. Enjoy the shops, see live entertainment, or revisit your favorite attractions until you are ready to leave.

# PART TEN

# EPCOT

## ▮ OVERVIEW

EPCOT IS MORE THAN TWICE AS BIG as either the Magic Kingdom or Disney-MGM Studios and, though smaller than the Animal Kingdom, has more territory to be covered on foot. Epcot rarely sees the congestion so common to the Magic Kingdom, but it has lines every bit as long as those at the Jungle Cruise or Space Mountain. Visitors must come prepared to do considerable walking among attractions and a comparable amount of standing in line.

Epcot's size means you can't see it all in one day without skipping an attraction or two and giving others a cursory glance. A major difference between Epcot and the other parks, however, is that some Epcot attractions can be savored slowly or skimmed, depending on personal interests. For example, the first section of General Motors' Test Track is a thrill ride, the second a collection of walk-through exhibits. Nearly all visitors take the ride, but many people, lacking time or interest, bypass the exhibits.

We have identified several Epcot attractions as "not to be missed." But part of the enjoyment of the park is that there's something for everyone. Ask your group. They're sure to have a variety of opinions as to which attraction is "best."

### OPERATING HOURS

EPCOT HAS TWO THEME AREAS: FUTURE World and World Showcase. Each has its own operating hours. Though schedules change throughout the year, Future World always opens before World Showcase in the morning and usually closes before World Showcase in the evening. Most of the year, World Showcase opens two hours later than Future World. For exact hours during your visit, call ☎ 407-824-4321.

# ARRIVING

PLAN TO ARRIVE AT THE TURNSTILES 30–40 minutes prior to official opening time. Give yourself an extra 10 minutes or so to park and make your way to the entrance.

If you are a guest at one of the Epcot resorts, it will take you about 20–30 minutes to walk from your hotel to the Future World section of Epcot via the International Gateway (back entrance of Epcot). Instead of walking, you can catch a boat from your Epcot resort hotel to the International Gateway and then walk about eight minutes to the Future World section. To reach the front (Future World) entrance of Epcot from the Epcot resorts, either take a boat from your hotel to Disney-MGM and transfer to an Epcot bus, take a bus to Downtown Disney and transfer to an Epcot bus, or best of all, take a cab.

*unofficial* **TIP**
Epcot has its own parking lot and, unlike at the Magic Kingdom, there's no need to take a monorail or ferry to reach the entrance.

Arriving at the park by private automobile is easy and direct. Trams serve the parking lot, or you can walk to the front gate. Monorail service connects Epcot with the Transportation and Ticket Center, the Magic Kingdom (transfer required), and Magic Kingdom resorts (transfer required).

| NOT TO BE MISSED AT EPCOT | |
|---|---|
| **World Showcase** | *The American Adventure* |
| | *IllumiNations* |
| **Future World** | Spaceship Earth |
| Living with the Land | *Honey, I Shrunk the Audience* |
| Test Track | Body Wars |
| *Cranium Command* | Mission: Space |

# GETTING ORIENTED

EPCOT'S THEME AREAS ARE DISTINCTLY DIFFERENT. Future World combines Disney creativity and major corporations' technological resources to examine where mankind has come from and where it's going. World Showcase features

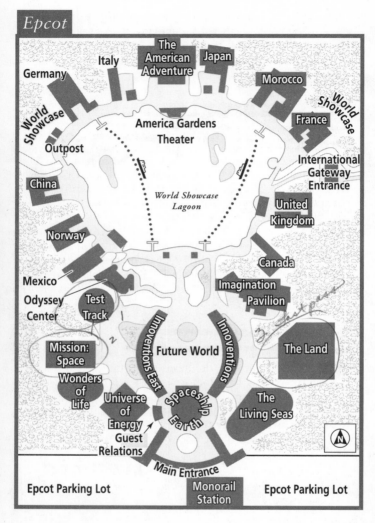

*Epcot*

Germany

Italy

The American Adventure

Japan

Morocco

World Showcase

France

World Showcase

America Gardens Theater

Outpost

International Gateway Entrance

China

World Showcase Lagoon

United Kingdom

Norway

Canada

Mexico

Imagination Pavilion

Odyssey Center

Test Track

Innoventions East

Innoventions

The Land

Mission: Space

Future World

Wonders of Life

The Living Seas

Universe of Energy

Spaceship Earth

Guest Relations

Main Entrance

Epcot Parking Lot

Monorail Station

Epcot Parking Lot

landmarks, cuisine, and culture of almost a dozen nations and is meant to be a sort of permanent World's Fair.

At Epcot, the architectural symbol is Spaceship Earth. This shiny, 180-foot geosphere is visible from almost everywhere in the park. Like Cinderella Castle at the Magic Kingdom, Spaceship Earth can help you keep track of where you are in Epcot. But it's in a high-traffic area and isn't centrally located, so it isn't a good meeting place.

Any of the distinctive national pavilions in World Showcase makes a good meeting place, but be specific. "Hey, let's meet in Japan!" sounds fun, but each pavilion is a mini-town with buildings, monuments, gardens, and plazas. You could wander awhile without finding your group. Pick a specific place in Japan—the sidewalk side of the pagoda, for example.

# FUTURE WORLD

GLEAMING, FUTURISTIC STRUCTURES OF immense proportions define the first theme area you encounter at Epcot. Broad thoroughfares are punctuated with billowing fountains—all reflected in shining, space-age facades. Everything, including landscaping, is sparkling clean and seems bigger than life. Pavilions dedicated to mankind's past, present, and future technological accomplishments form the perimeter of Future World. Front and center is Spaceship Earth, flanked by Innoventions East and West. Most Epcot services are concentrated in Future World's Entrance Plaza, near the main gate.

---

### FUTURE WORLD SERVICES

Epcot's service facilities in Future World include:

**Wheelchair & Stroller Rental**  Inside the main entrance and to the left, toward the rear of the Entrance Plaza

**Banking Services**  ATMs are outside the main entrance near the kennels, on the Future World bridge, and in World Showcase at the Germany pavilion.

**Storage Lockers**  Turn right at Spaceship Earth (lockers are cleaned out nightly).

**Lost & Found**  At the main entrance at the gift shop

**Live Entertainment & Parade Information**  At Guest Relations, left of Spaceship Earth

**Lost Persons**  At Guest Relations and the Baby Center on the World Showcase side of the Odyssey Center

**Dining Advance Reservation**  At Guest Relations

**Walt Disney World & Local Attraction Information**  At Guest Relations

**First Aid**  Next to the Baby Center on the World Showcase side of the Odyssey Center

**Baby Center/Baby-Care Needs**  On the World Showcase side of the Odyssey Center

---

## GUEST RELATIONS

GUEST RELATIONS, LEFT OF THE GEODESIC sphere, is Epcot's equivalent of the Magic Kingdom's City Hall. It serves as park headquarters and as Epcot's primary information center. Attendants staff information booths and take same-day advance reservation for Epcot restaurants. If you wish to eat in one of Epcot's sit-down restaurants, you can make your advance reservation at Guest Relations.

## Spaceship Earth

| APPEAL BY AGE | PRESCHOOL ★★★ | GRADE SCHOOL ★★★★ | TEENS ★★★½ |
|---|---|---|---|
| YOUNG ADULTS ★★★½ | | OVER 30 ★★★★ | SENIORS ★★★★ |

**What it is** Educational dark ride through past, present, and future. **Scope and scale** Headliner. **When to go** Before 10 a.m. or after 4 p.m. **Special comments** If lines are long when you arrive, try again after 4 p.m. **Author's rating** One of Epcot's best; not to be missed; ★★★★. **Duration of ride** About 16 minutes. **Average wait in line per 100 people ahead of you** 3 minutes. **Loading speed** Fast.

**DESCRIPTION AND COMMENTS** This ride spirals through the 18-story interior of Epcot's premier landmark, taking visitors past audio-animatronic scenes depicting mankind's developments in communications, from cave painting to printing to television to space communications and computer networks. The ride is well done and an amazing use of the geosphere's interior.

**TOURING TIPS** Because it's near Epcot's main entrance, Spaceship Earth is inundated with arriving guests throughout the morning. If you're interested in riding Test Track, postpone Spaceship Earth until, say, after 4 p.m. Spaceship Earth loads continuously and quickly. If the line runs only along the right side of the sphere, you'll board in less than 15 minutes.

## Innoventions

| APPEAL BY AGE | PRESCHOOL ★½ | GRADE SCHOOL ★★★½ | TEENS ★★★ |
|---|---|---|---|
| YOUNG ADULTS ★★★½ | | OVER 30 ★★★ | SENIORS ★★★ |

**What it is** Static and hands-on exhibits relating to products and technologies of the near future. **Scope and scale** Major diversion. **When to go** On your second day at Epcot or after seeing all major attractions. **Special comments** Most exhibits demand time and participation to be rewarding; not much gained here by a quick walk-through. **Author's rating** Vastly improved; ★★★½.

**DESCRIPTION AND COMMENTS** Innoventions consists of two huge, crescent-shaped, glass-walled structures separated by a central plaza. Dynamic, interactive, and forward-looking, Innoventions resembles a high-tech trade show. Products preview consumer and industrial goods of the near future. Electronics, communications, and entertainment technology play a prominent role. Exhibits, many of which are changed each year, demonstrate such products as virtual-reality games, high-definition TV, voice-activated appliances, future cars, medical diagnostic equipment, and Internet applications. Each of the major exhibit areas is sponsored by a different manufacturer or research lab, emphasizing the effect of the products or technology on daily living. The most popular Innoventions attraction is an arcade of video and simulator games. One of the coolest exhibits, however, is the demonstration area for the Segway Human Transporter, the much-publicized two-wheeled vehicle where riders look like they're standing on top of a push lawn mower.

Exhibits change periodically, and there is a definite trend toward larger, more elaborate exhibits, almost mini-attractions. The newer exhibits are certainly more compelling, but they require waiting in line to be admitted. Because the theater at each exhibit is quite small, you often wait as long for an Innoventions infomercial as for a real attraction elsewhere in the park.

**TOURING TIPS** Innoventions East and West provide visitors an opportunity to preview products of tomorrow in a fun, hands-on manner. Some exhibits are intriguing, while others are less compelling. We observed a wide range of reactions by visitors to the exhibits and can suggest only that you form your own opinion. Regarding touring strategy, spend time at Innoventions on your second day at Epcot. If you have only one day, visit later in the day if you have the time and endurance. Many exhibits, however, are technical and may not be compatible with your mood or energy toward the end of a long day. Also, you can't get much out of a walk-through; you have to invest time to understand what's going on.

## The Igloo

ATTACHED TO THE FOUNTAIN SIDE of Innoventions West is a tacky white igloo called Ice Station Cool. Inside, this Coca Cola–sponsored exhibit provides free unlimited samples of soft drinks from around the world. Some of the selections will taste like medicine to an American, but others will please. Because it's centrally located in Future World, it makes a good meeting or break place, and you can slake your thirst while you wait for the rest of your party to arrive.

## The Living Seas

| APPEAL BY AGE | PRESCHOOL ★★★ | GRADE SCHOOL ★★★ | TEENS ★★★ |
|---|---|---|---|
| YOUNG ADULTS ★★★ | OVER 30 ★★★ | | SENIORS ★★★★ |

**What it is** A huge saltwater aquarium, plus exhibits on oceanography, ocean ecology, and sea life. **Scope and scale** Major attraction. **When to go** Before 11:30 a.m. or after 5 p.m. **Author's rating** An excellent marine exhibit; ★★★½. **Average wait in line per 100 people ahead of you** 3½ minutes. **Loading speed** Fast.

**DESCRIPTION AND COMMENTS** The Living Seas is among Future World's most ambitious offerings. Scientists and divers conduct actual marine experiments in a 200-foot-diameter, 27-foot-deep main tank containing fish, mammals, and crustaceans in a simulation of an ocean ecosystem. Visitors can watch the activity through eight-inch-thick windows below the surface (including some in the Coral Reef restaurant). A two-part adventure consisting of a movie dramatizing the link between the ocean and man's survival and a simulated elevator descent to the bottom of the tank set you up for the underwater viewing.

The Living Seas' fish population is substantial, but the strength of this attraction lies in the dozen or so exhibits offered afterward. Visitors can view fish-breeding experiments, watch short films about sea life, and more. A delightful exhibit showcases clownfish (Nemo), regal blue tang (Dory), and other species featured in *Finding Nemo*. Other highlights include a haunting, hypnotic jellyfish tank, a seahorse aquarium, a stingray petting pool (really!), and a manatee tank.

**TOURING TIPS** Exhibits are the best part of The Living Seas. In the morning, they're often bypassed by guests rushing to stay ahead of the crowd. The Living Seas needs to be lingered over when you aren't in a hurry. Go in late afternoon or evening, or on your second day at Epcot.

## THE LAND PAVILION

**DESCRIPTION AND COMMENTS** The Land is a huge pavilion containing three attractions, several restaurants, and *Turtle Talk with Crush,* an animated interactive theater show. The original emphasis was on farming, but it now focuses on environmental concerns.

**TOURING TIPS** This is a good place for a fast-food lunch. If you're there to see the attractions, however, don't go during mealtimes.

### Living with the Land (FASTPASS)

| APPEAL BY AGE | PRESCHOOL ★★½ | GRADE SCHOOL ★★★ | TEENS ★★★½ |
| --- | --- | --- | --- |
| YOUNG ADULTS ★★★★ | OVER 30 ★★★★ | | SENIORS ★★★★ |

**What it is** Indoor boat-ride adventure through the past, present, and future of U.S. farming and agriculture. **Scope and scale** Major attraction. **When to go** Before 11 a.m., or use FASTPASS. **Special comments** Take the ride early in the morning, but save other Land attractions for later in the day. It's located on the pavilion's lower

level. **Author's rating** Interesting and fun; not to be missed; ★★★★.
**Duration of ride** About 12 minutes. **Average wait in line per 100
people ahead of you** 3 minutes. **Assumes** 15 boats operating.
**Loading speed** Moderate.

**DESCRIPTION AND COMMENTS** Boat ride takes visitors through
swamps, past inhospitable farm environments, and through a
futuristic, innovative greenhouse where real crops are grown
using the latest agricultural technologies. Inspiring and educational, with excellent effects and good narrative.

**TOURING TIPS** See this attraction before the lunch crowd hits The
Land restaurants, or use FASTPASS. If you really enjoy this ride
or have a special interest in the agricultural techniques
demonstrated, take the Behind the Seeds Greenhouse Tour.
It's a one-hour guided walk behind the scenes for an in-depth
examination of advanced and experimental growing methods.
It costs $12 for adults and $10 for children ages 3 to 9. Reservations are made on a space-available basis at the guided tour
waiting area near the entrance to Soarin'. This tour can also be
reserved in advance by calling.

## Soarin' (FASTPASS)

| APPEAL BY AGE | PRESCHOOL — | GRADE SCHOOL ★★★★★ | TEENS ★★★★½ |
|---|---|---|---|
| YOUNG ADULTS ★★★★★ | | OVER 30 ★★★★★ | SENIORS ★★★★ |

**What it is** Flight simulation ride. **Scope and scale** Super headliner.
**When to go** First 30 minutes the park is open or use FASTPASS. **Special
comments** Entrance on the lower level of The Land pavilion. May
induce motion sickness; 40-inch minimum-height requirement; switching off available (see page 75). **Author's rating** Exciting and mellow at
the same time; ★★★★½. Not to be missed. **Duration of ride** 5½ minutes. **Average wait in line per 100 people ahead of you** 4 minutes.
**Assumes** 2 concourses operating. **Loading speed** Moderate.

**DESCRIPTION AND COMMENTS** Soarin' is a thrill ride for all ages, exhil-
arating as a hank on the wing and as mellow as swinging in a
hammock. If you are fortunate enough to have experienced
"flying dreams" in your sleep, you'll have a sense of how
Soarin' feels.

Once you enter the main theater, you are secured in a seat
not unlike those on inverted roller coasters (where the coaster
is suspended from above). Once everyone is in place, the floor
drops away and you are suspended with your legs dangling.
Thus hung out to dry, you embark on a hang-glider tour with
IMAX images projected all around you, and with the flight
simulator moving in sync with the movie. The IMAX images
are well chosen and drop-dead beautiful. Special effects
include wind, sound, and even olfactory stimulation. The ride

itself is thrilling but perfectly smooth. We think Soarin' is a must-see for guests of any age who meet the height requirement. And yes, seniors we interviewed were crazy about it.

**TOURING TIPS** Soarin' joins Test Track and Mission: Space as an Epcot Super Headliner attraction. Its addition to the Epcot lineup will undoubtedly boost attendance, but also take some of the pressure off the park's other two big attractions. Keep in mind, however, that Test Track and Mission: Space serve up a little too much thrill for some guests. Soarin,' conversely, is an almost platonic ride for any age. Expressed differently, guests of all ages will want to ride. For that reason, and because it's new, we predict it will rise quickly to the top of the hit parade. Our advice: see it before 10:30 a.m. or use FAST-PASS. If you opt for the latter, don't expect there to be any left after 12:30 p.m. or so. Another strategy, if your group doesn't mind splitting up, is to use the singles line.

## The Circle of Life

| APPEAL BY AGE | PRESCHOOL ★★½ | GRADE SCHOOL ★★★ | TEENS ★★½ |
|---|---|---|---|
| YOUNG ADULTS ★★★ | OVER 30 ★★★ | | SENIORS ★★★ |

**What it is** Film exploring man's relationship with his environment. **Scope and scale** Minor attraction. **When to go** Before 11 a.m. or after 2 p.m. **Author's rating** Highly interesting and enlightening; ★★★½. **Duration of presentation** About 12½ minutes. **Preshow entertainment** None. **Probable waiting time** 10–15 minutes.

**DESCRIPTION AND COMMENTS** The featured attraction is *The Circle of Life,* starring Simba, Timon, and Pumbaa from Disney's animated feature *The Lion King.* This playful yet educational film spotlights the environmental interdependency of all creatures on earth, demonstrating how easily the ecological balance can be upset. The message is sobering, but one that enlightens.

**TOURING TIPS** Every visitor should see this film. To stay ahead of the crowd, see it in late afternoon. Long lines usually occur at mealtimes.

## IMAGINATION PAVILION

**DESCRIPTION AND COMMENTS** Multi-attraction pavilion on the west side of Innoventions West and down the walk from The Land. Outside is an "upside-down waterfall" and one of our favorite Future World landmarks, the "jumping water," a fountain that hops over the heads of unsuspecting passersby.

**TOURING TIPS** We recommend early-morning or late-evening touring. See the individual attractions for specifics.

## Journey into Imagination with Figment

| APPEAL BY AGE | PRESCHOOL ★★ | GRADE SCHOOL ★★ | TEENS ★★ |
|---|---|---|---|
| YOUNG ADULTS ★★★ | | OVER 30 ★★★ | SENIORS ★★★ |

**What it is** Dark fantasy-adventure ride. **Scope and scale** Major attraction wannabe. **When to go** Anytime. **Author's rating** ★★½. **Duration of ride** About 6 minutes. **Average wait in line per 100 people ahead of you** 2 minutes. **Loading speed** Fast.

DESCRIPTION AND COMMENTS This attraction replaced its dull and vacuous predecessor in the fall of 1999 and was retooled again in 2002 to add the ever-popular purple dragon, Figment. Drawing on the Imagination Institute theme from *Honey, I Shrunk the Audience* (in the same pavilion), the attraction takes you on a tour of the zany Institute. Sometimes you're a passive observer and sometimes you're a test subject as the ride provides a glimpse of the fictitious lab's inner workings. Stimulating all of your senses and then some, you are hit with optical illusions, an experiment where noise generates colors, a room that defies gravity, and other brain teasers. All along the way, Figment makes surprise appearances. After the ride, you can adjourn to an interactive exhibit area offering the latest in unique, hands-on imagery technology.

TOURING TIPS The standby wait for this attraction rarely exceeds 15 minutes. You can enjoy the interactive exhibit without taking the ride, so save it for later in the day.

## Honey, I Shrunk the Audience (FASTPASS)

| APPEAL BY AGE PRESCHOOL ★★★½ | GRADE SCHOOL ★★★★½ | TEENS ★★★★½ |
|---|---|---|
| YOUNG ADULTS ★★★★½ | OVER 30 ★★★★½ | SENIORS ★★★★ |

**What it is** 3-D film with special effects. **Scope and scale** Headliner. **When to go** Before 11:30 a.m., after 6 p.m., or use FASTPASS. **Special comments** Adults should not be put off by the sci-fi theme. The loud, intense show with tactile effects frightens some young children. **Author's rating** An absolute hoot! Not to be missed; ★★★★½. **Duration of presentation** About 17 minutes. **Preshow entertainment** 8 minutes. **Probable waiting time** 12 minutes (at suggested times).

DESCRIPTION AND COMMENTS *Honey, I Shrunk the Audience* is a 3-D offshoot of Disney's feature film, *Honey, I Shrunk the Kids. Honey, I Shrunk the Audience* features an array of special effects, including simulated explosions, smoke, fiber optics, lights, water spray, and moving seats. This attraction is played strictly for laughs, a commodity in short supply in Epcot entertainment.

TOURING TIPS The sound level is earsplitting, frightening some young children. Many adults report that the loud soundtrack is distracting, even uncomfortable. While *Honey, I Shrunk the Audience* is a huge hit, it overwhelms some preschoolers.

Though launched with little fanfare, *Honey, I Shrunk the Audience* has become one of Epcot's most popular attractions. Try to work it into your touring before 10:30 a.m. The show is located to the left of the Journey into Imagination ride; it isn't necessary to ride in order to enter the theater. If the wait is prohibitive (very rare), use FASTPASS. Avoid seats in the first several rows; if you're too close to the screen, the 3-D images don't focus properly.

## TEST TRACK

**DESCRIPTION AND COMMENTS** Test Track, presented by General Motors, contains the Test Track ride and TransCenter, a collection of transportation-themed stationary exhibits and mini-theater productions. The pavilion is the last on the left before crossing into the World Showcase.

Many readers tell us that Test Track "is one big commercial" for General Motors. We agree that promotional hype is more heavy-handed here than in most other business-sponsored attractions. But Test Track is one of the most creatively conceived and executed attractions in Walt Disney World.

### Test Track Ride (FASTPASS)

| APPEAL BY AGE | PRESCHOOL ★★★★ | GRADE SCHOOL ★★★★ | TEENS ★★★★ |
|---|---|---|---|
| YOUNG ADULTS ★★★★ | | OVER 30 ★★★★ | SENIORS ★★★★ |

**What it is** Automobile test-track simulator ride. **Scope and scale** Super headliner. **When to go** First 30 minutes the park is open, just before closing, or use FASTPASS. **Special comments** 40-inch height minimum. **Author's rating** Not to be missed; ★★★½. **Duration of ride** About 4 minutes. **Average wait in line per 100 people ahead of you** 4½ minutes. **Loading speed** Moderate to fast.

**DESCRIPTION AND COMMENTS** Visitors test a future-model car at high speeds through hairpin turns, up and down steep hills, and over rough terrain. The six-guest vehicle is a motion simulator that rocks and pitches. Unlike simulators at Star Tours, Body Wars, and Back to the Future (at Universal Studios), however, the Test Track model is affixed to a track and actually travels.

**TOURING TIPS** Some great technology is at work here. Test Track is so complex, in fact, that keeping it running is a constant challenge. When it's working properly, it's one of the park's better attractions.

If you use FASTPASS, be aware that the daily allocation of passes is often distributed by 12:30 or 1 p.m. If all the FAST-

PASSes are gone, another time-saving technique is to join the singles line. A singles line, thus far only available at Test Track, Mission: Space is a separate line for individuals who are alone or who do not object to riding alone. The objective of the singles line is to fill the odd spaces left by groups that don't fill up the ride vehicle. Because there are not many singles, and because most groups are unwilling to split up, singles lines are usually much shorter than the regular line and can save you a bunch of time if you don't mind riding by yourself.

## WONDERS OF LIFE PAVILION
### (open seasonally)

**DESCRIPTION AND COMMENTS** This multifaceted pavilion deals with the human body, health, and medicine. Housed in a 100,000-square-foot, gold-domed structure, Wonders of Life focuses on the capabilities of the human body and the importance of keeping fit.

### Body Wars

| APPEAL BY AGE | PRESCHOOL ★★★ | GRADE SCHOOL ★★★★ | TEENS ★★★★ |
| --- | --- | --- | --- |
| YOUNG ADULTS ★★★★ | | OVER 30 ★★★½ | SENIORS ★★½ |

**What it is** Flight-simulator ride through the human body. **Scope and scale** Headliner. **When to go** Anytime. **Special comments** Not recommended for pregnant women or people prone to motion sickness; 40-inch height minimum. **Author's rating** Anatomy made fun; not to be missed; ★★★★. **Duration of ride** 5 minutes. **Average wait in line per 100 people ahead of you** 4 minutes. **Assumes** All simulators operating. **Loading speed** Moderate to fast.

**DESCRIPTION AND COMMENTS** This thrill ride through the human body was developed along the lines of Disney-MGM Studios' Star Tours space-simulation ride. The story is that you're a passenger in a miniature capsule injected into a human body to pick up a sci-

Motion Sickness WARNING!

entist who has been inspecting a splinter in the patient's finger. The scientist, however, is sucked into the circulatory system, and you hurtle through the body to rescue her. The simulator creates a visually graphic experience as it seems to career at fantastic speeds through human organs. The story is more than a little silly, but we nevertheless rate Body Wars as "not to be missed."

**TOURING TIPS** Once one of Epcot's premier attractions, Body Wars no longer draws large crowds on a regular basis. Be aware that

Body Wars makes a lot of people motion sick; it isn't unusual for a simulator to be taken off-line for attendants to clean up a previous rider's mess. If you're at all susceptible to motion sickness, reconsider riding. If you're on Body Wars and become nauseated, fix your gaze on something other than the screen and as far away as possible (the ceiling or side and back walls). Without the visual effects, the ride isn't rough enough to disturb most guests. If you get queasy, restrooms are nearby as you get off the ride. Star Tours is just as wild but makes very few people sick. Successfully riding Star Tours doesn't necessarily mean you'll tolerate Body Wars. Conversely, if Body Wars makes you ill, you can't assume that Star Tours will, too.

### Cranium Command

| APPEAL BY AGE | PRESCHOOL ★★ | GRADE SCHOOL ★★★★ | TEENS ★★★★ |
|---|---|---|---|
| YOUNG ADULTS ★★★★½ | | OVER 30 ★★★★½ | SENIORS ★★★★½ |

**What it is** Audio-animatronic theater show about the brain. **Scope and scale** Major attraction. **When to go** Before 11 a.m. or after 3 p.m. **Author's rating** Funny, outrageous, and educational; not to be missed; ★★★★½. **Duration of presentation** About 20 minutes. **Preshow entertainment** Explanatory lead-in to feature presentation. **Probable waiting time** Less than 10 minutes at times suggested.

DESCRIPTION AND COMMENTS *Cranium Command* is Epcot's great sleeper attraction. Stuck on the backside of the Wonders of Life pavilion and far less promoted than Body Wars, this humorous Epcot offering is bypassed by many guests. Characters called "Brain Pilots" are trained to operate human brains. The show consists of a day in the life of one of these Cranium Commanders as he tries to pilot the brain of an adolescent boy. Epcot and Walt Disney World could use a lot more of this type of humor.

TOURING TIPS To understand the program, you need to see the pre-show cartoon. If you arrive in the waiting area while it's in progress, be sure you see enough to get a sense of the story before you enter the theater. While most preschoolers enjoy *Cranium Command,* many don't really understand it.

### The Making of Me

| APPEAL BY AGE | PRESCHOOL ★½ | GRADE SCHOOL ★★★½ | TEENS ★★½ |
|---|---|---|---|
| YOUNG ADULTS ★★★ | | OVER 30 ★★★ | SENIORS ★★★ |

**What it is** Humorous movie about human conception and birth. **Scope and scale** Minor attraction. **When to go** Early in the morning or after 4:30 p.m. **Author's rating** Sanitized sex education; ★★★.

**Duration of presentation** 14 minutes. **Preshow entertainment**
None. **Probable waiting time** 25 minutes or more, unless you go at
suggested times.

**DESCRIPTION AND COMMENTS** This lighthearted and very sensitive
movie about human conception, gestation, and birth was considered a controversial addition to Wonders of Life, but most
viewers agree it's tasteful and creative. The plot's main character goes back in time to watch his parents date, fall in love,
marry, and, yes, conceive and give birth to him.

Sexual material is well handled, with emphasis on loving
relationships, not plumbing. Parents of children younger than
age 7 tell us the sexual information went over their children's
heads for the most part. In older children, however, the film
precipitates questions. You be the judge.

**TOURING TIPS** *The Making of Me* is excellent and should be moved
from its tiny space to a larger theater. Of course, we've been
saying that for years.

## Mission: Space (FASTPASS)

| APPEAL BY AGE | PRESCHOOL — | GRADE SCHOOL ★★★★½ | TEENS ★★★★½ |
|---|---|---|---|
| YOUNG ADULTS ★★★★½ | | OVER 30 ★★★★ | SENIORS ★★★½ |

**What it is** Space-flight simulation ride. **Scope and scale** Super
headliner. **When to go** First 30 minutes the park is open, or use
FASTPASS. **Special comments** Not recommended for pregnant
women or people prone to motion sickness; 44-inch minimum-height
requirement. **Author's rating** Impressive; ★★★★. **Duration of ride**
About 5 minutes plus pre-show. **Average wait in line per 100 people
ahead of you** 4 minutes.

Motion
Sickness

WARNING!

**DESCRIPTION AND COMMENTS** Mission: Space,
among other things, is Disney's reply to all
the cutting-edge attractions introduced over
the past several years by cross-town rival
Universal. The first truly groundbreaking Disney attraction since the Tower of Terror,
Mission: Space is one of the hottest tickets at Walt Disney
World.

Guests enter the NASA Mission: Space Training Center
where they are first introduced to the Mission: Space deep-
space exploration program and then divided into groups for in-
troductory space-flight training. After flight orientation, they
are strapped into a space capsule for a simulated flight, where,
of course, the unexpected happens. Interactive computer con-
trols aboard the capsule allow guests to carry out routine flight

tasks and to respond to the emergency. The capsules are small and the ride amazingly realistic. Each capsule accommodates a crew consisting of group commander, pilot, navigator, and engineer, with a guest functioning in each role. In contrast to the pre-opening hype, the crew's skill and finesse (or more often, lack thereof) in handling their respective responsibilities have no effect on the outcome of the flight. The queuing area and pre-show are pretty dazzling. En route to the main event guests pass space hardware, astronaut tributes and memorials, a cutaway of a huge spacewheel showing crew working and living compartments, and a manned Mission Control where cast members actually operate the attraction.

The post-show area features an electronic game called Mission: Space Race that almost three dozen guests, divided into two teams, can play at once. The winning team beats the other team's spaceship back from Mars to the home base. Individuals on each team are responsible for certain tasks essential to the mission and make their ship fly faster by hitting correct keyboard buttons. Making the game even more unique is that folks at home can play in real time by logging onto **www.disneyspacerace.com.**

**TOURING TIPS** Be sure to make a restroom stop before you get in line; you'll feel like your bladder has been to Mars and back for real before you get out of this attraction. In addition to a FASTPASS return line, there is a singles line to expedite traffic flow and loading (yeah!). By our calculations, Mission: Space should be able to handle about 1,600 guests per hour if it is operating at capacity with no breakdowns. This is respectable, but not a huge number for an attraction of its scope and popularity, so expect long waits unless you ride immediately after the park opens or use FASTPASS. If you intend to use FASTPASS, assume that all the FASTPASSes for the day will be distributed by about noon.

## Universe of Energy: Ellen's Energy Adventure

| APPEAL BY AGE | PRESCHOOL ★★★ | GRADE SCHOOL ★★★★ | TEENS ★★★½ |
|---|---|---|---|
| YOUNG ADULTS ★★★★ | OVER 30 ★★★★ | | SENIORS ★★★★ |

**What it is** Combination ride/theater presentation about energy. **Scope and scale** Major attraction. **When to go** Before 11:15 a.m. or after 4:30 p.m. **Special comments** Don't be dismayed by long lines; 580 people enter the pavilion each time the theater changes audiences. **Author's rating** The most unique theater in Walt Disney World; ★★★★. **Duration of presentation** About 26½ minutes. **Preshow entertainment** 8 minutes. **Probable waiting time** 20–40 minutes.

**DESCRIPTION AND COMMENTS** Audio-animatronic dinosaurs and the unique traveling theater make this Exxon pavilion one of Future World's most popular. Because this is a theater with a ride component, the line doesn't move while the show is in progress. When the theater empties, however, a large chunk of the line will disappear as people are admitted for the next show. Visitors are seated in what appears to be an ordinary theater while they watch a film about energy sources. Then the theater seats divide into six 97-passenger traveling cars that glide among the swamps and reptiles of a prehistoric forest. Special effects include the feel of warm, moist air from the swamp, and the smell of sulphur from an erupting volcano.

The accompanying film is a humorous and upbeat flick starring Ellen DeGeneres and Bill Nye that sugarcoats the somewhat ponderous discussion of energy. For kids, Universe of Energy remains a toss-up. The dinosaurs frighten some preschoolers, and kids of all ages lose the thread during the educational segments.

**TOURING TIPS** This attraction draws large crowds beginning early in the morning. Because Universe of Energy can operate more than one show at a time, lines are generally tolerable. If you decide to skip the show, at least check out the great dinosaur topiaries outside the pavilion.

## The "Mom, I Can't Believe It's Disney!" Fountain

| APPEAL BY AGE | PRESCHOOL ★★★★★ | GRADE SCHOOL ★★★★★ | TEENS ★★★★ |
|---|---|---|---|
| YOUNG ADULTS ★★★★ | OVER 30 ★★★★ | | SENIORS ★★★★★ |

**What it is** Combination fountain and shower. **When to go** When it's hot. **Scope and scale** Diversion. **Special comments** Secretly installed by Martians during *IllumiNations*. **Author's rating** Yes!! ★★★★. **Duration of Experience** Indefinite. **Probable waiting time** None.

**DESCRIPTION AND COMMENTS** This simple fountain on the walkway linking Future World to World Showcase isn't much to look at, but it offers a truly spontaneous experience—rare in Walt Disney World, where everything is controlled, from the snow peas in your stir fry to how frequently the crocodile yawns in the Jungle Cruise.

Spouts of water erupt randomly from the sidewalk. You can frolic in the water or let it cascade down on you or blow up your britches. On a broiling Florida day, when you think you might suddenly combust, fling yourself into the fountain and do decidedly un-Disney things. Dance, skip, sing, jump, splash, cavort, roll around, stick your toes down the spouts, or catch the water in your mouth as it descends. You can do all of this with your clothes on or, depending on your age, with your clothes off. It's hard to imagine so much personal freedom at Disney World and almost unthinkable to contemplate soggy people slogging and squishing around the park, but there you have it. Hurrah!

**TOURING TIPS** We don't know if the fountain's creator has been drummed out of the corps by the Disney Tribunal of People-Who-Sit-on-Sticks [probably], but we're grateful for his courage in introducing one thing that's not super-controlled. We do know your kids will be right in the middle of this thing before your brain sounds the alert. Our advice: Pack a pair of dry shorts and turn the kids loose. You might even want to bring a spare pair for yourself. Or maybe not—so much advance planning would stifle the spontaneity.

# WORLD SHOWCASE

WORLD SHOWCASE, EPCOT'S SECOND theme area, is an ongoing World's Fair encircling a picturesque 40-acre lagoon. The cuisine, culture, history, and architecture of almost a dozen countries are permanently displayed in individual national pavilions spaced along a 1.2-mile promenade. Pavilions replicate familiar landmarks and present representative street scenes from the host countries.

World Showcase features some of the most lovely gardens in the United States. Located in Germany, France, England, Canada, and to a lesser extent, China, they are sometimes tucked away and out of sight of pedestrian traffic on the World Showcase promenade.

Most adults enjoy World Showcase, but many children find it boring. To make it more interesting to children, most Epcot retail shops sell Passport Kits for about $10. Each kit contains a blank passport and stamps for every World Showcase country. As kids accompany their folks to each country, they tear out the appropriate stamp and stick it in the passport. The kit also contains basic information on the nations and a Mickey Mouse button. Disney has built a lot of profit into this little product, but I guess that isn't the issue. More important, parents tell us the Passport Kit helps get the kids through World Showcase with a minimum of impatience, whining, and tantrums.

*unofficial* **TIP**
To get your kids interested in World Showcase, buy them a Passport Kit and let them collect stamps from each Epcot country.

Children also enjoy "Kidcot Fun Stops," a program Disney designed to make World Showcase more interesting for the 5–12 crowd. So simple and uncomplicated that you can't believe Disney people thought it up, the Fun Stops usually are nothing more than a large table on the sidewalk at each pavilion. Each table is staffed by a Disney cast member who stamps passports and supervises children in modest craft projects relating to the host country. Reports from parents about the Fun Stops have been uniformly positive.

Moving clockwise around the promenade, here are the nations represented and their attractions.

## MEXICO PAVILION

**DESCRIPTION AND COMMENTS** Pre-Columbian pyramids dominate the architecture of this exhibit. One forms the pavilion's facade, and the other overlooks the restaurant and plaza alongside the boat ride, El Río del Tiempo, inside the pavilion.

**TOURING TIPS** Romantic and exciting testimony to Mexico's charms, the pyramids contain a large number of authentic and valuable artifacts. Many people zip past these treasures without stopping to look. The village scene inside the pavilion is beautiful and exquisitely detailed. The retail shop that formerly occupied most of the left half of the inner pavilion has been replaced with an open, cheerful, two floor–space housing Mexico's Kidcot stop, plus hands-on exhibits of Mexico's food, culture, and geography. Be sure to send a video postcard of yourself cliff-diving in Acapulco to your friends back home.

### El Río del Tiempo

| APPEAL BY AGE | PRESCHOOL ★★ | | GRADE SCHOOL ★★ |
|---|---|---|---|
| TEENS ★½ | YOUNG ADULTS ★★ | OVER 30 ★★ | SENIORS ★½ |

**What it is** Indoor scenic boat ride. **Scope and scale** Minor attraction. **When to go** Before 11 a.m. or after 3 p.m. **Author's rating** Light and relaxing; ★★. **Duration of ride** About 7 minutes (plus 1½-minute wait to disembark). **Average wait in line per 100 people ahead of you** 4½ minutes. **Assumes** 16 boats in operation. **Loading speed** Moderate.

**DESCRIPTION AND COMMENTS** El Río del Tiempo (The River of Time) cruises among audio-animatronic and cinematic scenes depicting the history of Mexico from the ancient Mayan, Toltec, and Aztec civilizations to modern times. Special effects include fiber-optic projections that simulate fireworks near the ride's end. Though tranquil and relaxing, El Río del Tiempo is not particularly interesting and definitely is not worth a long wait.

TOURING TIPS The ride tends to get crowded during early afternoon.

## NORWAY PAVILION

DESCRIPTION AND COMMENTS The Norway pavilion is complex, beautiful, and architecturally diverse. Surrounding a courtyard is an assortment of traditional Scandinavian buildings, including a replica of the 14th-century Akershus Castle, a wooden stave church, red-tiled cottages, and replicas of historic buildings representing the traditional designs of Bergen, Alesund, and Oslo. Attractions include an adventure boat ride in the mold of Pirates of the Caribbean, a movie about Norway, and a gallery of art and artifacts in the stave church. For smaller children there is a Viking-ship play area. The pavilion houses Restaurant Akershus, a sit-down eatery (advance reservations required) that serves koldtboard (cold buffet) at lunch and dinner. In the morning the restaurant hosts the Princesses character breakfast, one of the most popular in Walt Disney World. An open-air café and a bakery cater to those on the run. Shoppers find abundant native handicrafts.

### Maelstrom (FASTPASS)

| APPEAL BY AGE | PRESCHOOL ★★★½ | GRADE SCHOOL ★★★½ | TEENS ★★★ |
| --- | --- | --- | --- |
| YOUNG ADULTS ★★★ | OVER 30 ★★★ | | SENIORS ★★★ |

**What it is** Indoor adventure boat ride. **Scope and scale** Major attraction. **When to go** Before noon, after 4:30 p.m., or use FASTPASS. **Author's rating** Too short, but has its moments; ★★★. **Duration of ride** 4½ minutes, followed by a 5-minute film with a short wait in between; about 14 minutes for the whole show. **Average wait in line per 100 people ahead of you** 4 minutes. **Assumes** 12 or 13 boats operating. **Loading speed** Fast.

DESCRIPTION AND COMMENTS In one of Disney World's shorter water rides, guests board dragon-headed ships for a voyage through the fabled rivers and seas of Viking history and legend. They brave trolls, rocky gorges, waterfalls, and a storm at sea. A second-generation Disney water ride, the Viking voyage assembles an impressive array of special effects, combining visual, tactile, and auditory stimuli in a fast-paced and often humorous odyssey. Afterward, guests see a five-minute film on Norway. We don't have any major problems with Maelstrom, but a vocal minority of our readers consider the ride too brief and resent having to sit through what they characterize as a travelogue.

**TOURING TIPS** Sometimes, several hundred guests from a recently concluded screening of *Reflections of China* arrive at Maelstrom en masse. Should you encounter this horde, postpone Maelstrom. If you don't want to see the Norway film, not to worry. You will be given the opportunity to exit before the film begins.

## CHINA PAVILION

**DESCRIPTION AND COMMENTS** A half-sized replica of the Temple of Heaven in Beijing identifies this pavilion. Gardens and reflecting ponds simulate those found in Suzhou, and an art gallery features a lotus blossom gate and formal saddle roof line. The China pavilion offers two restaurants: a fast-food eatery and a full-service establishment (advance reservations required) that serves lamentably lackluster Chinese food in a lovely setting.

### Reflections of China

| APPEAL BY AGE | PRESCHOOL ★★ | GRADE SCHOOL ★★½ | TEENS ★★★ |
|---|---|---|---|
| YOUNG ADULTS ★★★½ | | OVER 30 ★★★★ | SENIORS ★★★★ |

**What it is** Film about the Chinese people and country. **Scope and scale** Major attraction. **When to go** Anytime. **Special comments** Audience stands throughout performance. **Author's rating** This beautifully produced film was introduced in 2003; ★★★½. **Duration of presentation** About 14 minutes. **Preshow entertainment** None. **Probable waiting time** 10 minutes

**DESCRIPTION AND COMMENTS** Pass through the Hall of Prayer for Good Harvest to view the Circle-Vision 360 film *Reflections of China*. Warm and appealing, it's a brilliant (albeit politically sanitized) introduction to the people and natural beauty of China.

**TOURING TIPS** The pavilion is truly beautiful—serene yet exciting. *Reflections of China* plays in a theater where guests must stand, but the film can usually be enjoyed anytime without much waiting. If you're touring World Showcase in a counterclockwise rotation and plan next to go to Norway and ride Maelstrom, position yourself on the far left of the theater (as you face the attendant's podium). After the show, be one of the first to exit. Hurry to Maelstrom as fast as you can to arrive ahead of the several hundred other *Reflections of China* patrons who will be right behind you.

## GERMANY PAVILION

**DESCRIPTION AND COMMENTS** A clock tower adorned with boy and girl figures rises above the platz (plaza) marking the Germany pavilion. Dominated by a fountain depicting St. George's victory over the dragon, the platz is encircled by buildings done in traditional German architecture. The main attraction is the Biergarten, a buffet restaurant (advance reservations required) serving German food and beer. Yodeling, folk dancing, and oompah-band music are included during mealtimes.

Also at Germany, be sure to check out the large and elaborate model railroad located just beyond the restrooms as you walk from Germany toward Italy.

**TOURING TIPS** The pavilion is pleasant and festive. Tour anytime.

## ITALY PAVILION

**DESCRIPTION AND COMMENTS** The entrance to Italy is marked by a 105-foot-tall campanile (bell tower) said to mirror the tower in St. Mark's Square in Venice. Left of the campanile is a replica of the 14th-century Doge's Palace, also in the famous square. Other buildings are composites of Italian architecture. For example, L'Originale Alfredo di Roma Ristorante is Florentine. Visitors can watch pasta being made in this popular restaurant, which specializes in fettuccini Alfredo. The pavilion has a waterfront on the lagoon where gondolas are tied to striped moorings.

**TOURING TIPS** Streets and courtyards in the Italy pavilion are among the most realistic in World Showcase. You really feel as if you're in Italy. Because there's no film or ride, tour at any hour.

## UNITED STATES PAVILION

### *The American Adventure*

| APPEAL BY AGE | PRESCHOOL ★★ | GRADE SCHOOL ★★★ | TEENS ★★★ |
| --- | --- | --- | --- |
| YOUNG ADULTS ★★★★ | OVER 30 ★★★★½ | SENIORS ★★★★★ | |

**What it is** Patriotic mixed-media and audio-animatronic theater presentation on U.S. history. **Scope and scale** Headliner. **When to go** Anytime. **Author's rating** Disney's best historic/patriotic attraction; not to be missed; ★★★★. **Duration of presentation** About 29 minutes. **Preshow entertainment** Voices of Liberty chorale singing. **Probable waiting time** 16 minutes.

**DESCRIPTION AND COMMENTS** The United States pavilion, generally referred to as The American Adventure, consists (not surprisingly) of a fast-food restaurant and a patriotic show.

*The American Adventure* is a composite of everything Disney does best. Located in an imposing brick structure reminiscent of Colonial Philadelphia, the 29-minute production is a stirring, but sanitized, rendition of American history narrated by an audio-animatronic Mark Twain (who carries a smoking cigar) and Ben Franklin (who climbs a set of stairs to visit Thomas Jefferson). Behind a stage (almost half the size of a football field) is a 28- by 55-foot rear-projection screen (the largest ever used) on which motion-picture images are interwoven with action on stage.

Though the production stimulates patriotic emotion in some viewers, others find it overstated and boring.

**TOURING TIPS** Architecturally, the United States Pavilion isn't as interesting as most other pavilions. But the presentation, our researchers believe, is the very best patriotic attraction in the Disney repertoire. It usually plays to capacity audiences from around 1:30 to 3:30 p.m., but it isn't hard to get into. Because of the theater's large capacity, the wait during busy times of day seldom approaches an hour, and averages 25–40 minutes. Because of its theme, the presentation is decidedly less compelling to non-Americans.

The adjacent Liberty Inn serves a quick, nonethnic, fast-food meal.

## JAPAN PAVILION

**DESCRIPTION AND COMMENTS** The five-story, blue-roofed pagoda, inspired by a 17th-century shrine in Nara, sets this pavilion apart. A hill garden behind it encompasses waterfalls, rocks, flowers, lanterns, paths, and rustic bridges. The building on the right (as one faces the entrance) was inspired by the ceremonial and coronation hall at the Imperial Palace at Kyoto. It contains restaurants and a large retail store. Through the center entrance and to the left is the Bijutsu-kan Gallery, exhibiting some exquisite Japanese artifacts.

**TOURING TIPS** Tasteful and elaborate, the pavilion creatively blends simplicity, architectural grandeur, and natural beauty. Tour anytime.

## MOROCCO PAVILION

**DESCRIPTION AND COMMENTS** The bustling market, winding streets, lofty minarets, and stuccoed archways re-create the romance and intrigue of Marrakesh and Casablanca. Attention to detail makes Morocco one of the most exciting World Showcase pavilions. It also has a museum of Moorish art and the Restaurant Marrakesh, which serves some unusual and difficult-to-find North African specialties.

**TOURING TIPS** Morocco has neither a ride nor theater; tour anytime.

# FRANCE PAVILION

**DESCRIPTION AND COMMENTS** Naturally, a replica of the Eiffel Tower (a big one) is this pavilion's centerpiece. In the foreground, streets recall *La Belle Époque,* France's "beautiful time" between 1870 and 1910. The sidewalk café and restaurant are very popular, as is the pastry shop. You won't be the first visitor to buy a croissant to tide you over until your next real meal.

## *Impressions de France*

| APPEAL BY AGE | PRESCHOOL ★½ | GRADE SCHOOL ★★½ | TEENS ★★★ |
|---|---|---|---|
| YOUNG ADULTS ★★★★ | OVER 30 ★★★★ | | SENIORS ★★★★ |

**What it is** Film essay on the French people and country. **Scope and scale** Major attraction. **When to go** Anytime. **Author's rating** Exceedingly beautiful film; not to be missed; ★★★½. **Duration of presentation** About 18 minutes. **Preshow entertainment** None. **Probable waiting time** 12 minutes (at suggested times).

**DESCRIPTIONS AND COMMENTS** *Impressions de France* is an 18-minute movie projected over 200 degrees onto five screens. Unlike at China and Canada, the audience sits to view this well-made film introducing France's people, cities, and natural wonders.

**TOURING TIPS** Detail and the evocation of a bygone era enrich the atmosphere of this pavilion. Streets are small and become quite congested when visitors queue for the film.

# UNITED KINGDOM PAVILION

**DESCRIPTION AND COMMENTS** A variety of period architecture attempts to capture Britain's city, town, and rural atmospheres. One street alone has a thatched-roof cottage, a four-story timber-and-plaster building, a pre-Georgian plaster building, a formal Palladian exterior of dressed stone, and a city square with a Hyde Park bandstand (whew!).

The pavilion is mostly shops. The Rose & Crown Pub and Dining Room is the only World Showcase full-service restaurant with dining on the water side of the promenade. For fast food try Harry Ramsden Fish & Chips.

**TOURING TIPS** There are no attractions, hence minimal congestion; tour anytime. Advance reservations aren't required to enjoy the pub section of the Rose & Crown, making it a nice place to stop for a mid-afternoon beer. Speaking of which, if you can't make up your mind, a beer sampler is available for about $10. Included are six-ounce servings of Bass Ale, Harp Irish Lager, Tennent Scottish Lager, Guinness Stout, and Boddington Crème Ale. In the category of dubious distinctions, the

Rose & Crown Pub is the only place at Epcot where smoking is allowed indoors.

## CANADA PAVILION

Canada's cultural, natural, and architectural diversity is reflected in this large and impressive pavilion. Thirty-foot-tall totem poles embellish a Native American village at the foot of a magnificent château-style hotel. Nearby is a rugged stone building said to be modeled after a famous landmark near Niagara Falls and reflecting Britain's influence on Canada. Le Cellier, a steakhouse on the pavilion's lower level, accepts advance reservations but also welcomes walk-ins.

### O Canada!

| APPEAL BY AGE | PRESCHOOL ★★ | GRADE SCHOOL ★★½ | TEENS ★★★ |
|---|---|---|---|
| YOUNG ADULTS ★★★½ | OVER 30 ★★★★ | | SENIORS ★★★★ |

**What it is** Film essay on the Canadian people and their country. **Scope and scale** Major attraction. **When to go** Anytime. **Special comments** Audience stands during performance. **Author's rating** Makes you want to catch the first plane to Canada! ★★★½. **Duration of presentation** About 18 minutes. **Preshow entertainment** None. **Probable waiting time** 10 minutes.

DESCRIPTION AND COMMENTS  *O Canada!* showcases Canada's natural beauty and population diversity and demonstrates the immense pride Canadians have in their country. Visitors leave the theater through Victoria Gardens inspired by the famed Butchart Gardens of British Columbia.

TOURING TIPS  *O Canada!,* a large-capacity theater attraction (guests must stand), gets fairly heavy late-morning attendance because Canada is the first pavilion encountered as one travels counterclockwise around World Showcase Lagoon.

# LIVE ENTERTAINMENT
# *in* EPCOT

LIVE ENTERTAINMENT IN EPCOT IS MORE diverse than it is in the Magic Kingdom. In World Showcase, it reflects the nations represented. Future World provides a perfect setting for new and experimental offerings. Information about live entertainment on the day you visit is contained in the Epcot guidemap you obtain upon entry or at Guest Relations.

Here are some performers and performances you're apt to encounter:

**IN FUTURE WORLD** A roving brass band, a musical crew of drumming janitors, socializing robots (EpBOTS), and gymnasts in *Alien* attire striking statuesque poses work near the front entrance and at Innoventions Plaza (between the two Innoventions buildings and by the fountain) according to the *Times Guide.*

**INNOVENTIONS FOUNTAIN SHOW** Numerous times each day, the fountain between the two Innoventions buildings comes alive with pulsating, arching plumes of water synchronized to a musical score.

**DISNEY CHARACTERS** Once believed to be inconsistent with Epcot's educational image, Disney characters have now been imported in significant numbers. In a new program called Disney Characters on Holiday, a dozen or so characters roll around the World Showcase in a British double-decker bus, stopping at times and places listed in the park map entertainment schedule. At each stop, the characters sing a song or two and then wallow into the crowd for autographs and photos.

Characters also appear in live shows at the American Gardens Theatre and at the Showcase Plaza between Mexico and Canada. Times are listed in the *Times Guide,* in the Epcot guidemap available upon entry, and at Guest Relations. Finally, The Garden Grill Restaurant in the Land pavilion offers character meals.

**AMERICAN GARDENS THEATRE** The site of Epcot's premier live performances is in a large amphitheater near *The American Adventure,* facing World Showcase Lagoon. International talent plays limited engagements there. Many shows spotlight the music, dance, and costumes of the performer's home country. Other programs feature Disney characters.

**ILLUMINATIONS** An after-dark program of music, fireworks, erupting fountains, special lighting, and laser technology is performed on World Showcase Lagoon (see pages 199–202).

**AROUND WORLD SHOWCASE** Impromptu performances take place in and around the World Showcase pavilions. They include a strolling mariachi group in Mexico; street actors in Italy; a fife-and-drum corps or singing group (The Voices of Liberty) at *The American Adventure;* traditional songs, drums, and dances in Japan; street comedy and a Beatles impersonation band in the United Kingdom; white-faced mimes in France; and bagpipes in Canada, among others. Street entertainment occurs about every half hour (though not necessarily on the hour or half hour).

**KIDCOT FUN ZONES** In the World Showcase there are Kidcot Fun Zones, where younger children can hear a story or make some small craft representative of the host nation. The Fun Zones are quite informal, usually set up right on the walkway; during busy times of year, you'll find them at each country.

**DINNER AND LUNCH SHOWS** Restaurants in World Showcase serve healthy portions of live entertainment to accompany the victuals. Find folk dancing and an oompah band in Germany, singing waiters in Italy and Germany, and belly dancers in Morocco. Shows are performed only at dinner in Italy, but at both lunch and dinner in Germany and Morocco. Priority seating is required.

## THE BEST WAYS TO SEE *ILLUMINATIONS*

*ILLUMINATIONS* IS EPCOT'S GREAT OUTDOOR spectacle, integrating fireworks, laser lights, neon, and music in a stirring tribute to the nations of the world. It's the climax of every Epcot day when the park is open late. Don't miss it.

### Getting out of Epcot after *IllumiNations*
### (Read This before Selecting a Viewing Spot)

Decide how quickly you want to leave the park after the show, then pick your vantage point. *IllumiNations* ends the day at Epcot. When it's over, only a couple of gift shops remain open. Because there's nothing to do, everyone leaves at once. This creates a great snarl at Package Pick-up, the Epcot monorail station, and the Disney bus stop. It also pushes to the limit the tram system hauling guests to their cars in the parking lot. Stroller return, however, is extraordinarily efficient and doesn't cause any delay.

If you're staying at an Epcot resort (Swan, Dolphin, and Yacht and Beach Club resorts, and BoardWalk Inn and Villas), watch *IllumiNations* from somewhere on the southern (*The American Adventure*) half of World Showcase Lagoon and then leave through the International Gateway between France and the United Kingdom. You can walk or take a boat back to your hotel from the International Gateway. If you have a car and are visiting Epcot in the evening for dinner and *IllumiNations,* park at the Yacht or Beach clubs. After the show, duck out the International Gateway and be on the road to your hotel in 15 minutes. We should warn you that there is a manned security gate at the entrances to most of the Epcot resorts, including the Yacht and Beach clubs. You will, of course, be admitted if you have legitimate business, such as dining at one of the hotel restaurants, or, if you park at the BoardWalk Hotel and Villas (requiring a slightly longer walk to Epcot), going to the clubs and restaurants at Disney's BoardWalk. If you're staying at any other Disney hotel and don't have a car, the fastest way home is to join the mass exodus through the main gate after *IllumiNations* and catch a bus or the monorail.

Those who have a car in the Epcot lot have a more problematic situation. If you want to beat the crowd, find a viewing spot at the end of World Showcase Lagoon nearest Future World (and the exits). Leave as soon as *IllumiNations* concludes, trying to exit ahead of the crowd. Be forewarned that thousands of people will be doing exactly the same thing. To get a good vantage point anywhere between Mexico and Canada on the northern end of the lagoon, you'll have to stake out your spot 45–90 minutes before the show. Conceivably, you may squander more time holding your spot before *IllumiNations* than you would if you watched from the less congested southern end of the lagoon and took your chances with the crowd upon departure.

*unofficial* **TIP**
Everyone in your party should be told not to exit through the turnstiles until all noses have been counted.

More groups get separated, and more children lost, after *IllumiNations* than at any other time. In summer, you will be walking in a throng of up to 30,000 people. If you're heading for the parking lot, anticipate this congestion and preselect a point in the Epcot entrance area where you can meet in the event that someone gets separated from the group. We recommend the fountain just inside the main entrance. It can be a nightmare if the group gets split up and you don't know whether the others are inside or outside the park.

For those with a car, the main problem is reaching it. Once there, traffic leaves the parking lot pretty well. If you paid close attention to where you parked, consider skipping the tram and walking. If you walk, watch your children closely and hang on to them for all you're worth. The parking lot is pretty wild at this time of night, with hundreds of moving cars.

## Good Locations for Viewing *IllumiNations* and Other World Showcase Lagoon Performances

The best place to be for any presentation on World Showcase Lagoon is in a seat on the lakeside veranda of the Cantina de San Angel in Mexico. Come early (*at least* 90 minutes before *IllumiNations*) and relax with a cold drink or snack while you wait for the show.

The Rose & Crown Pub in the United Kingdom also has lagoonside seating. Because of a small wall, however, the view isn't quite as good as from the Cantina. If you want to combine dinner on the Rose & Crown's veranda with *Illu- miNations*, make a dinner advance reservation for about 1 hour and 15 minutes before show time. Report a few minutes early for your seating and tell the Rose & Crown host that you want a table outside where you can view *IllumiNations* during or after dinner. Our experience is that the Rose & Crown staff will bend over backward to accommodate you. If you aren't able to obtain a table outside, eat inside, then hang out until show time. When the lights dim, indicating the start of *IllumiNations*, you will be allowed to join the diners on the terrace to watch the show.

Because most guests run for the exits after a presentation, and because islands in the southern *(The American Adventure)* half of the lagoon block the view from some places, the most popular spectator positions are along the northern waterfront from Norway and Mexico on around to Canada and the United Kingdom. For those who are late finishing dinner or don't want to spend 45 minutes standing by a rail, here are some good viewing spots along the southern perimeter (moving counterclockwise from the United Kingdom to Germany) that often go unnoticed until 10–20 minutes before show time:

1. **International Gateway Island**  The pedestrian bridge across the canal near International Gateway spans an island that offers great viewing. This island normally fills 30 minutes or more before show time.

*unofficial* **TIP** It's important not to position yourself under a tree, awning, or anything else that blocks your overhead view.

2. **Second-Floor** (Restaurant-Level) Deck of the Mitsukoshi Building in Japan  An Asian arch slightly blocks your sightline, but this covered deck offers a great vantage point, especially if the weather is iffy. Only the Cantina de San Angel in Mexico is more protected.

3. **Gondola Landing at Italy**  An elaborate waterfront promenade offers excellent viewing positions. Claim your spot at least 30 minutes before show time.

4. **The Boat Dock Opposite Germany**  Another good vantage point, the dock generally fills 30 minutes before *IllumiNations*.

5. **Waterfront Promenade by Germany**  Views are good from the 90-foot-long lagoonside walkway between Germany and China.

*unofficial* **TIP**
Although the northern end of the lagoon unquestionably offers excellent viewing, it's usually necessary to claim a spot 40–60 minutes before *IllumiNations* begins.

None of the above viewing locations are reserved for *Unofficial Guide* readers, and on busier nights, good spots go early. But we still won't hold down a slab of concrete for two hours before *IllumiNations* as some people do. Most nights, you can find an acceptable vantage point 15–30 minutes before the show. Because most of the action is significantly above ground level, you don't need to be right on the rail or have an unobstructed view of the water.

If *IllumiNations* is a top priority for you and you want to be absolutely certain of getting a good viewing position, claim your place an hour or more before show time.

### *IllumiNations* Cruise

For a really good view, you can charter a pontoon boat for $120. Captained by a Disney cast member, the boat holds up to ten guests. Your captain will take you for a little cruise and then position the boat in a perfect place to watch *IllumiNations*. Optional food and beverage items are available through Yacht Club Private Dining at ☎ 407-934-3160. Cruises depart from the BoardWalk and Yacht and Beach Club docks. A major indirect benefit of the charter is that you can enjoy *IllumiNations* without fighting the mob afterwards. Because this is a private charter rather than a tour, only your group will be aboard. Life jackets are provided, but you can wear them at your discretion. Because there are few boats, charters sell out fast. To reserve, call ☎ 407-WDW-PLAY at exactly 7 a.m. 90 days before the day you want to charter. Because the Disney reservations system counts days in a somewhat atypical manner, we recommend phoning about 95 days out to have a Disney agent specify the exact morning to call for reservations. Similar charters are available on the Seven Seas Lagoon to watch the Magic Kingdom fireworks.

# ■ EPCOT TOURING PLANS

OUR EPCOT TOURING PLANS ARE FIELD-TESTED, step-by-step itineraries for seeing all major attractions at Epcot with a minimum of waiting in line. They're designed to keep you ahead of the crowds while the park is filling in the morning, and to place you at the less crowded attractions during Epcot's busier hours. They assume you would be happier doing a little extra walking rather than a lot of extra standing in line.

Touring Epcot is much more strenuous and demanding than touring the other theme parks. Epcot requires about twice as much walking. Our plans will help you avoid crowds and bottlenecks on days of moderate to heavy attendance, but they can't shorten the distance you have to walk. (Wear comfortable shoes.) On days of lighter attendance, when crowd conditions aren't a critical factor, the plans will help you organize your tour. We offer four touring plans:

*unofficial* **TIP**
Unlike the Magic Kingdom, Epcot has no effective in-park transportation; wherever you want to go, it's always quicker to walk.

**EPCOT ONE-DAY TOURING PLAN** This plan packs as much as possible into one long day and requires a lot of hustle and stamina.

**AUTHOR'S SELECTIVE EPCOT ONE-DAY TOURING PLAN** This plan eliminates some lesser attractions (in the author's opinion) and offers a somewhat more relaxed tour if you have only one day.

**EPCOT TWO-DAY SUNRISE/STARLIGHT TOURING PLAN** This plan combines the easy touring of early morning on one day with Epcot's festivity and live pageantry at night on the second day. The first day requires some backtracking and hustle but is much more laid-back than either one-day plan.

**EPCOT TWO-DAY EARLY RISER TOURING PLAN** This is the most efficient Epcot touring plan, eliminating 90% of the backtracking and extra walking required by the others while still providing a comprehensive tour.

## PRELIMINARY INSTRUCTIONS FOR ALL EPCOT TOURING PLANS

1. Call ☎ 407-824-4321 in advance for the hours of operation on the day of your visit.
2. Make advance reservations at the Epcot full-service restaurant(s) of your choice in advance of your visit.

### Epcot One-Day Touring Plan
**FOR** Adults and children ages 8 or older
**ASSUMES** Willingness to experience all major rides and shows

THIS PLAN REQUIRES A LOT OF WALKING and some backtracking in order to avoid long waits in line. A little extra walking and some early-morning hustle will spare you two to three hours of standing in line. You might not complete the tour. How far you get depends on how quickly you move from attraction to attraction, how many times you rest and eat, how quickly the park fills, and what time it closes.

This plan is not recommended for families with very young children. If you're touring with young children and have only one day, use the Author's Selective Epcot One-Day Touring Plan. Break after lunch and relax at your hotel, returning to the park in late afternoon. If you can allocate two days to Epcot, use one of the Epcot two-day touring plans.

1. Arrive at the parking lot 40 minutes before official opening time.

2. Proceed to the plaza behind Spaceship Earth and then along crescent-shaped Innoventions East building on your left until you see an open passage through the building. Turn left through this passage. After emerging on the far side of Innoventions East, turn right to Test Track. Ride Test Track. Do not use FASTPASS.

3. Mission: Space is next door to Test Track. Enjoy. Do not use FASTPASS.

4. Obtaining FASTPASSes for Soarin' should be your next step. Soarin' is located in the Land pavilion on the far side of Innoventions West (to your right after passing Spaceship Earth).

5. Ride Living with the Land. Save other attractions in the pavilion for later.

6. Exit the Land pavilion and bear right to the Imagination pavilion. Take the Journey into Imagination ride.

7. In the Imagination pavilion, see *Honey, I Shrunk the Audience*.

8. Return to the Land and see *The Circle of Life*.

9. Ride Soarin' using the FASTPASSes obtained in Step 4.

10. Exit the Land to the left and experience The Living Seas.

11. Head through Innoventions West toward the front entrance of the park. Ride Spaceship Earth (in the geodesic sphere).

12. Exiting Spaceship Earth, proceed to the Mission: Space side of Future World and visit the Universe of Energy. If you haven't made advance reservations for dinner, you can make them now at guest relations (to the left of Spaceship Earth) en route to the Universe of Energy.

13. Exit the Universe of Energy and bear left to the Wonders of Life pavilion. Ride Body Wars (open seasonally).

14. In the Wonders of Life pavilion, see *Cranium Command* (open seasonally).

15. Depart Future World and proceed to the World Showcase section of the park.

16. Initiate a clockwise rotation around the World Showcase Lagoon. Starting at Mexico, ride El Río del Tiempo. If you are primarily interested in the attractions, try to limit your perusal of the dozens of shops. The street scenes at each World Showcase nation, however, are what make this section of Epcot special. Even when there is not a ride or a show, we recommend you spend some time enjoying the architecture, gardens, and street entertainment. The World Showcase is definitely a smell-the-roses kind of place, so try to relax and not hurry through.

17. Exiting Mexico, bear left to Norway. Ride Maelstrom.

18. Continuing clockwise around the lagoon, proceed to China. See *Reflections of China*.

19. Continuing clockwise, tour Germany.

20. Visit Italy next door.

21. Proceed clockwise to The American Adventure. See the show.

22. Continue around the lagoon and tour Japan.

23. Next to Japan, visit Morocco.

24. Continue to France and see the movie.

25. Next, cross the bridge to the United Kingdom.

26. Proceed to Canada and see the movie.

27. This concludes the touring plan. Check your watch to see if you're approaching your reservation time for dinner. If you plan to stay for *IllumiNations,* give yourself at least 30 minutes to find a good viewing spot. Unless an unusual holiday schedule is in effect, everything at Epcot closes after *IllumiNations* except for a few shops. Thirty or forty thousand people bolt for the exits at once. Suggestions for coping with this exodus begin on page 199.

## Author's Selective Epcot One-Day Touring Plan

**FOR** All parties

**ASSUMES** Willingness to experience major rides and shows

THIS TOURING PLAN INCLUDES only what the author believes is the best Epcot has to offer. However, exclusion of an attraction doesn't mean it isn't worthwhile.

Families with children younger than age 8 using this touring plan should review Epcot attractions in the Small Child Fright-Potential Chart (pages 76–80). Rent a stroller for any child small enough to fit in one, and take your young children back to the hotel for a nap after lunch. If you can

s to see Epcot, try one of the Epcot two-day

rking lot 40 minutes before official opening

...he plaza behind Spaceship Earth and then along crescent-shaped Innoventions East building on your left until you see an open passage through the building. Turn left through this passage. After emerging on the far side of Innoventions East, turn right to Test Track. Ride Test Track. Do not use FASTPASS.

3. Mission: Space is next door to Test Track. Enjoy. Do not use FASTPASS.

4. Obtaining FASTPASSes for Soarin' should be your next step. Soarin' is located in the Land pavilion on the far side of Innoventions West (to your right after passing Spaceship Earth).

5. Ride Living with the Land. Save other attractions in the pavilion for later.

6. Exit the Land pavilion and bear right to the Imagination pavilion. Take the Journey into Your Imagination ride.

7. In the Imagination pavilion, see *Honey, I Shrunk the Audience.*

8. Return to the Land and ride Soarin' using the FASTPASSes obtained in Step 4.

9. Exit the Land to the left and experience the Living Seas.

10. Head through Innoventions West toward the front entrance of the park. Ride Spaceship Earth (in the geodesic sphere).

11. Exiting Spaceship Earth, proceed to the Mission: Space side of Future World and visit the Universe of Energy. If you haven't made advance reservations for dinner, you can make them now at Guest Relations (to the left of Spaceship Earth) en route to the Universe of Energy.

12. Exit the Universe of Energy and bear left to the Wonders of Life pavilion. Ride Body Wars (open seasonally).

13. In the Wonders of Life pavilion see *Cranium Command* (open seasonally).

14. Depart Future World and proceed to the World Showcase section of the park.

15. Initiate a counterclockwise rotation around the World Showcase Lagoon. If you are primarily interested in the attractions, try to limit your perusal of the dozens of shops. The street scenes at each World Showcase nation, however, are what make this section of Epcot special. Even when there is not a ride or a show, we recommend you spend some time enjoying

the architecture, gardens, and street entertainment. The World Showcase is definitely a smell-the-roses kind of place, so try to relax and not hurry through.

16. Continue counterclockwise around the World Showcase Lagoon through Great Britain. Stop at France and see the film.

17. Continue on, visiting Morocco and Japan along the way.

18. At The American Adventure, enjoy the show.

19. Stroll through Italy and Germany and then cross the bridge to China. See the *Reflections of China* film.

20. Bear right on exiting China and proceed next door to Norway. At Norway, ride Maelstrom.

21. Bear right and check out Mexico. Try the boat ride inside the pyramid if you're so inclined.

22. Check your watch. Is your dinner reservation soon? Suspend touring and go to the restaurant when it's time. Check the daily entertainment schedule for the time of *IllumiNations*. Give yourself at least 30 minutes after dinner to locate a good viewing spot.

23. This concludes the touring plan. Unless an unusual holiday schedule is in effect, everything at Epcot closes after *IllumiNations* except for a few shops. Thirty or forty thousand people bolt for the exits at once. Suggestions for coping with this exodus begin on page 199.

## Epcot Two-Day Sunrise/Starlight Touring Plan

**FOR** All parties

THIS TOURING PLAN is for visitors who want to tour Epcot comprehensively over two days. Day One takes advantage of early morning touring opportunities. Day Two begins in late afternoon and continues until closing.

Many readers spend part of their Disney World arrival day traveling, checking into their hotel, and unpacking. They aren't free to go to the theme parks until the afternoon. The second day of the Epcot Two-Day Sunrise/Starlight Touring Plan is ideal for people who want to commence their Epcot visit later in the day.

Families with children younger than age 8 using this plan should review Epcot attractions in the Small Child Fright-Potential Chart (pages 76–80). Rent a stroller for any child small enough to fit into one. Break off Day One no later than 2:30 p.m. and return to your hotel for rest. If you missed attractions in Day One, add them to your itinerary on Day Two.

**DAY ONE**

1. Arrive at the parking lot 40 minutes before official opening time.

2. Proceed to the plaza behind Spaceship Earth and the crescent-shaped Innoventions East building on your left until you see an open passage through the building. Turn left through this passage. After emerging on the far side of Innoventions East, turn right to Test Track. Ride Test Track. If the wait at Test Track when you arrive exceeds 30 minutes, obtain FAST-PASSes and return later to ride.

3. Mission: Space is next door to Test Track. Enjoy. If the wait exceeds 35 minutes, use FASTPASS or try the single-rider line.

4. If you want to make a reservation for lunch or dinner do it now at Guests Relations near Spaceship Earth.

5. Cross to the opposite side of Future World passing through Innoventions East and Innoventions West en route. Proceed to the Land pavilion and enjoy Soarin' and the boat ride.

6. Leaving the other Land attractions for later, exit the pavilion, turning right to the Imagination pavilion. Take the Journey into Imagination ride first, and then see the 3-D movie *Honey, I Shrunk the Audience.*

7. Departing the Imagination pavilion, turn right and proceed to the World Showcase section of Epcot.

8. Turn left and proceed clockwise around the World Showcase Lagoon. Experience the El Río del Tiempo boat ride in Mexico. The ride is in the far-left corner of the interior courtyard and isn't very well marked. Consign any purchases to Package Pick-up for collection when you leave the park.

9. Continue left to Norway. Ride Maelstrom. Use FASTPASS if the wait exceeds 20 minutes. Note: Check your watch. Is your lunch reservation soon? Suspend touring and go to the restaurant when it's time. After lunch, resume the touring plan where you left off.

10. Continue left to China. See *Reflections of China.*

11. Visit Germany and Italy. Enjoy the settings; there are no rides or films. If you don't have a restaurant reservation, Sommerfest (fast food) at Germany serves tasty bratwurst, soft pretzels, desserts, and Beck's beer on draft.

12. Continue clockwise to The American Adventure. See the show. If you don't have a restaurant reservation, the Liberty Inn (left side of The American Adventure) serves hamburgers, hot dogs, and chicken sandwiches.

13. Visit Japan and Morocco. Consign any purchases to Package Pick-up for collection when you leave the park.

14. This concludes the touring plan for Day One. Attractions and pavilions not included today will be experienced tomorrow. If you're full of energy and wish to continue touring, follow the Epcot One-Day Touring Plan for Steps 11–13. If you've had enough, exit through the International Gateway or leave through the main entrance. To reach the main entrance without walking around the lagoon, catch a boat at the dock near Morocco.

**DAY TWO**

1. Enter Epcot about 1 p.m. Get a park guide map and the daily entertainment schedule/*Times Guide* at Guest Relations.

2. While at Guest Relations, make a dinner reservation, if you haven't done so already. You can eat your evening meal in any Epcot restaurant without interrupting the sequence and efficiency of the touring plan. We recommend a 7 p.m. reservation. The timing of the seating is important if you want to see *IllumiNations,* held over the lagoon at 9 p.m. If your preferred restaurants and seatings are filled, try for a dinner reservation at Morocco or Norway. Because these nations' delightful ethnic dishes are little known to most Americans, reservations may be available.

3. Ride Spaceship Earth.

4. Cut left through Innoventions East and return to the Wonders of Life pavilion. See *Cranium Command* (open seasonally).

5. In the same pavilion, experience Body Wars (open seasonally).

6. Exiting the Wonders of Life pavilion, turn right to the Universe of Energy and see the show.

7. Pass through Innoventions East and West and proceed to The Living Seas. For maximum efficiency, be one of the last people to enter the theater (where you sit) from the preshow area (where you stand). Sit as close to the end of a middle row as possible. This will position you to be first on the ride that follows the theater presentation. Afterward, enjoy the exhibits of Sea Base Alpha.

8. Exit right from The Living Seas to the Land. See *The Circle of Life,* featuring characters from *The Lion King.* Note: Check your watch. Is your dinner reservation soon? Suspend touring and go to the restaurant when it's time. After dinner, check the daily entertainment schedule for the time of *IllumiNations.* Don't miss it. Give yourself at least a half hour after dinner to find a good viewing spot along the perimeter of World Showcase Lagoon. For details on the best spots, see pages 200–202.

9. Leave Future World and walk counterclockwise around World Showcase Lagoon to Canada. See *O Canada!*

10. Turn right and visit the United Kingdom.

11. Turn right and proceed to France. See the film.

12. This concludes the touring plan. Enjoy your dinner and *Illumi-Nations*. If you have time, shop or revisit your favorite attractions.

13. Unless a holiday schedule is in effect, everything at Epcot closes after *IllumiNations* except for a few shops. Thirty thousand or more people bolt for the exits at once.

## Epcot Two-Day Early Riser Touring Plan

**FOR** All parties

THE TWO-DAY EARLY RISER TOURING PLAN is the most efficient Epcot touring plan, eliminating much of the backtracking and crisscrossing required by the other plans. It takes advantage of easy touring made possible by morning's light crowds. Most folks will complete each day of the plan by midafternoon. While the plan doesn't include *IllumiNations* or other evening festivities, these activities plus dinner at an Epcot restaurant can be added to the itinerary at your discretion.

Families with children younger than age 8 using this plan should review Epcot attractions in the Small Child Fright-Potential Chart (pages 76–80). Rent a stroller for any child small enough to fit.

### DAY ONE

1. Arrive at the parking lot 40 minutes before official opening time. As soon as the park opens ride Soarin' at the Land pavilion.

2. Also in the Land pavilion, ride Living with the Land.

3. Also in the Land pavilion, see *The Circle of Life*.

4. Go to Guest Relations and make a reservation for the Epcot full-service restaurant of your choice if you did not make them in advance.

5. Tour Innoventions East on the same side of Future World as Guest Relations.

6. Exit Innoventions East on the Mission: Space side of Future World. Bear left and continue to the Universe of Energy. Enjoy the show.

7. Bear left on leaving the Universe of Energy and proceed to the Wonders of Life pavilion. See *Cranium Command* (open seasonally).

8. Ride Body Wars, also in the Wonders of Life pavilion (open seasonally).

9. Depart Future World and enter the World Showcase section of the park. Proceed counterclockwise around the World Showcase Lagoon to Canada. See the film *O Canada!*

10. Exit Canada to the right and explore the United Kingdom. If you're a beer lover, the Rose *&* Crown Pub serves a great beer sampler. advance reservations are not required.

11. Continue counterclockwise and across the bridge to France. See the film *Impressions de France.*

12. At this juncture, the only thing remaining on the touring plan is to explore the interactive exhibits of Innoventions West, across the central plaza from Innoventions East. If you're inclined, you can continue around the lagoon, explore the various pavilions, and even try a couple of the attractions that are scheduled for Day Two. Be sure to return to Future World and Innoventions West by about 5 p.m., since Future World attractions sometimes close as early as 6 or 7 p.m.

13. Return to Future World and check out the exhibits of Innoventions.

14. This concludes Day One of the touring plan. If you linger over exhibits at The Living Seas and Innoventions East and West, it may be late in the day when you finish, and you might consider staying for dinner and *IllumiNations*. If you toured more briskly, you probably will complete the plan by about 4 p.m., even with a full-service lunch.

**DAY TWO**

1. Arrive 40 minutes prior to official opening time. When admitted to the park, proceed to the plaza behind Spaceship Earth and then along the crescent-shaped Innoventions East building on your left until you see an open passage through the building. Turn left through this passage. After emerging on the far side of Innoventions East, turn right to Test Track. If you are held up by a rope barrier anywhere along the route from the park entrance to Test Track, don't worry. Just stay put and proceed to Test Track when permitted. Similarly, if you get to Test Track and it's not operating yet, remain in place and be patient. If you do not want to experience Test Track, skip ahead to Step 2. If the wait at Test Track when you arrive exceeds 35 minutes, obtain FASTPASSes and return later to ride.

2. Mission: Space is next door to Test Track. Enjoy. If the wait exceeds 35 minutes, use FASTPASS.

3. After Test Track, retrace your steps and head for the giant geodesic sphere, Spaceship Earth. Ride.

4. After Spaceship Earth, cross to the opposite side of Future

World, passing through Innoventions West en route. Proceed to the Living Seas.

5. Proceed to the Imagination pavilion. Take the Journey into Your Imagination ride first, and then see the 3-D movie *Honey, I Shrunk the Audience*. After the movie, check out the exhibits at the Image Works, also in the Imagination pavilion.

6. Departing the Imagination pavilion, turn right and proceed to the World Showcase section of Epcot.

7. Turn left and proceed clockwise around World Showcase Lagoon. Experience the El Río del Tiempo boat ride at Mexico. The ride is in the far-left corner of the interior courtyard and isn't very well marked. Consign any purchases to Package Pick-up for collection when you leave the park.

8. Go left to Norway. Ride Maelstrom. Use FASTPASS if the wait exceeds 20 minutes.

9. Go left to China. See *Reflections of China*.

10. Visit Germany and Italy. Enjoy the settings; there are no rides or films. If you don't have a restaurant reservation, Sommerfest (fast food) at Germany serves tasty bratwurst, soft pretzels, desserts, and Beck's beer on draft.

11. Continue clockwise to The American Adventure. See the show. If you don't have a restaurant reservation, the Liberty Inn (left side of The American Adventure) serves hamburgers, hot dogs, and chicken sandwiches.

12. Visit Japan and Morocco. Consign any purchases to Package Pick-up for collection when you leave the park.

13. This concludes Day Two of the touring plan. If you futzed around in World Showcase shops and it's late in the day, consider staying for dinner and *IllumiNations*. If you caught *IllumiNations* after Day One, consider exiting Epcot through the International Gateway (between the United Kingdom and France) and exploring the restaurants, shops, and clubs of Disney's BoardWalk. The BoardWalk is a five-minute walk from the International Gateway.

# PART ELEVEN

# THE ANIMAL KINGDOM

AT 500 ACRES, DISNEY'S ANIMAL KINGDOM is five times the size of the Magic Kingdom and more than twice the size of Epcot. But like Disney-MGM Studios, most of the Animal Kingdom's vast geography is only accessible on guided tours or as part of attractions. The Animal Kingdom features six sections or "lands": The Oasis, Discovery Island, DinoLand U.S.A., Camp Minnie-Mickey, Africa, and Asia.

Its size notwithstanding, the Animal Kingdom features a limited number of attractions. To be exact, there are six rides, several walk-through exhibits, an indoor theater, four amphitheaters, a conservation exhibit, and a children's playground.

The Animal Kingdom continues to receive mixed reviews. Guests complain loudly about the park layout and the necessity of backtracking through Discovery Island in order to access the various theme areas. Congested walkways, lack of shade, and insufficient air-conditioning also rank high on the gripe list. However, most of the attractions (with one or two notable exceptions) are well received. Also praised are the natural habitat animal exhibits as well as the park architecture and landscaping.

## ARRIVING

THE ANIMAL KINGDOM IS SITUATED OFF Osceola Parkway in the southwest corner of Walt Disney World, and is not too far from Blizzard Beach, the Coronado Springs Resort, and the All-Star resorts. The Animal Kingdom Lodge is about a mile away from the park on its northwest

# Disney's Animal Kingdom

1. The Boneyard
2. Character Greeting Area
3. Conservation Station
4. Dinosaur
5. Expedition Everest
6. *Festival of the Lion King*
7. *Flights of Wonder*
8. Gibbon Pool
9. Guest Relations
10. Harambe Village
11. Kali River Rapids
12. Kilimanjaro Safaris
13. Maharaja Jungle Trek
14. Main Entrance
15. Pangani Forest
    Exploration Trail
16. *Pocahontas and Her
    Forest Friends*
17. Primeval Whirl
18. Rafiki's Planet Watch
19. Rainforest Cafe
20. Theater in the Wild
21. Ticket Booths
22. Tree of Life/*It's Tough to
    Be a Bug!*
23. TriceraTop Spin
24. Wildlife Express (Train)

**Africa**

**Camp Minnie-Mickey**

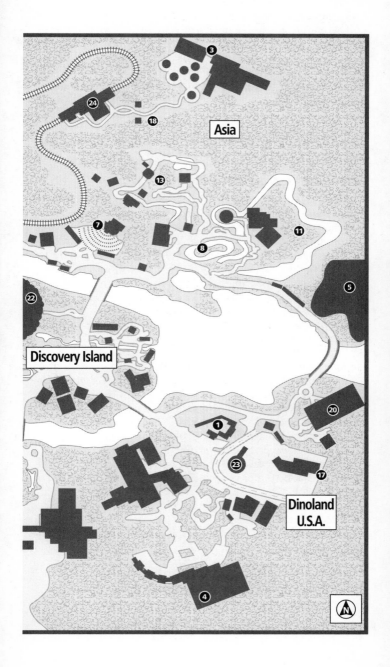

side. From I-4, take Exit 64B, US 192, to the so-called Walt Disney World main entrance (World Drive) and follow the signs to the Animal Kingdom. The Animal Kingdom has its own 6,000-car pay parking lot with close-in parking for the disabled. Once parked, you can walk to the entrance or catch a ride on one of Disney's trademark trams. The park is connected to other Walt Disney World destinations only by the Disney bus system.

## OPERATING HOURS

THE ANIMAL KINGDOM, NOT UNEXPECTEDLY, hosted tremendous crowds during its early years. Consequently, Disney management has done a fair amount of fiddling and experimenting with operating hours and opening procedures. Disney changed Animal Kingdom opening time to correspond to that of the other parks. Thus, you can expect a 9 a.m. opening during less busy times of the year and an 8 a.m. opening during holidays and high season. The Animal Kingdom usually closes well before the other parks—as early as 5 p.m., in fact, during off-season. More common is a 6 or 7 p.m. closing.

Park opening procedures at the Animal Kingdom vary. Sometimes guests arriving prior to the official opening time are admitted to The Oasis and Discovery Island. The remainder of the park is roped off until official opening time. The rest of the time, those arriving early are held at the entrance turnstiles.

During the financial turmoil of the last few years, Disney laid off a number of cast members and trotted out several cost-cutting initiatives. One of these is to delay the opening of the Asia section of the park, as well as the Boneyard playground, the Wildlife Express train, Rafiki's Planet Watch, and Conservation Station until an hour after the rest of the Animal Kingdom opens. It's not clear whether these delayed openings will be temporary or permanent, or seasonal or year-round.

On holidays and other days of projected heavy attendance, Disney will open the park 30 or 60 minutes early.

Many guests wrap up their tour and leave by 3:30 or 4 p.m. Lines for the major rides and the 3-D movie in the Tree of Life will usually thin appreciably between 4 p.m. and closing time. If you arrive at 2 p.m. and take in a couple of stage shows (described later), waits should be tolerable by the time you hit the Tree of Life and the rides. As an added bonus for late-afternoon touring, the animals tend to be more active.

The Animal Kingdom has joined the other three major theme parks in the Extra Magic Hours early-entry program. Though participation in the program will probably be a good idea after Expedition Everest opens in 2006, it's counterproductive now. Our testing has shown that the additional attendance on early-entry days totally nullifies any advantage associated with being admitted an hour early. The time required to see the same set of attractions surpasses the time required on a non-early-entry day.

Likewise, the Animal Kingdom takes part in the evening Extra Magic Hours rotation when a designated park remains open three hours beyond the official closing time for Disney resort guests. Because most of the park's animals go to bed early, however, you're pretty much relegated to rides and shows. Until Expedition Everest opens in 2006, the Animal Kingdom will be a rather dull place at night.

*unofficial* **TIP**
Our advice is to arrive, admission in hand, 30 minutes before official opening during the summer and holiday periods, and 20 minutes before official opening the rest of the year.

---

**ANIMAL KINGDOM SERVICES**

Most of the park's service facilities are located inside the main entrance and on Discovery Island as follows:

**Wheelchair & Stroller Rentals** Inside the main entrance to the right

**Banking Services** ATMs are located at the main entrance and on Discovery Island.

**Storage Lockers** Inside the main entrance to the left

**Lost & Found** Inside the main entrance to the left

**Guest Relations/Information** Inside the main entrance to the left

**Live Entertainment/Parade Information** Included in the park guidemap available free at Guest Relations

**Lost Persons** Lost persons can be reported at Guest Relations and at Baby Services on Discovery Island.

**First Aid** On Discovery Island, next to the Creature Comforts Shop

**Baby Center/Baby-Care Needs** On Discovery Island, next to the Creature Comforts Shop

**Film & Cameras** Just inside the main entrance at Garden Gate Gifts, on Discovery Island at Wonders of the Wild, and in Africa at Duka La Filimu

| NOT TO BE MISSED AT THE ANIMAL KINGDOM | |
|---|---|
| **Discovery Island** | *It's Tough to Be a Bug!* |
| **Camp Minnie-Mickey** | *Festival of the Lion King* |
| **Africa** | Kilimanjaro Safaris |
| **DinoLand U.S.A.** | Dinosaur |
| **Asia** | Expedition Everest (opens 2006) |

# GETTING ORIENTED

AT THE ENTRANCE PLAZA ARE TICKET kiosks fronting the main entrance. To your right before the turnstiles are the kennel and an ATM. Passing through the turnstiles, wheelchair and stroller rentals are to your right. Guest Relations, the park headquarters for information, handout park maps, entertainment schedules (*Times Guide*), missing persons, and lost and found, is to the left. Nearby are restrooms, public phones, and rental lockers. Beyond the entrance plaza you enter The Oasis, a lushly vegetated network of converging pathways winding through a landscape punctuated with streams, waterfalls, and misty glades, and inhabited by what Disney calls "colorful and unusual animals."

The park is arranged somewhat like the Magic Kingdom, in a hub-and-spoke configuration. The lush, tropical Oasis serves as Main Street, funneling visitors to Discovery Island at the center of the park. Dominated by the park's central icon, the 14-story hand-carved Tree of Life, Discovery Island is the park's retail and dining center. From Discovery Island, guests can access the respective theme areas, known as Africa, Camp Minnie-Mickey, Asia, and DinoLand U.S.A. Discovery Island additionally hosts a theater in the Tree of Life, and a number of short nature trails.

# THE OASIS

THOUGH THE FUNCTIONAL PURPOSE of The Oasis is the same as that of Main Street in the Magic Kingdom (i.e., to funnel guests to the center of the park), it also serves as what Disney calls a "transitional experience." In plain English, this means that it sets the stage and gets you into the right mood to enjoy the Animal Kingdom. You will know the minute you pass through the turnstiles that this is not just another Main Street. Where Main Street, Hollywood Boulevard, and the Epcot entrance plaza direct you like an arrow straight into the heart of the respective parks, The Oasis immediately envelops you in an environment that is replete with choices. There is not one broad thoroughfare, but rather multiple paths. Each will deliver you to Discovery Island at the center of the park, but which path you choose and what you see along

❊ *unofficial* **TIP**
The lush exhibits are designed for the animals' comfort, so you must be patient and look closely if you want to see these creatures.

the way is up to you. There is nothing obvious about where you are going, no Cinderella Castle or giant golf ball to beckon you. There is instead a lush, green, canopied landscape with streams, grottos, and waterfalls, an environment that promises adventure without revealing its nature.

The natural-habitat zoological exhibits in The Oasis are representative of those throughout the park. Although extraordinarily lush and beautiful, the exhibits are primarily designed for the comfort and well-being of the animals. A sign will identify the animal(s) in each exhibit, but there's no guarantee the animals will be immediately visible. Because most habitats are large and provide ample terrain for the occupants to hide, you must linger and concentrate, looking for small movements in the vegetation. When you do spot the animal, you may only make out a shadowy figure, or perhaps only a leg or a tail will be visible. In any event, don't expect the animals to stand out like a lump of coal in the snow. Animal-watching Disney-style requires a sharp eye and a bit of effort.

**TOURING TIPS** The Oasis is a place to linger and appreciate, and although this is exactly what the designers intended, it will be largely lost on Disney-conditioned guests who blitz through at warp speed to queue up for the big attractions. If you are a blitzer in the morning, plan to spend some time in The Oasis on your way out of the park. The Oasis usually opens 30 minutes before and closes 30–60 minutes after the rest of the park.

# DISCOVERY ISLAND

DISCOVERY ISLAND IS AN ISLAND OF tropical greenery and whimsical equatorial African architecture, executed in vibrant hues of teal, yellow, red, and blue. Connected to the other lands by bridges, the island is the hub from which guests can access the park's various theme areas. A village is arrayed in a crescent around the base of the Animal Kingdom's signature landmark, the Tree of Life. Towering 14 stories above the village, the Tree of Life is this park's version of Cinderella Castle or Spaceship Earth. Flanked by pools, meadows, and exotic gardens populated by a diversity of birds and animals, the Tree of Life houses a theater attraction inspired by the Disney/Pixar film *A Bug's Life*.

*unofficial* **TIP**
It is here, in Discovery Island, that you will find the First Aid and Baby-Care Centers.

As you enter Discovery Island via the bridge from The Oasis and the main entrance, you will see the Tree of Life directly ahead at the 12 o'clock position, with the village at its base in a semicircle. The bridge to Asia is to the right of the tree at the 2 o'clock position, with the bridge to DinoLand U.S.A. at roughly 4 o'clock. The bridge connecting The Oasis to Discovery Island is at the 6 o'clock position; the bridge to Camp Minnie-Mickey is at 8 o'clock; and the bridge to Africa is at 11 o'clock.

Discovery Island is the park's central shopping, dining, and services headquarters. For the best selection of Disney trademark merchandise, try the Island Mercantile or Wonders of the Wild shops. Counter-service food and snacks are available, but there are no full-service restaurants on Discovery Island (the only full-service restaurant in the park is the Rainforest Cafe, located to the left of the main entrance).

### The Tree of Life/*It's Tough to Be a Bug!* (FASTPASS)

| APPEAL BY AGE | PRESCHOOL ★★★½ | GRADE SCHOOL ★★★½ | TEENS ★★½ |
|---|---|---|---|
| YOUNG ADULTS ★★★ | | OVER 30 ★★★ | SENIORS ★★★ |

**What it is** 3-D theater show. **Scope and scale** Major attraction. **When to go** Before 10:30 a.m., after 4 p.m., or use FASTPASS. **Special comments** The theater is inside the tree. **Author's rating** Zany and frenetic; ★★★★. **Duration of presentation** Approximately 7½ minutes. **Probable waiting time** 12–30 minutes.

**DESCRIPTION AND COMMENTS** The Tree of Life, apart from its size, is quite a work of art. Although from afar it is certainly magnificent and imposing, it is not until you examine the tree at close range that you truly appreciate its rich detail. What appears to be ancient gnarled bark is, in fact, hundreds of carvings depicting all manner of wildlife, each integrated seamlessly into the trunk, roots, and limbs of the tree. A stunning symbol of the interdependence of all living things, the Tree of Life is the most visually compelling structure to be found in any Disney park.

In sharp contrast to the grandeur of the tree is the subject of the attraction housed within its trunk. Called *It's Tough to Be a Bug!*, this humorous 3-D film is about the difficulties of being a very small creature. *It's Tough to Be a Bug!* also contrasts with the relatively serious tone of the Animal Kingdom in general, standing virtually alone in providing some much needed levity and whimsy. *It's Tough to Be a Bug!* is similar to *Honey, I Shrunk the Audience* at Epcot in that it combines a 3-D film with an arsenal of tactile and visual special effects. We rate the Bugs as not to be missed.

**TOURING TIPS** Because it's situated in the most eye-popping structure in the park, and also because there aren't that many attractions anyway, you can expect *It's Tough to Be a Bug!* to be mobbed most of the day. We recommend going in the morning after Kilimanjaro Safaris, Kali River Rapids, and Dinosaur. If you miss the *Bugs* in the morning, try again in the late afternoon or use FASTPASS.

Be advised that *It's Tough to Be a Bug!* is very intense and that the special effects will do a number on young children as well as anyone who is squeamish about insects.

# CAMP MINNIE-MICKEY

THIS LAND IS DESIGNED TO BE THE Disney characters' Animal Kingdom headquarters. A small land, Camp Minnie-Mickey is about the size of Mickey's Toontown Fair but has a rustic and woodsy theme like a summer camp. In addition to a character meeting and greeting area, Camp Minnie-Mickey is  home to two live stage productions featuring Disney characters.

Situated in a cul-de-sac, Camp Minnie-Mickey is a pedestrian's nightmare. Lines for the two stage shows and from the character greeting areas spill out into the congested walkways, making movement almost impossible. To compound the problem, hundreds of parked strollers clog the paths, squeezing the flow of traffic to a trickle. Meanwhile, hordes of guests trying to enter Camp Minnie-Mickey collide with guests trying to exit on the bridge connecting the camp to Discovery Island. To make matters worse, Disney positions vendor carts on the approaches to the bridge. It's a planning error of the first order, one that seems totally avoidable in a theme park with as much usable acreage as the Animal Kingdom.

## Character Trails

**DESCRIPTION AND COMMENTS** Characters can be found at the end of each of several "character trails" named Jungle, Forest, or some such, and Mickey and Minnie. Each trail has its own private reception area and, of course, its own queue. Jungle Characters features characters from *The Lion King* and *The Jungle Book,* and the other trail generally offers characters from Disney's latest movie. The Minnie trail leads to Minnie and the Mickey trail to Mickey. One or two characters are present in the Forest and Jungle greeting areas, while Minnie and Mickey each work solo. Sometimes other characters such as Goofy or Daisy work solo in place of the Jungle and Forest characters.

**TOURING TIPS** Characters usually appear an hour after the rest of the park opens. Waiting in line to see the characters can be very time-consuming. We recommend visiting early in the morning or late in the afternoon. Because there are fewer attractions at the Animal Kingdom than at the other parks, expect to find a disproportionate number of guests in Camp Minnie-Mickey. If the place is really mobbed, you may want to consider meeting the characters in one of the other parks. Ditto for the stage shows.

### Festival of the Lion King

| APPEAL BY AGE | PRESCHOOL ★★★★ | GRADE SCHOOL ★★★★½ | TEENS ★★★★ |
| --- | --- | --- | --- |
| YOUNG ADULTS ★★★★ | | OVER 30 ★★★★ | SENIORS ★★★★ |

**What it is** Theater-in-the-round stage show. **Scope and scale** Major attraction. **When to go** Before 11 a.m. or after 4 p.m. **Special comments** Performance times are listed in the handout park map or *Times Guide.* **Author's rating** Upbeat and spectacular, not to be missed; ★★★★. **Duration of presentation** 25 minutes. **Preshow entertainment** None. **Probable waiting time** 20–35 minutes.

**DESCRIPTION AND COMMENTS** This energetic production, inspired by Disney's *Lion King* feature, is part stage show, part parade, part circus. Guests are seated in four sets of bleachers surrounding the stage and organized into separate cheering sections, which are called on to make elephant, warthog, giraffe, and lion noises (you won't be alone if you don't know how to make a giraffe or warthog noise). There is a great deal of parading around, some acrobatics, and a lot of singing and dancing. By our count, every tune from *The Lion King* is belted out and reprised several times. No joke—if you don't know the words to all the songs by the end of the show, you must have been asleep.

**TOURING TIPS** This show is both popular and difficult to see. Your best bet is to go to the first show in the morning or to one of the last two performances in the evening. To see the show during the more crowded middle of the day, you'll need to queue up at least 35–45 minutes before show time. To minimize standing in the hot sun, refrain from hopping in line until the Disney people begin directing guests to the far-right queue. If you have small children or short adults in your party, sit higher up in the bleachers. The first five rows in particular have very little rise, making it difficult for those in rows two through five to see.

### Pocahontas and Her Forest Friends

| APPEAL BY AGE | PRESCHOOL ★★★½ | GRADE SCHOOL ★★★½ | TEENS ★★★ |
| YOUNG ADULTS ★★★½ | OVER 30 ★★★ | . | SENIORS ★★★ |

**What it is** Conservation-theme stage show. **Scope and scale** Major attraction. **When to go** Before 11 a.m. or after 4 p.m. **Special comments** Performance times are listed in the daily entertainment schedule/*Times Guide.*. **Author's rating** A little sappy; ★★½. **Duration of presentation** 15 minutes. **Preshow entertainment** None. **Probable waiting time** 20–30 minutes.

DESCRIPTION AND COMMENTS This show featuring Pocahontas addresses the role of man in protecting the natural world. Various live creatures of the forest, including a raccoon, a snake, and a turkey, as well as a couple of audio-animatronic trees (Grandmother Willow and Twig), assist Pocahontas in making the point. The presentation is gushy and overacted but has its moments nonetheless.

TOURING TIPS Because the theater is relatively small, and because Camp Minnie-Mickey stays so mobbed, the *Pocahontas* show is hard to get into. Among other problems, its queuing area adjoins that of *Festival of the Lion King* next door. If you approach when a lot of guests are waiting, which is almost always, it's hard to figure out which show you're lining up for. To avoid the hassle, try to catch *Pocahontas* before 11 a.m. or after 3 p.m. Regardless of time of day, arrive about 20–30 minutes before show time and ask a Disney cast member to steer you to the correct line.

# AFRICA

AFRICA IS THE LARGEST OF THE ANIMAL Kingdom's lands, and guests enter through Harambe, Disney's idealized and immensely sanitized version of a modern, rural African town. There is a market (with modern cash registers), and counter-service food is available. What distinguishes Harambe is its understatement. Far from the stereotypical great-white-hunter image of an African town, Harambe is definitely (and realistically) not exotic. The buildings, while interesting, are quite plain and architecturally simple. Though certainly better maintained and more aseptic than the real McCoy, Disney's Harambe would be a lot more at home in Kenya than the Magic Kingdom's Main Street would be in Missouri.

Harambe serves as the gateway to the African veldt habitat, the Animal Kingdom's largest and most ambitious zoological exhibit. Access to the veldt is via the Kilimanjaro Safaris attraction, located at the end of Harambe's main drag near the fat-trunked baobab tree. Harambe is also the departure point for the train to Rafiki's *Planet Watch* and Conservation Station, the park's veterinary headquarters.

## Kilimanjaro Safaris (FASTPASS)

| APPEAL BY AGE | PRESCHOOL ★★★★ | GRADE SCHOOL ★★★★★ | TEENS ★★★★½ |
| --- | --- | --- | --- |
| YOUNG ADULTS ★★★★½ | OVER 30 ★★★★½ | | SENIORS ★★★★★ |

**What it is** Truck ride through an African wildlife reservation. **Scope and scale** Super headliner. **When to go** As soon as the park opens, in the 2 hours before closing, or use FASTPASS. **Author's rating** Truly exceptional; ★★★★★. **Duration of ride** About 20 minutes. **Average wait in line per 100 people ahead of you** 4 minutes. **Assumes** Full-capacity operation with 18-second dispatch interval. **Loading speed** Fast.

DESCRIPTION AND COMMENTS The park's premier zoological attraction, Kilimanjaro Safaris offers an exceptionally realistic, albeit brief, imitation of an actual African photo safari. Thirty-two guests at a time board tall, open safari vehicles and are dispatched into a simulated African veldt habitat. Animals such as zebra, wildebeest, impala, Thomson's gazelle, giraffe, and even rhinos roam apparently free, while predators such as lions, as well as potentially dangerous large animals like hippos, are separated from both prey and guests by all-but-invisible, natural-appearing barriers. Although the animals have more than 100 acres of savanna, woodland, streams, and rocky hills to call home, careful placement of water holes, forage, and salt licks ensure that the critters are hanging out by the road when safari vehicles roll by.

A scripted narration provides a story line about finding Big Red and Little Red, a mother elephant and her baby, while an on-board guide points out and identifies the various animals encountered. Toward the end of the ride, the safari chases poachers who have just wounded Big Red. If the attraction has a shortcoming, it is the rather strident story line about the poachers and Big Red, which, while thought-provoking, is somewhat distracting when you are trying to spot and enjoy the wildlife. Also, because the story is repeated on every trip, it really gets on your nerves after the first couple of times.

TOURING TIPS Until the Expedition Everest roller coaster opens in 2006, Kilimanjaro Safaris is the Animal Kingdom's top draw. In fact, we've not seen an attraction in any Disney park that so completely channels guest traffic. While Space Mountain, Test Track, and Tower of Terror attract throngs of early-morning guests, there remain a substantial number of additional guests who head for other attractions. At the Animal Kingdom, however, as many as 90% of those on hand at opening head straight for the safari, and later-arriving guests do exactly the same thing. Over the first couple of years, Disney tried any number of ploys to lure guests elsewhere, but to no avail. So, if you want to see Kilimanjaro Safaris without a long wait, be one of the first through the turnstiles and make a beeline for Africa (or use FASTPASS). If you are held up en route by a rope barrier or by cast members, stay put until you are permitted to continue on to the attraction.

Waits for the Kilimanjaro Safaris diminish in late afternoon, sometimes as early 3:30 p.m., but more commonly somewhat later. As noted above, Kilimanjaro Safaris is a FASTPASS attraction. If the wait exceeds 30 minutes when you arrive, by all means use FASTPASS. The downside to FASTPASS, and the reason we prefer that you ride as soon as the park opens, is that there aren't many other attractions in Africa to occupy your attention while you wait for your FASTPASS return time. This means you will probably be touring somewhere far removed when it's time to backtrack to Safaris. The best way to avoid this disruption is to see the attraction first thing in the morning.

If you want to take photos on your safari, be advised that the vehicle doesn't stop very often, so be prepared to snap while under way. Also, don't worry about the ride itself: it really isn't very rough. Finally, the only thing that a young child might find intimidating is crossing an "old bridge" that pretends to collapse under your truck.

## Pangani Forest Exploration Trail

| APPEAL BY AGE | PRESCHOOL ★★½ | GRADE SCHOOL ★★★ | TEENS ★★½ |
|---|---|---|---|
| YOUNG ADULTS ★★★ | OVER 30 ★★★ | | SENIORS ★★★ |

**What it is** Walk-through zoological exhibit. **Scope and scale** Major attraction. **When to go** Before 10 a.m. and after 2:30 p.m.. **Author's rating** ★★★. **Duration of tour** About 20–25 minutes.

**DESCRIPTION AND COMMENTS** Because guests disembark from the safari at the entrance to the Pangani Forest Exploration Trail, many guests try the trail immediately after the safari. Winding between the domain of two troops of lowland gorillas, it's hard to see what, if anything, separates you from the primates. Also on the trail are a hippo pool with an underwater viewing area, and a naked mole rat exhibit (I promise I'm not making this up). A highlight of the trail is an exotic bird aviary so craftily designed that you can barely tell you're in an enclosure.

**TOURING TIPS** The Pangani Forest Exploration Trail is lush, beautiful, and jammed to the gills with people much of the time. Guests exiting the safari can choose between returning to Harambe or walking the Pangani Forest Exploration Trail. Not unexpectedly, many opt for the trail. Thus, when the safari is operating at full tilt, it spews hundreds of guests every couple of minutes onto the Exploration Trail. The one-way trail in turn becomes so clogged that nobody can move or see much of anything. After a minute or two, however, you catch the feel of the mob moving forward in small lurches. From then on you shift, elbow, grunt, and wriggle your way along, every so often coming to an animal exhibit. Here you endeavor to work your way close to the rail but are opposed by people trapped against the rail who are trying to rejoin the surging crowd. The animals, as well as their natural-habitat enclosures, are pretty nifty if you can fight close enough to see them.

Clearly this attraction is either badly designed, misplaced, or both. Your only real chance for enjoying it is to walk through before 10 a.m. (i.e., before the safari hits full stride) or after 2:30 p.m.

Another strategy, especially if you're more into the wildlife than the thrill rides, is to head for Kilimanjaro Safaris as soon as the park opens and get a FASTPASS instead of riding. Early in the morning, the return window will be short, just short enough, in fact, for an uncrowded, leisurely tour of the Pangani Forest Exploration Trail before you go on safari.

## Rafiki's *Planet Watch*

Rafiki's *Planet Watch* showed up on park maps in 2001. It's not a "land" and not really an attraction, either. Our best guess is that Disney is using the name as an umbrella for Conservation Station, the petting zoo, and the environmental exhibits accessible from Harambe via the Wildlife Express train. Presumably, Disney hopes that invoking Rafiki (a beloved character from *The Lion King*) will stimulate guests to make the effort to check out things in this far-flung outpost of the park. As for your kids seeing Rafiki, don't bet on it. The closest likeness we've seen here is a two-dimensional wooden cutout.

## Wildlife Express Train

| APPEAL BY AGE | PRESCHOOL ★★★ | GRADE SCHOOL ★★★ | TEENS ★½ |
|---|---|---|---|
| YOUNG ADULTS ★★½ | | OVER 30 ★★½ | SENIORS ★★½ |

**What it is** Scenic railroad ride to Rafiki's *Planet Watch* and Conservation Station. **Scope and scale** Minor attraction. **When to go** Anytime. **Special comments** Opens 30 minutes after the rest of the park. **Author's rating** Ho hum; ★★. **Duration of ride** About 5–7 minutes one way. **Average wait in line per 100 people ahead of you** 9 minutes. **Loading speed** Moderate.

**DESCRIPTION AND COMMENTS** A transportation ride that snakes behind the African wildlife reserve as it makes its loop connecting Harambe to Rafiki's *Planet Watch* and Conservation Station. En route, you see the nighttime enclosures for the animals that populate the Kilimanjaro Safaris. Similarly, returning to Harambe, you see the backstage areas of Asia. Regardless which direction you're heading, the sights are not especially interesting.

**TOURING TIPS** Most guests will embark for Rafiki's *Planet Watch* and Conservation Station after experiencing the Kilimanjaro Safaris and the Pangani Forest Exploration Trail. Thus, the train begins to get crowded between 10 and 11 a.m. Though you may catch a glimpse of several species from the train, it can't compare to Kilimanjaro Safaris for seeing the animals.

## Habitat Habit!

Listed on the park map as an attraction is Habitat Habit!, located on the pedestrian path between the train station and Conservation Station. Habitat Habit! consists of a tiny collection of signs (about coexistence with wildlife) and a few cotton-top tamarins. To call it an attraction is absurd.

## Conservation Station and Affection Section

| APPEAL BY AGE | PRESCHOOL ★★½ | GRADE SCHOOL ★★ | TEENS ★½ |
|---|---|---|---|
| YOUNG ADULTS ★★½ | OVER 30 ★★½ | | SENIORS ★★½ |

**What it is** Behind-the-scenes walk-through educational exhibit and petting zoo. **Scope and scale** Minor attraction. **When to go** Anytime. **Special comments** Opens 30 minutes after the rest of the park. **Author's rating** Evolving; ★★★. **Probable waiting time** None.

**DESCRIPTION AND COMMENTS** Conservation Station is the Animal Kingdom's veterinary and conservation headquarters. Located on the perimeter of the African section of the park, Conservation Station is, strictly speaking, a backstage, working facility. Here guests can meet wildlife experts, observe some of the Station's ongoing projects, and learn about the behind-the-scenes operations of the park. The Station includes, among other things, a rehabilitation area for injured animals and a nursery for recently born (or hatched) critters. Vets and other experts are on hand to answer questions.

While there are several permanent exhibits, including Affection Section (an animal petting area), what you see at Conservation Station will largely depend on what's going on when you arrive. On the days we visited, there wasn't enough happening to warrant waiting in line twice (coming and going) for the train.

You can access Conservation Station by taking the Wildlife Express train directly from Harambe. To return to the center of the park, continue the loop from Conservation Station back to Harambe.

**TOURING TIPS** Conservation Station is interesting, but you have to invest a little effort and it helps to be inquisitive. Because it's so removed from the rest of the park, you'll never bump into Conservation Station unless you take the train.

# ASIA

CROSSING THE ASIA BRIDGE FROM Discovery Island, you enter Asia through the village of Anandapur, a veritable collage of Asian themes inspired by the architecture and ruins of India, Thailand, Indonesia, and Nepal. Situated near the bank of the Chakranadi River (translation: the river that runs in circles) and surrounded by lush vegetation, Anandapur provides access to a gibbon exhibit and to Asia's two feature attractions, the Kali River Rapids whitewater raft ride and the Maharaja Jungle Trek. Also in Asia is *Flights of Wonder*, an educational production about birds.

Coming to Asia in 2006 is a super-headliner roller coaster called Expedition Everest (yep, another mountain, and at 200 feet, the tallest in Florida). You'll board an old mountain railway destined for the foot of Mount Everest that ends up racing both forwards and backwards through caverns and frigid canyons en route to paying a social call on the abominable snowman. Expedition Everest is being billed as a "family thrill ride," which means simply that it will be more like Big Thunder Mountain Railroad than the Rock 'n' Roller Coaster.

## Expedition Everest (FASTPASS)
## (scheduled opening Spring 2006)

**What it Is** High-speed, outdoor roller coaster through Nepalese mountain village. **Scope and scale** Super headliner. **When to go** Before 9:30 a.m., after 4 p.m., or use FASTPASS. **Special comments** Contains some of the park's most stunning visual elements. **Author's rating** Not open at press time. **Duration of ride** Not open at press time. **Average wait in line per 100 people ahead of you** About 3 minutes. **Assumes** 2 tracks operating. **Loading speed** Moderate to fast.

**DESCRIPTION AND COMMENTS** The first true roller coaster in Disney's Animal Kingdom, Expedition Everest is almost certain to be the park's top draw the minute it opens. You're led through an elaborate waiting area modeled after a Nepalese village, after which you board an old mining train headed for the top of Mount Everest. All along the way, townspeople warn you of a terrible creature that protects the mountain from outsiders. The warnings are ignored (as if you had a choice!), resulting in a high-speed encounter with the Abominable Snowman himself. The mountain is the highest in Florida (don't forget the oxygen!).

The ride track consists of tight turns, hills, and dips, rather than loops or inversions. But with a top speed reported to be around 50 miles per hour—almost twice as fast as Space Mountain—expect to see the usual warnings for children and seniors. Disney promises some truly special effects for Expedition Everest, including icy winds, bad smells, and one of the largest, most sophisticated animatronic figures ever made.

**TOURING TIPS** Ride Everest first thing in the morning, during evening Extra Magic Hours, or use FASTPASS. If using FAST-PASS, try to catch Asia's *Flights of Wonder* and the Maharaja Jungle Trek before your return. If the FASTPASS return time is more than two hours away, head to DinoLand U.S.A. after completing those attractions to minimize backtracking.

## Kali River Rapids (FASTPASS)

**APPEAL BY AGE    PRESCHOOL ★★★★    GRADE SCHOOL ★★★★    TEENS ★★★★
YOUNG ADULTS ★★★½    OVER 30 ★★★½    SENIORS ★★★**

**What it is** Whitewater raft ride. **Scope and scale** Headliner. **When to go** Before 10:30 a.m., after 4:30 p.m., or use FASTPASS. **Special comments** You are guaranteed to get wet; opens 30 minutes after the rest of the park; height requirement is 38 inches tall; switching off available. **Author's rating** Short but scenic; ★★★½. **Duration of ride** About 5 minutes. **Average wait in line per 100 people ahead of you** 5 minutes. **Loading speed** Moderate.

**DESCRIPTION AND COMMENTS** Whitewater raft rides have been a hot-weather favorite of theme-park patrons for more than 20 years. The ride itself consists of an unguided trip down a man-made river in a circular rubber raft with a platform seating 12 people mounted on top. The raft essentially floats free in the current and is washed downstream through rapids and waves. Because the river is fairly wide, with numerous currents, eddies, and obstacles, there is no telling exactly where the raft will drift. Thus, each trip is different and exciting. At the end of the ride, a conveyor belt hauls the raft up to be unloaded and prepared for the next group of guests.

What distinguishes Kali River Rapids from other theme-park raft rides is Disney's trademark attention to visual detail. Where many raft rides essentially plunge down a concrete ditch, Kali River Rapids flows through a dense rain forest, past waterfalls, temple ruins, and bamboo thickets, emerging into a cleared area where greedy loggers have ravaged the forest, and finally drifting back under the tropical canopy as the river cycles back to Anandapur. Along the way, your raft runs a gauntlet of raging cataracts, log jams, and other dangers.

**TOURING TIPS** This attraction is hugely popular, especially on hot summer days. Ride Kali River Rapids before 10 a.m., after 4:30 p.m., or use FASTPASS. You can expect to get wet and probably drenched on this ride. Our recommendation is to wear shorts to the park and bring along a jumbo-size trash bag as well as a smaller plastic bag. Before boarding the raft, take off your socks and punch holes in your jumbo bag for your head. Though you can also cut holes for your arms, you will probably stay drier with your arms inside the bag. Use the smaller plastic bag to wrap around your shoes. If you are worried about mussing your hairdo, bring a third bag for your head.

Other tips for staying dry (make that drier) include wearing as little as the law and Disney allow and storing a change of clothes in a park rental locker. Sandals are the perfect footwear for water rides. As a last-ditch effort to keep your shoes moderately dry (if you don't have sandals), try to prop your feet up above the bottom of the raft.

## Maharaja Jungle Trek

| APPEAL BY AGE | PRESCHOOL ★★★ | GRADE SCHOOL ★★★½ | TEENS ★★★ |
|---|---|---|---|
| YOUNG ADULTS ★★★½ | | OVER 30 ★★★½ | SENIORS ★★★★ |

**What it is** Walk-through zoological exhibit. **Scope and scale** Headliner. **When to go** Anytime. **Special comments** Opens 30 minutes after the rest of the park. **Author's rating** A standard-setter for natural habitat design; ★★★★. **Duration of tour** About 20–30 minutes.

**DESCRIPTION AND COMMENTS** The Maharaja Jungle Trek is a zoological nature walk similar to the Pangani Forest Exploration Trail, but with an Asian setting and Asian animals. You start with Komodo dragons and then work up to Malayan tapirs. Next is a cave with fruit bats. Ruins of the maharaja's palace provide the setting for Bengal tigers. From the top of a parapet in the palace you can view a herd of blackbuck antelope and Asian deer. The trek concludes with an aviary.

Labyrinthine, overgrown, and elaborately detailed, the temple ruin would be a compelling attraction even without the animals. Throw in a few bats, bucks, and Bengals and you're in for a treat.

**TOURING TIPS** The Jungle Trek does not get as jammed up as the Pangani Forest Exploration Trail and is a good choice for mid-day touring when most other attractions are crowded. The downside, of course, is that the exhibit showcases tigers, tapirs, and other creatures that might not be as active in the heat of the day [as proverbial mad dogs and Englishmen].

### Flights of Wonder

| APPEAL BY AGE | PRESCHOOL ★★★★ | GRADE SCHOOL ★★★★ | TEENS ★★★½ |
|---|---|---|---|
| YOUNG ADULTS ★★★★ | | OVER 30 ★★★★ | SENIORS ★★★★ |

**What it is** Stadium show about birds. **Scope and scale** Major attraction. **When to go** Anytime. **Special comments** Performance times are listed in the handout park map or *Times Guide*. **Author's rating** Unique; ★★★★. **Duration of presentation** 30 minutes. **Preshow entertainment** None. **Probable waiting time** 20 minutes.

**DESCRIPTION AND COMMENTS** Both interesting and fun, *Flights of Wonder* is well paced and showcases a surprising number of different bird species. The show has been rescripted, abandoning an improbable plot for a more straightforward educational presentation. The focus of *Flights of Wonder* is on the natural talents and characteristics of the various species, so don't expect to see any parrots riding bicycles. The natural behaviors, however, far surpass any tricks learned from humans. Overall, the presentation is fascinating and exceeds most guests' expectations.

**TOURING TIPS** *Flights of Wonder* plays at the stadium located near the Asia Bridge on the walkway into Asia. Though the stadium is covered, it's not air-conditioned, thus, early-morning and late-afternoon performances are more comfortable. To play it safe, arrive about 10–15 minutes before show time.

# DINOLAND U.S.A.

THIS MOST TYPICALLY DISNEY OF THE Animal Kingdom's lands is a cross between an anthropological dig and a quirky roadside attraction. Accessible via the bridge from Discovery Island, DinoLand U.S.A. is home to a children's play area, a nature trail, a 1,500-seat amphitheater, a couple of natural history exhibits, and Dinosaur, one of the Animal Kingdom's two thrill rides.

### Dinosaur (FASTPASS)

| APPEAL BY AGE | PRESCHOOL † | GRADE SCHOOL ★★★★½ | TEENS ★★★★½ |
|---|---|---|---|
| YOUNG ADULTS ★★★★½ | | OVER 30 ★★★★½ | SENIORS ★★★½ |

† Sample size too small for an accurate rating.

**What it is** Motion-simulator dark ride. **Scope and scale** Super headliner. **When to go** Before 10:30 a.m., in the hour before closing, or use

FASTPASS. **Special comments** Must be 40 inches tall to ride. Switching-off option provided (see page 75). **Author's rating** Really improved; ★★★★½. **Duration of ride** 3⅓ minutes. **Average wait in line per 100 people ahead of you** 3 minutes. **Assumes** Full-capacity operation with 18-second dispatch interval. **Loading speed** Fast.

**DESCRIPTION AND COMMENTS** Dinosaur, formerly known as Count-down to Extinction, is a combination track ride and motion simulator. In addition to moving along a cleverly hidden track, the ride vehicle also bucks and pitches (the simulator part) in sync with the visuals and special effects encountered. The plot has you traveling back in time on a mission of rescue and con-servation. Your objective, believe it or not, is to haul back a living dinosaur before the species becomes extinct. Whoever is operating the clock, however, cuts it a little close, and you arrive on the prehistoric scene just as a giant asteroid is hurl-ing toward Earth. General mayhem ensues as you evade carnivorous predators, catch Barney, and make your escape before the asteroid hits.

Elaborate even by Disney standards, the attraction pro-vides a tense, frenetic ride embellished by the entire Imagineering arsenal of high-tech gimmickry. Although the ride is jerky, it's not too rough for seniors. The menacing dinosaurs, however, along with the intensity of the experi-ence, make Dinosaur a no-go for younger children.

Dinosaur, to our surprise and joy, has been refined and cranked up a couple of notches on the intensity scale. The lat-est version is darker, more interesting, and much zippier.

**TOURING TIPS** We recommend that you ride early after experienc-ing Kilimanjaro Safaris. If you bump into a long line, use FASTPASS.

## TriceraTop Spin

| APPEAL BY AGE | PRESCHOOL ★★★★ | GRADE SCHOOL ★★★ | TEENS ★★ |
|---|---|---|---|
| YOUNG ADULTS ★★ | OVER 30 ★★ | | SENIORS ★★ |

**What it is** Hub-and-spoke midway ride. **Scope and scale** Minor attraction. **When to go** First 90 minutes the park is open and in the hour before park closing. **Author's rating** Dumbo's prehistoric forebear; ★★. **Duration of ride** 1½ minutes. **Average wait in line per 100 people ahead of you** 10 minutes. **Loading speed** Slow.

**DESCRIPTION AND COMMENTS** Another Dumbo-like ride. Here you spin around a central hub until a dinosaur pops out of the top of the hub. You'd think with the collective imagination of the Walt Disney Company, they'd come up with something a little more creative.

**TOURING TIPS** An attraction for the children, except they won't appreciate the long wait for this slow-loading ride.

## Primeval Whirl (FASTPASS)

| APPEAL BY AGE | PRESCHOOL ★★★ | GRADE SCHOOL ★★★★½ | TEENS ★★★½ |
|---|---|---|---|
| YOUNG ADULTS ★★★ | | OVER 30 ★★★ | SENIORS ★★ |

**What it is** Small coaster. **Scope and scale** Minor attraction. **When to go** During the first 2 hours the park is open, in the hour before park closing, or use FASTPASS. **Special comments** 48-inch minimum height. Switching-off option provided (see page 75). **Author's rating** Wild Mouse on steroids; ★★★. **Duration of ride** Almost 2½ minutes. **Average wait in line per 100 people ahead of you** 4½ minutes. **Loading speed** Slow.

**DESCRIPTION AND COMMENTS** Primeval Whirl is a small coaster with short drops and curves, and it runs through the jaws of a dinosaur, among other things. What makes this coaster different is that the cars also spin. Because guests cannot control the spinning, the cars spin and stop spinning according to how the ride is programmed. Sometimes the spin is braked to a jarring halt after half a revolution, and sometimes it's allowed to make one or two complete turns. The complete spins are fun, but the screeching-stop half-spins are almost painful. If you subtract the time it takes to rachet up the first hill, the actual ride time is about 90 seconds.

**TOURING TIPS** Like Space Mountain, the ride is duplicated side by side, but with only one queue. When running smoothly, about 700 people per side can whirl in an hour; a goodly number for this type of attraction, but not enough to preclude long waits on busy-to-moderate days. If you want to ride, try to get on before 11 a.m. or use FASTPASS.

## Theater in the Wild

| APPEAL BY AGE | PRESCHOOL ★★★ | GRADE SCHOOL ★★★ | TEENS ★★★ |
|---|---|---|---|
| YOUNG ADULTS ★★★ | | OVER 30 ★★½ | SENIORS ★★½ |

**What it is** Open-air venue for live stage shows. **Scope and scale** Major attraction. **When to go** Anytime. **Special comments** Performance times are listed in the handout park map or *Times Guide*. **Author's rating** For *Tarzan Rocks*, ★★½. **Duration of presentation** 25–35 minutes. **Preshow entertainment** None. **Probable waiting time** 20–30 minutes.

**DESCRIPTION AND COMMENTS** The Theater in the Wild is a 1,500-seat covered amphitheater. The largest stage production facility in the Animal Kingdom, the theater can host just about any type of stage show. The most recent production, a rock musical production based on Disney's animated *Tarzan* movie, is said to be closing. Its successor has not been announced.

**TOURING TIPS** To get a seat, show up 20–25 minutes in advance for morning and late-afternoon shows, and 30–35 minutes in advance for shows scheduled between noon and 4:30 p.m. Access to the theater is via a relatively narrow pedestrian path. If you arrive as the previous show is letting out, you will feel like a salmon swimming upstream.

## The Boneyard

| APPEAL BY AGE | PRESCHOOL ★★★★½ | | GRADE SCHOOL ★★★★½ |
|---|---|---|---|
| TEENS — | YOUNG ADULTS — | OVER 30 — | SENIORS — |

**What it is** Elaborate playground. **Scope and scale** Diversion. **When to go** Anytime. **Special comments** Opens 30 minutes after the rest of the park. **Author's rating** Stimulating fun for children; ★★★½. **Duration of visit** Varies. **Probable waiting time** None.

**DESCRIPTION AND COMMENTS** This attraction is an elaborate playground, particularly appealing to kids ages 10 and younger, but visually appealing to all ages. Arranged in the form of a rambling open-air dig site, The Boneyard offers plenty of opportunity for exploration and letting off steam. Playground equipment consists of the skeletons of Triceratops, Tyrannosaurus rex, Brachiosaurus, and the like, on which children can swing, slide, and climb. In addition, there are sand pits where little ones can scrounge around for bones and fossils.

**TOURING TIPS** Not the cleanest Disney attraction, but certainly one where younger children will want to spend some time. Aside from getting dirty, or at least sandy, be aware that The Boneyard gets mighty hot in the Florida sun. Keep your kids well hydrated and drag them into the shade from time to time. If your children will let you, save the playground until after you have experienced the main attractions. Because The Boneyard is so close to the center of the park, it's easy to stop in whenever your kids get itchy. While the little ones clamber around on giant femurs and ribs, you can sip a tall cool one in the shade (still keeping an eye on them, of course).

Be aware that The Boneyard rambles over about a half-acre and is multistoried. It's pretty easy to lose sight of a small child in the playground. Fortunately, there's only one entrance and exit.

# LIVE ENTERTAINMENT *in the* ANIMAL KINGDOM

**STAGE SHOWS** Stage shows are performed daily at the Theater in the Wild in DinoLand U.S.A., at Grandmother Willow's Grove and at the Lion King Theater in Camp Minnie-Mickey, and at the stadium in Asia. Presentations at Camp Minnie-Mickey and DinoLand U.S.A. feature the Disney characters.

**STREET PERFORMERS** Street performers can be found most of the time at Discovery Island, at Harambe in Africa, at Anandapur in Asia, and in DinoLand U.S.A.

**AFTERNOON PARADE** Mickey's Jammin' Jungle Parade is comparable to the parades at the other parks, complete with floats, Disney characters (especially those from the *Lion King, Jungle Book, Tarzan,* and *Pocahontas*), skaters, acrobats, and stilt walkers.

> *unofficial* **TIP**
> During the afternoon parade, avoid anything in Harambe around the bridge.

Though subject to change, the parade starts in Africa, crosses the bridge to Discovery Island, proceeds counterclockwise around the island, and then crosses the bridge to Asia. In Asia, the parade turns left and follows the walkway paralleling the river back to Africa. The walking path between Africa and Asia has several small cutouts that offer good views of the parade and excellent sun protection. As it's used primarily as a walkway, the path is also relatively uncrowded. The paths on Discovery Island also get very crowded, and it's easier to lose members of your party there.

**KIDS' DISCOVERY CLUB** Informal, creative activity stations offer kids ages 4–8 a structured learning experience as they tour the Animal Kingdom. Set up along walkways in six theme areas, Discovery Club stations are manned by cast members who supervise a different activity at each station. A souvenir logbook, available free, is stamped at each station when the child completes the craft or exercise. Children enjoy collecting the stamps and noodling the puzzles in the logbook while in attraction lines.

**ANIMAL ENCOUNTERS** Throughout the day, knowledgeable Disney staff conduct impromptu short lectures on specific animals at the park. Look for a cast member in safari garb holding a bird, reptile, or small mammal.

**GOODWILL AMBASSADORS** A number of Asian and African natives are on-hand throughout the park. Both gracious and knowledgeable, they are delighted to discuss their country and its wildlife. Look for them in Harambe and along the Pangani Forest Exploration Trail in Africa, and in Anandapur and along the Maharaja Jungle Trek in Asia. They can also be found near the main entrance and at The Oasis.

# ANIMAL KINGDOM TOURING PLANS

TOURING THE ANIMAL KINGDOM IS not as complicated as touring the other parks because it offers a smaller number of attractions. Also, most Animal Kingdom rides, shows, and zoological exhibits are oriented to the entire family, thus eliminating differences of opinion regarding how to spend the day. At the Animal Kingdom, the whole family can pretty much see and enjoy everything together.

 *unofficial* **TIP**
For the time being, the limited number of attractions in the Animal Kingdom can work to your advantage.

Since there are fewer attractions than at the other parks, expect the crowds at the Animal Kingdom to be more concentrated. If a line seems unusually long, ask an Animal Kingdom cast member what the estimated wait is. If the wait exceeds your tolerance, try the same attraction again after 3 p.m., while a show is in progress at the Theater in the Wild in DinoLand U.S.A., or while some special event is going on.

## BEFORE YOU GO

1. Call ☎ 407-824-4321 before you go to learn the park's hours of operation.
2. Purchase your admission prior to arrival.

## EXPEDITION EVEREST AND THE ANIMAL KINGDOM TOURING PLANS

EXPEDITION EVEREST, THE NEW super-headliner attraction at the Animal Kingdom, will open in 2006, but nobody (including Disney) is sure when. Its targeted for opening in January or February but project insiders say sometime in the August to October period is more realistic. Because Expedition Everest will totally alter guest traffic patterns in the park, we present two Animal Kingdom one-day touring plans. If Expedition Everest is not open during your visit, use Plan A. If when you go, Expedition Everest is operating, use Plan B.

## Animal Kingdom One-Day Touring Plan A (Expedition Everest Not Open)

The Animal Kingdom One-Day Touring Plan A assumes a willingness to experience all major rides and shows. Be forewarned that Dinosaur, Primeval Whirl, and Kali River Rapids are sometimes frightening to children under age 8. Similarly, the theater attraction at the Tree of Life might be too intense for some preschoolers. When following the touring plan, simply skip any attraction you do not wish to experience.

1. Arrive at the turnstiles 40 minutes before the official opening time during summer and holiday periods, and 30 minutes before the official opening time the rest of the year. At the entrance plaza, pick up a park map and daily entertainment schedule. Wait at the entrance turnstiles to be admitted.

2. When admitted through the turnstiles, move quickly through the Oasis without stopping and cross the bridge into Discovery Island. Turn left after the bridge and walk clockwise around the Tree of Life until you reach the bridge to Africa. Cross the bridge and continue straight ahead to the entrance of Kilimanjaro Safaris. Experience Kilimanjaro Safaris. Unless the wait exceeds 30 minutes, do not use FASTPASS.

3. After the safari, head back toward the Africa bridge to Discovery Island, but turn left before crossing. Follow the walkway along the river to Asia. In Asia, ride Kali River Rapids.

   As a cost-cutting measure, Disney delayed the opening of Asia until 30 minutes after the rest of the park. If Asia is not yet open when you arrive or if the weather is cool (or you just don't feel like getting wet), proceed to Steps 4–6. Return to Kali River Rapids after seeing *It's Tough to Be a Bug!* (Step 6). If the wait is more than 30 minutes for the raft ride when you return, use FASTPASS.

4. Following the raft trip, return to the entrance of Asia and turn left over the Asia bridge into Discovery Island. Pass the Beastly Bazaar and Flame Tree Barbecue, and then turn left and cross the bridge into DinoLand U.S.A. After passing beneath the brontosaurus skeleton, angle left to Primeval Whirl. Ride. Note: If you have children ages 8 and younger in your party, they will want to ride TriceraTop Spin (a children's ride

straight and to the left) after entering DinoLand. Ride Triceratop Spin first, then Primeval Whirl.

5. Follow the signs to Dinosaur. Ride.

6. Next, retrace your steps to Discovery Island, bearing left after you cross the DinoLand bridge. See *It's Tough to Be a Bug!* in the Tree of Life. If the wait exceeds 30 minutes, use FAST-PASS.

7. By now you will have most of the Animal Kingdom's potential bottlenecks behind you. Check your daily entertainment schedule for shows at the Theater in the Wild in DinoLand U.S.A., for *Flights of Wonder* in Asia, and for *Festival of the Lion King* and *Pocahontas* in Camp Minnie-Mickey. Plan the next part of your day around eating lunch and seeing these four shows. Before 11 a.m., arrive about 15 to 20 minutes prior to show time. During the middle of the day (11 a.m. to 4 p.m.), you will need to queue up as follows:

| | |
|---|---|
| **For the Theater in the Wild:** | 30 minutes before show time |
| **For the Caravan Stage:** | 15 minutes before show time |
| **For Pocahontas:** | 25–30 minutes before show time |
| **For the Lion King Theater:** | 25–35 minutes before show time |

There is almost always 90 minutes between the first showing of *Flights of Wonder* and the second showing of *Festival of the Lion King.* For example, the first showing of *Flights* is usually at 10:30 a.m., and the second *Festival* is usually at noon. A good sequence for Step 7 is *Flights of Wonder,* lunch (at Flame Tree Barbecue), then *Festival of the Lion King.* If interested in seeing the Theater in the Wild show or *Pocahontas,* you will still have several afternoon shows to choose from. We've successfully tested this version of Step 7 at least six times. It does require a bit of clock management during lunch (no more than 45 minutes), but it's a solid sequence for hopping from show to show with little downtime or backtracking between.

8. Between shows, check out the Boneyard in DinoLand U.S.A. and the zoological exhibits around the Tree of Life and in the Oasis. The best time to meet the characters at Camp Minnie-Mickey is while performances are under way at the two Camp Minnie-Mickey amphitheaters.

9. Return to Asia and take the Maharaja Jungle Trek.

10. Return to Africa and take the Wildlife Express train to Rafiki's *Planet Watch* and Conservation Station. Tour the exhibits. If you want to experience Kilimanjaro Safaris again, obtain a FASTPASS before boarding the train.

11. Depart Rafiki's *Planet Watch* and Conservation Station and catch the train back to Harambe.

12. In Harambe, walk the Pangani Forest Exploration Trail.
13. Shop, snack, or repeat any attractions you especially enjoyed.
14. This concludes the touring plan. Be sure to allocate some time to visit the zoological exhibits in the Oasis on your way out of the park.

## Animal Kingdom One-Day Touring Plan B (Expedition Everest Is Operating)

1. Arrive at the turnstiles 40 minutes before official opening June 15 to August 15 and during all holiday periods. At other times arrive at the turnstiles 30 minutes early.
2. As soon as the park opens, experience Expedition Everest in Asia. If wait exceeds 30 minutes, use FASTPASS.
3. Ride Kali River Rapids.
4. Walk the Maharaja Jungle Trek.
5. Obtain FASTPASSes for the Kilimanjaro Safaris in Africa.
6. Take the Wildlife Express train to Rafiki's *Planet Watch* and Conservation Station.
7. Catch the train back to Harambe.
8. Eat lunch and walk the Pangani Forest Exploration Trail
9. Experience the Kilimanjaro Safaris in Africa, using FASTPASSes obtained in Step 5.
10. Work in the following shows: *Flights of Wonder, Pocahontas, Festival of the Lion King,* and the show at the Theater in the Wild according to the daily *Times Guide.*
11. See *It's Tough to Be a Bug!* If wait exceeds 30 minutes, use FASTPASS.
12. Check out the exhibits at the Tree of Life and the Boneyard in DinoLand U.S.A.
13. Ride Primeval Whirl. If you have small children, ride TriceraTop Spin.
14. Ride Dinosaur.
15. Shop, snack, or repeat any attractions you especially enjoyed.
16. Visit the zoological exhibits in the Oasis and exit the Animal Kingdom.

# PART TWELVE

# DISNEY-MGM STUDIOS

DISNEY-MGM STUDIOS IS ABOUT THE SIZE of the Magic Kingdom and about half as large as the sprawling Epcot. Unlike the other parks, Disney-MGM is a working motion-picture and television production facility. This means, among other things, that about half of it has controlled access, with guests permitted only on guided tours or observation walkways.

When Epcot opened in 1982, Disney patrons expected a futuristic version of the Magic Kingdom. What they got was humanistic inspiration and a creative educational experience. Since then, Disney has tried to inject more magic, excitement, and surprise into Epcot. Remembering the occasional disappointment of those early Epcot guests, Disney fortified the Studios with action, suspense, surprise, and, of course, special effects. The formula proved so successful that it was trotted out again at the new Animal Kingdom theme park. If you want to learn about the history and technology of movies and television, Disney-MGM Studios will teach you plenty. If you just want to be entertained, you won't leave disappointed.

It's impossible to see all of Epcot or the Magic Kingdom in one day. Disney-MGM Studios, however, is more manageable. There's much less ground to cover by foot. Trams carry guests through much of the backlot and working areas, and attractions in the open-access parts are concentrated in an area about the size of Main Street, Tomorrowland, and Frontierland com-

*unofficial* **TIP**
After 3:30 or 4 p.m., lines for most attractions are manageable, and the park is cooler and more comfortable.

bined. Someday, no doubt, as Disney-MGM develops and grows, you'll need more than a day to see everything. For now, the Studios is a nice one-day outing.

Because Disney-MGM is smaller, it's more affected by large crowds. Our touring plans will help you stay a step ahead of the mob and minimize waiting in line. Even when the park is crowded, however, you can see almost everything in a day.

---

**NOT TO BE MISSED AT DISNEY-MGM STUDIOS**

Star Tours

Disney-MGM Studios Backlot Tour

*Indiana Jones Epic Stunt Spectacular*

*Jim Henson's Muppet-Vision 3-D*

*Fantasmic!*

*Voyage of the Little Mermaid*

*The Twilight Zone* Tower of Terror

Rock 'n' Roller Coaster

*Lights! Motors! Action! Extreme Stunt Show*

---

Because Disney-MGM Studios can be seen in three-fourths of a day, many guests who arrive early in the morning run out of things to do by 3:30 or 4 p.m. and leave the park. Their departure greatly thins the crowd and makes the Studios ideal for evening touring. The *Indiana Jones Epic Stunt Spectacular* and productions at other outdoor theaters are infinitely more enjoyable during the evening than in the sweltering heat of the day. A drawback to touring the Studios at night is that there won't be much activity on the production soundstages.

In 1998, the Studios launched *Fantasmic!* (see pages 252–253), arguably the most spectacular nighttime entertainment event in the Disney repertoire. Staged nightly (weather permitting) in its own theater behind the Tower of Terror, *Fantasmic!* is rated as "not to be missed." Unfortunately, evening crowds have increased substantially at the studios because of *Fantasmic!* Some guests stay longer at Disney-MGM and others arrive after dinner from other parks expressly to see the show. Although crowds thin in the late afternoon, they build again as performance time approaches, making *Fantasmic!* a challenge to get into. Also adversely affected are the Tower of Terror and the Rock 'n'

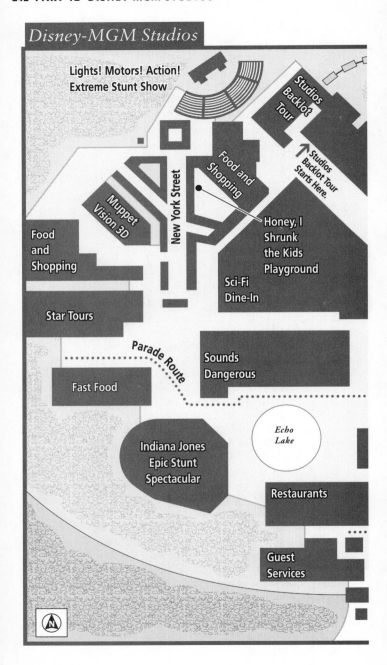

*Disney-MGM Studios*

Lights! Motors! Action!
Extreme Stunt Show

Studios
Backlot
Tour

Food and
Shopping

Studios
Backlot Tour
Starts Here.

Muppet
Vision 3D

New York Street

Honey, I
Shrunk
the Kids
Playground

Food
and
Shopping

Sci-Fi
Dine-In

Star Tours

Parade Route

Sounds
Dangerous

Fast Food

Echo
Lake

Indiana Jones
Epic Stunt
Spectacular

Restaurants

Guest
Services

N

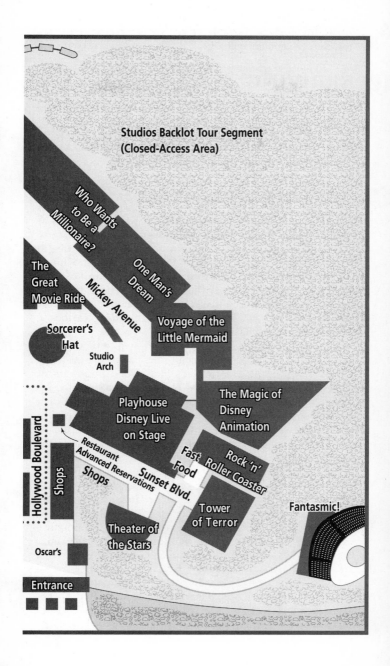

Studios Backlot Tour Segment
(Closed-Access Area)

Who Wants to Be a Millionaire?

One Man's Dream

The Great Movie Ride

Mickey Avenue

Voyage of the Little Mermaid

Sorcerer's Hat

Studio Arch

The Magic of Disney Animation

Playhouse Disney Live on Stage

Hollywood Boulevard

Restaurant Advanced Reservations

Shops

Fast Food

Rock 'n' Roller Coaster

Shops

Sunset Blvd.

Tower of Terror

Fantasmic!

Theater of the Stars

Oscar's

Entrance

Roller Coaster, both situated near the entrance to *Fantas-mic!* Crowd levels throughout the remainder of the park, however, are generally light.

# ARRIVING

DISNEY-MGM STUDIOS HAS ITS OWN PAY parking lot and is served by the Disney transportation system. Most larger hotels outside the World shuttle guests to the Studios. If you drive, Disney's ubiquitous trams will transport you to the ticketing area and entrance gate.

# GETTING ORIENTED

GUEST RELATIONS, ON YOUR LEFT as you enter, serves as the park headquarters and information center, similar to City Hall in the Magic Kingdom and Guest Relations at Epcot and the Animal Kingdom. Go there for a schedule of live performances, lost persons, Package Pick-up, lost and found (on the right side of the entrance), general informa-tion, or in an emergency. If you haven't received a map of the Studios, get one here. To the right of the entrance are locker, stroller, and wheelchair rentals.

About one-half of the complex is set up as a theme park. As at the Magic Kingdom, you enter the park and pass down a main street. Only this time it's Hollywood Boulevard of the 1930s and 1940s. At the end of Hollywood Boulevard is a replica of Hollywood's famous Chinese Theater. Lording over the plaza in front of the theater is a 122-foot-tall replica of the sorcerer hat Mickey Mouse wore in the animated clas-sic *Fantasia*. Besides providing photo ops, the hat is the park's most central landmark, making it a good meeting place if your group becomes separated.

Though modest in size, the open-access areas of the Stu-dios are confusingly arranged (a product of the park's hurried expansion in the early 1990s). As you face the hat, two guest areas—Sunset Boulevard and the Animation Courtyard—branch off Hollywood Boulevard to the right. Branching left off Hollywood Boulevard is the Echo Lake area. The open-access backlot wraps around the back of Echo Lake, the Chinese Theater, and the Animation Court-yard. You can experience all attractions here and in the other open-access sections of the park according to your tastes and time. Still farther to the rear is the limited-access backlot, consisting of the working sound-stages, technical facilities, wardrobe shops, administrative offices, animation studios, and backlot sets. These are accessible to visitors on a guided tour by tram and foot.

At the corner of Hollywood and Sunset Boulevards is a large display listing current waiting times for all Disney-MGM Studios attractions. It's updated continuously throughout the day.

**unofficial TIP**
We've found the waiting times listed to be slightly overstated. If the display says the wait for Star Tours is 45 minutes, for example, you probably will have to wait about 35–40 minutes.

---

**HOLLYWOOD BOULEVARD SERVICES**

Most of the park's service facilities are on Hollywood Boulevard, including:

**Wheelchair & Stroller Rental**  Right of the entrance at Oscar's

**Banking Services**  An ATM is outside the park to the right of the turnstiles.

**Storage Lockers**  Rental lockers are right of the main entrance, to the left of Oscar's.

**Lost & Found**  At Package Pick-up, right of the entrance

**Live Entertainment/Parade Information/Character Information**  Available free at Guest Relations and elsewhere in the park

**Lost Persons**  Report lost persons at Guest Relations.

**Walt Disney World & Local Attraction Information**  At Guest Relations

**First Aid**  At Guest Relations

**Baby Center/Baby-Care Needs**  At Guest Relations. Oscar's sells baby food and other necessities.

**Film**  At The Darkroom on the right side of Hollywood Boulevard, just beyond Oscar's

---

# ATTRACTIONS

## HOLLYWOOD BOULEVARD

HOLLYWOOD BOULEVARD IS A PALM-LINED re-creation of Hollywood's main drag during the city's golden age. Architecture is streamlined moderne with art deco embellishments. Most service facilities are here, interspersed with eateries and shops. Merchandise includes Disney trademark items, Hollywood and movie-related souvenirs, and one-of-a-kind collectibles obtained from studio auctions and estate sales. Hollywood characters and roving performers entertain on the boulevard, and daily parades and other happenings pass this way.

## SUNSET BOULEVARD

SUNSET BOULEVARD, EVOKING THE 1940S, is a major addition to Disney-MGM Studios. The first right off Hollywood Boulevard, Sunset Boulevard provides another venue for dining, shopping, and street entertainment.

### *The Twilight Zone* Tower of Terror (FASTPASS)

| APPEAL BY AGE | PRE-SCHOOL ★★★ | GRADE SCHOOL ★★★★★ | TEENS ★★★★★ |
|---|---|---|---|
| YOUNG ADULTS ★★★★★ | OVER 30 ★★★★★ | | SENIORS ★★★★½ |

**What it is** Sci-fi-theme indoor thrill ride. **Scope and scale** Super headliner. **When to go** Before 9:30 a.m., after 6 p.m., or use FASTPASS. **Special comments** Must be 40 inches tall to ride; switching-off option offered. **Author's rating** Walt Disney World's best attraction; not to be missed; ★★★★★. **Duration of ride** About 4 minutes plus preshow. **Average wait in line per 100 people ahead of you** 4 minutes. **Assumes** All elevators operating. **Loading speed** Moderate.

**DESCRIPTION AND COMMENTS** The Tower of Terror is a new species of Disney thrill ride, though it borrows elements of The Haunted Mansion at the Magic Kingdom. The story is that you're touring a once-famous Hollywood hotel gone to ruin. As at Star Tours, the queuing area integrates guests into the adventure as they pass through the hotel's once-opulent public rooms. From the lobby, guests are escorted into the hotel's library, where Rod Serling, speaking on an old black-and-white television, greets the guests and introduces the plot.

The Tower of Terror is a whopper at 13-plus stories tall. Breaking tradition in terms of visually isolating themed areas, you can see the entire Studios from atop the tower, but you have to look quick.

The ride vehicle, one of the hotel's service elevators, takes guests to see the haunted hostelry. The tour begins innocuously, but about the fifth floor things get pretty weird. Guests are subjected to a full range of eerie effects as they cross into the Twilight Zone. The climax of the adventure occurs when the elevator reaches the top floor (the 13th, of course) and the cable snaps.

The Tower has great potential for terrifying young children and rattling more mature visitors. If you have teenagers in your party, use them as experimental probes. If they report back that they really, really liked the Tower of Terror, run as fast as you can in the opposite direction.

**TOURING TIPS** This one ride is worth your admission to Disney-MGM Studios. Because of its height, the Tower is a veritable beacon, visible from outside the park and luring curious guests as soon as they enter. Because of its popularity with school kids, teens, and young adults, you can count on a foot race to the attraction, as well as to the nearby Rock 'n' Roller Coaster, when the park opens. Expect the Tower to be mobbed most of the day. Experience it first thing in the morning, in the evening before the park closes, or use FASTPASS.

If you're on hand when the park opens and want to ride Tower of Terror first, position yourself on the far right side of Sunset Boulevard as close to the rope barrier as possible. Once in position, wait for the rope to drop. When the park opens, cast members will walk the rope up the street toward Rock 'n' Roller Coaster and Tower of Terror. Just stay on the far right sidewalk and you'll be among the first to make the right turn to the entrance of the tower. Usually the Disney people get out of the way and allow you to run the last 100 feet or so. Also, be aware that about 65% of the folks waiting for the rope walk will head for Rock 'n' Roller Coaster. If you are not positioned on the far right, it will be almost impossible to move through the throng of coaster enthusiasts to make a right turn into Tower of Terror.

To save time, when you enter the library waiting area, stand in the far back corner across from the door where you entered and at the opposite end of the room from the TV. When the doors to the loading area open, you'll be one of the first admitted.

If you have young children (or anyone) who are apprehensive about this attraction, ask the attendant about switching off (page 75).

A good strategy for riding both Tower of Terror and Rock 'n' Roller Coaster with minimum waits is to rush first thing after opening to Rock 'n' Roller Coaster and obtain FASTPASSes, then line up for the Tower of Terror. Most days, by the time you finish experiencing the Tower of Terror, it will be time to use your FASTPASS for Rock 'n' Roller Coaster.

## Rock 'n' Roller Coaster (FASTPASS)

| APPEAL BY AGE | PRE-SCHOOL ★★★ | GRADE SCHOOL ★★★★ | TEENS ★★★★ |
|---|---|---|---|
| YOUNG ADULTS ★★★★ | OVER 30 ★★★★ | | SENIORS ★★★ |

**What it is** Rock music–themed roller coaster. **Scope and scale** Headliner. **When to go** Before 10 a.m. or in the hour before closing. **Special comments** Must be 48 inches tall to ride; children younger than age 7 must ride with an adult. Switching-off option provided (page 75). **Author's rating** Disney's wildest American coaster; not to be missed; ★★★★. **Duration of ride** Almost 1½ minutes. **Average wait in line per 100 people ahead of you** 2½ minutes. **Assumes** All trains operating. **Loading speed** Moderate to fast.

Motion Sickness

WARNING!

**DESCRIPTION AND COMMENTS** This is Disney's answer to the roller-coaster proliferation at Universal's Islands of Adventure and Busch Gardens theme parks. Exponentially wilder than Space Mountain or Big Thunder Mountain in the Magic Kingdom, the Rock 'n' Roller Coaster is an attraction for fans of cutting-edge thrill rides. Although the rock icons and synchronized music add measurably to the experience, the ride itself, as opposed to sights and sounds along the way, is the focus. The Rock 'n' Roller Coaster offers loops, corkscrews, and drops that make Space Mountain seem like the Jungle Cruise. What really makes this metal coaster unusual, however, is that first, it's in the dark (like Space Mountain, only with Southern California nighttime scenes instead of space), and second, you're launched up the first hill like a jet off a carrier deck. By the time you crest the hill, you'll have gone from 0 to 57 miles per hour in less than three seconds. When you enter the first loop, you'll be pulling five g's. By comparison, that's two more g's than astronauts experience at lift-off on a space shuttle.

**TOURING TIPS** This ride is not for everyone. If Space Mountain or Big Thunder push your limits, stay away from the Rock 'n' Roller Coaster. It's eye-catching, and it's definitely a zippy, albeit deafening, ride. Expect long lines except in the first 30 minutes after opening and during the late-evening performance of *Fantasmic!*. Ride first thing in the morning or use FASTPASS.

If you're on hand when the park opens, position yourself on the far left side of Sunset Boulevard as close to the rope barrier as possible. If there's already a crowd at the rope, you can usually work yourself forward by snaking along the wall of the Beverly Sunset Shop. Once in position, wait for the rope drop. When the park opens, cast members will walk the rope up the street toward Rock 'n' Roller Coaster and Tower of Terror. Stay on the far left sidewalk and you'll be among the first to make the left turn to the entrance of the coaster. Usually the Disney people get out of the way and allow you to run the last 100 feet or so.

A good strategy for riding both Tower of Terror and Rock 'n' Roller Coaster with minimum waits is to rush first thing after opening to Rock 'n' Roller Coaster and obtain FAST-

PASSes, then line up for the Tower of Terror. Most days, by the time you finish experiencing the Tower of Terror, it'll be time to use your FASTPASS for Rock 'n' Roller Coaster.

## The Great Movie Ride

| APPEAL BY AGE | PRE-SCHOOL ★★½ | GRADE SCHOOL ★★★½ | TEENS ★★★½ |
|---|---|---|---|
| YOUNG ADULTS ★★★★ | | OVER 30 ★★★★ | SENIORS ★★★ |

**What it is** Movie-history indoor adventure ride. **Scope and scale** Headliner. **When to go** Before 11 a.m. or after 4:30 p.m. **Special comments** Elaborate, with several surprises. **Author's rating** Unique; ★★★½. **Duration of ride** About 19 minutes. **Average wait in line per 100 people ahead of you** 2 minutes. **Assumes** All trains operating. **Loading speed** Fast.

DESCRIPTION AND COMMENTS   Entering through a re-creation of Hollywood's Chinese Theater, guests board vehicles for a fast-paced tour through soundstage sets from classic films including *Casablanca, Tarzan, The Wizard of Oz, Aliens,* and *Raiders of the Lost Ark.* Each set is populated with new-generation Disney audio-animatronic (robot) characters, as well as an occasional human, all augmented by sound and lighting effects. One of Disney's larger and more ambitious dark rides, The Great Movie Ride encompasses 95,000 square feet and showcases some of the most famous scenes in filmmaking. Life-sized audio-animatronic sculptures of stars, including Gene Kelly, John Wayne, James Cagney, and Julie Andrews, inhabit some of the largest sets ever constructed for a Disney ride.

TOURING TIPS   The Great Movie Ride draws large crowds (and lines) from midmorning on. As an interval-loading, high-capacity ride, lines disappear quickly. Even so, waits can exceed an hour after midmorning. (Actual waits usually run about one-third shorter than the time posted. If the chalkboard indicates an hour's wait, your actual time will be around 40 minutes.)

## Star Tours (FASTPASS)

| APPEAL BY AGE | PRE-SCHOOL ★★★★ | GRADE SCHOOL ★★★★ | TEENS ★★★★ |
|---|---|---|---|
| YOUNG ADULTS ★★★★ | | OVER 30 ★★★★ | SENIORS ★★★★ |

**What it is** Indoor space flight–simulation ride. **Scope and scale** Headliner. **When to go** First 90 minutes after opening. **Special comments** Expectant mothers and anyone prone to motion sickness are advised against riding. Too intense for many children younger than age 8. Must be 40 inches tall to ride. **Author's rating** Not to be missed; ★★★★. **Duration of ride** About 7 minutes. **Average wait in line per 100 people ahead of you** 5 minutes. **Assumes** All simulators operating. **Loading speed** Moderate to fast.

**DESCRIPTION AND COMMENTS** Based on the *Star Wars* movie series, this attraction was Disney's first modern simulator ride. Guests ride in a flight simulator modeled after those used for training pilots and astronauts. You're supposedly on a vacation outing in space, piloted by a droid (android, aka humanoid, aka robot) on his first flight with real passengers. Mayhem ensues almost immediately. Scenery flashes by, and the simulator bucks and pitches. You could swear you were moving at the speed of light. After several minutes of this, the droid somehow lands the spacecraft.

**TOURING TIPS** Star Tours hasn't been as popular at Disney-MGM Studios as it has been at Disneyland in California. Except on unusually busy days, waits rarely exceed 35–45 minutes. For the first couple of hours the park is open, expect a wait of 25 minutes or less. Even so, see Star Tours before 11 a.m. or use FASTPASS. If you have young children (or anyone) who are apprehensive about this attraction, ask the attendant about switching off (page 75).

Star Tours is near the exit of the 2,000-seat stadium that houses *Indiana Jones*. When an *Indiana Jones* performance lets out, Star Tours is temporarily inundated. Ditto for *Muppet-Vision 3-D* nearby. If you arrive in the midst of this mayhem, come back later.

### Sounds Dangerous

| APPEAL BY AGE | PRE-SCHOOL ★★½ | GRADE SCHOOL ★★★½ | TEENS ★★★ |
|---|---|---|---|
| YOUNG ADULTS ★★★ | OVER 30 ★★★ | | SENIORS ★★★★ |

**What it is** Show demonstrating sound effects. **Scope and scale** Minor attraction. **When to go** Before 11 a.m. or after 4 p.m. **Author's rating** Funny and informative; ★★★. **Duration of presentation** 12 minutes. **Preshow entertainment** Video introduction to sound effects. **Probable waiting time** 15–30 minutes.

**DESCRIPTION AND COMMENTS** *Sounds Dangerous,* a film presentation starring Drew Carey as a blundering detective, is the vehicle for a crash course on movie and TV sound effects. Funny, educational, well paced, and (for once) not hawking some Disney flick or product, *Sounds Dangerous* is both entertaining and worthwhile. Earphones worn throughout the show make the various sounds seem very real, indeed . . . perhaps too real for some younger children during a part of the show when the theater is plunged into darkness.

**TOURING TIPS** Because the theater is relatively small, long waits (partially in the hot sun) are common here. Another thing: *Sounds Dangerous* is periodically inundated by guests coming from a just-concluded performance of the *Indiana Jones Epic Stunt Spectacular*. This is not the time to get in line. Wait at least 30 minutes and try again.

## Indiana Jones Epic Stunt Spectacular (FASTPASS)

| APPEAL BY AGE | PRE-SCHOOL ★★★ | GRADE SCHOOL ★★★★ | TEENS ★★★★ |
|---|---|---|---|
| YOUNG ADULTS ★★★★ | | OVER 30 ★★★★ | SENIORS ★★★★ |

**What it is** Movie-stunt demonstration and action show. **Scope and scale** Headliner. **When to go** First 3 morning shows or last evening show. **Special comments** Performance times posted on a sign at the entrance to the theater. **Author's rating** Done on a grand scale; ★★★★. **Duration of presentation** 30 minutes. **Preshow entertainment** Selection of "extras" from audience. **Probable waiting time** None.

**DESCRIPTION AND COMMENTS** Coherent and educational, though somewhat unevenly paced, the popular production show-cases professional stunt men and women who demonstrate dangerous stunts with a behind-the-scenes look at how it's done. Sets, props, and special effects are very elaborate.

**TOURING TIPS** The Stunt Theater holds 2,000 people; capacity audiences are common. The first performance is always the easiest to see. If the first show is at 9:30 a.m. or earlier, you can usually walk in, even if you arrive five minutes late. If the first show is scheduled for 9:45 a.m. or later, arrive 20 or so min-utes early. For the second performance, show up about 20–35 minutes ahead of time. For the third and subsequent shows, arrive 30–45 minutes early or use FASTPASS. If you plan to tour during late afternoon and evening, attend the last sched-uled performance. If you want to beat the crowd out of the stadium, sit on the far right (as you face the staging area) and near the top. To be chosen from the audience to be an "extra" in the stunt show, arrive early, sit down front, and display unmitigated enthusiasm.

## Theater of the Stars
### Beauty and the Beast–Live on Stage

| APPEAL BY AGE | PRE-SCHOOL ★★★★ | GRADE SCHOOL ★★★★ | TEENS ★★★ |
|---|---|---|---|
| YOUNG ADULTS ★★★ | | OVER 30 ★★★★ | SENIORS ★★★★ |

**What it is** Live Hollywood-style musical, usually featuring Disney characters; performed in an open-air theater. **Scope and scale** Major attraction. **When to go** Anytime; evenings are cooler. **Special**

**comments** Performances are listed in the daily *Times Guide.*. **Author's rating** Excellent; ★★★★. **Duration of presentation** 25 minutes. **Preshow entertainment** None. **Probable waiting time** 20–30 minutes.

**DESCRIPTION AND COMMENTS** The *Theater of the Stars* combines Disney characters with singers and dancers in upbeat and humorous Hollywood musicals. The *Beauty and the Beast* show, in particular, is outstanding. The theater offers a clear field of vision from almost every seat. Best, a canopy protects the audience from the Florida sun (or rain). The theater still gets mighty hot in the summer, but you should make it through a performance without suffering heatstroke.

**TOURING TIPS** Unless you visit during the cooler months, see this show in the late afternoon or the evening. The production is so popular that you should show up 25–35 minutes early to get a seat.

### Fantasmic!

| APPEAL BY AGE | PRE-SCHOOL ★★★★ | | GRADE SCHOOL ★★★★★ | TEENS ★★★★½ |
|---|---|---|---|---|
| YOUNG ADULTS ★★★★½ | | OVER 30 ★★★★½ | | SENIORS ★★★★½ |

**What it is** Mixed-media nighttime spectacular. **Scope and scale** Super headliner. **When to go** Only staged in the evening. **Special comments** Disney's best nighttime event. **Author's rating** Not to be missed; ★★★★★. **Duration of presentation** 25 minutes. **Probable waiting time** 50–90 minutes for a seat; 35–40 minutes for standing room.

**DESCRIPTION AND COMMENTS** *Fantasmic!* is a mixed-media show presented one or more times each evening when the park is open late. Located off Sunset Boulevard behind the Tower of Terror, *Fantasmic!* is staged on an island opposite a 6,900-seat amphitheater. By far the largest theater facility ever created by Disney, the amphitheater can accommodate an additional 3,000 standing guests for an audience of nearly 10,000.

*Fantasmic!* is far and away the most unique outdoor spectacle ever attempted in any theme park. Starring Mickey Mouse in his role as the Sorcerer's Apprentice from *Fantasia,* the production uses lasers, images projected on a shroud of mist, fireworks, lighting effects, and music in combinations so stunning you can scarcely believe what you are seeing. The plot is simple: good versus evil. The story gets lost in all the special effects at times, but no matter, it is the spectacle, not the story line, that is so overpowering.

**TOURING TIPS** *Fantasmic!* provides a whole new dimension to nighttime at Disney-MGM Studios. As a day-capping event, it is to the Studios what *IllumiNations* is to Epcot. While it's hard to imagine running out of space in a 10,000-person stadium, it happens almost every day. On evenings when there are two performances, the second show will always be less crowded. If you attend the first (or only) scheduled performance, show up at least an hour in advance. If you opt for the second show, arrive 50 minutes early.

Rain and wind conditions sometimes cause *Fantasmic!* to be cancelled. Unfortunately, Disney officials usually do not make a final decision about whether to proceed or cancel until just before show time. We have seen guests wait stoically for over an hour with no assurance that their patience and sacrifice would be rewarded. We do not recommend arriving more than a few minutes before show time on rainy or especially windy nights. On nights like these, pursue your own agenda until ten minutes or so before show time and then head to the stadium to see what happens.

We suggest you spend a little time preparing your younger children for what they will see. Also, make sure to hang on to your children after *Fantasmic!* and to give them explicit instructions for regrouping in the event you are separated.

### Voyage of the Little Mermaid (FASTPASS)

| APPEAL BY AGE | PRE-SCHOOL ★★★★ | GRADE SCHOOL ★★★★ | TEENS ★★★½ |
|---|---|---|---|
| YOUNG ADULTS ★★★★ | | OVER 30 ★★★★ | SENIORS ★★★★ |

**What it is** Musical stage show featuring characters from the Disney movie *The Little Mermaid*. **Scope and scale** Major attraction. **When to go** Before 9:45 a.m., just before closing, or use FASTPASS. **Author's rating** Romantic, lovable, and humorous in the best Disney tradition; not to be missed; ★★★★. **Duration of presentation** 15 minutes. **Preshow entertainment** Taped ramblings about the décor in the preshow holding area. **Probable waiting time** Before 9:30 a.m., 10–30 minutes; after 9:30 a.m., 35–70 minutes.

**DESCRIPTION AND COMMENTS** *Voyage of the Little Mermaid* is a winner, appealing to every age. Cute without being silly or saccharine, and infinitely lovable, the *Little Mermaid* show is the most tender and romantic entertainment offered anywhere in Walt Disney World. The story is simple and engaging, the special effects impressive, and the Disney characters memorable.

**TOURING TIPS** Because it's well done and located at a busy pedestrian intersection, *Voyage of the Little Mermaid* plays to capacity crowds all day. FASTPASS has helped redistribute crowds at *Voyage of the Little Mermaid*. At least 40–50% of each audience is drawn from the standby line. As a rough approximation, guests in the front third of the queuing area will usually make it into the next performance, and quite often folks in the front half of the queuing area will be admitted. Those in the back half of the queuing area will probably have to wait through two showings before being admitted.

### Jim Henson's Muppet-Vision 3-D

| APPEAL BY AGE | PRE-SCHOOL ★★★★½ | GRADE SCHOOL ★★★★★ | TEENS ★★★★½ |
| YOUNG ADULTS ★★★★½ | OVER 30 ★★★★½ | | SENIORS ★★★★½ |

**What it is** 3-D movie starring the Muppets. **Scope and scale** Major attraction. **When to go** Before 11 a.m. or after 3 p.m. **Author's rating** Uproarious; not to be missed; ★★★★½. **Duration of presentation** 17 minutes. **Preshow entertainment** Muppets on television. **Probable waiting time** 12 minutes.

DESCRIPTION AND COMMENTS *Muppet-Vision 3-D* provides a total sensory experience, with wild 3-D action augmented by auditory, visual, and tactile special effects. If you're tired and hot, this zany presentation will make you feel brand new. Arrive early and enjoy the hilarious video preshow.

TOURING TIPS This production is very popular. Before noon, waits are about 20 minutes. Also, watch for throngs arriving from just-concluded performances of the *Indiana Jones Epic Stunt Spectacular.* If you encounter a long line, try again later.

### Honey, I Shrunk the Kids Movie Set Adventure

| APPEAL BY AGE | PRE-SCHOOL ★★★★½ | GRADE SCHOOL ★★★½ | TEENS ★★ |
| YOUNG ADULTS ★★½ | OVER 30 ★★★ | | SENIORS ★★½ |

**What it is** Small but elaborate playground. **Scope and scale** Diversion. **When to go** Before 11 a.m. or after dark. **Special comments** Opens an hour later than the rest of the park. **Author's rating** Great for young children, more of a curiosity for adults; ★★½. **Duration of presentation** Varies. **Average wait in line per 100 people ahead of you** 20 minutes.

DESCRIPTION AND COMMENTS This elaborate playground appeals particularly to kids age 11 and younger. The story is that you have been "miniaturized" and have to make your way through a yard full of 20-foot-tall blades of grass, giant ants, dog poop (just kidding), lawn sprinklers, and other oversized features.

TOURING TIPS This imaginative playground has tunnels, slides, rope ladders, and a variety of oversized props. All surface areas are padded, and Disney personnel are on-hand to help keep children in some semblance of control.

While this Movie Set Adventure undoubtedly looked good on paper, the actual attraction has problems that are hard to "miniaturize." First, it isn't nearly large enough to accommodate the children who would like to play. Only 240 people are allowed "on the set" at a time, and many of these are supervising parents or curious adults who hopped in line without knowing what they were waiting for. Frequently by 10:30 or 11 a.m., the playground is full, with dozens waiting outside (some impatiently).

Also, there's no provision for getting people to leave. Kids play as long as parents allow. This creates uneven traffic flow and unpredictable waits. If it weren't for the third flaw, that the attraction is poorly ventilated (as hot and sticky as an Everglades swamp), there's no telling when anyone would leave.

If you visit during warmer months and want your children to experience the playground, get them in and out before 11 a.m. By late morning, this attraction is way too hot and crowded for anyone to enjoy. Access the playground via the Streets of America, or via Mickey Avenue.

### Lights! Motors! Action! Extreme Stunt Show (FASTPASS)

| APPEAL BY AGE | PRE-SCHOOL ★★ | | GRADE SCHOOL ★★★★ | | TEENS ★★★★ |
|---|---|---|---|---|---|
| YOUNG ADULTS ★★★½ | | OVER 30 ★★★½ | | SENIORS ★★★½ | |

**What it is** Auto stunt show. **Scope and scale** Headliner. **When to go** First show of the day or after 4 p.m. **Author's rating** Good stunt work, slow pace; ★★★½. **Duration of presentation** 25–30 minutes. **Preshow entertainment** Selection of audience "volunteers."

DESCRIPTION AND COMMENTS    This show, which originated at Disneyland Paris, features cars and motorcycles in a blur of chases, crashes, jumps, and explosions. The secrets behind the special effects are explained after each stunt sequence, with replays and different camera views shown on an enormous movie screen; the replays also serve to pass the time needed in placing the next stunt's props into position. While the stunt driving is excellent, the show plods along between tricks, and you will probably have had your fill by the time the last stunt ends. Expect about 6 to 8 minutes of real action in a show that runs 25 to 30 minutes. Because of this, small children may become restless during the show.

TOURING TIPS    The auto stunt show, located at the end of the Streets of America, is scheduled to present 3 to 5 shows daily. As a new attraction, it will be popular, but its remote location (the most distant attraction from the park entrance) will help distribute and moderate the crowds. Seating will be in a 3,000-person stadium, so we don't think it will be difficult to find a seat except on the busiest days.

## Streets of America

| APPEAL BY AGE | PRE-SCHOOL ★½ | GRADE SCHOOL ★★★ | TEENS ★★★ |
|---|---|---|---|
| YOUNG ADULTS ★★★ | | OVER 30 ★★★ | SENIORS ★★★ |

**What it is** Walk-through backlot movie set. **Scope and scale** Diversion. **When to go** Anytime. **Author's rating** Interesting, with great detail; ★★★. **Duration of presentation** Varies. **Average wait in line per 100 people ahead of you** No waiting.

**DESCRIPTION AND COMMENTS** Guests can stroll an elaborate urban street set and appreciate its rich detail.

**TOURING TIPS** There's never a wait to enjoy the Streets of America; save it until you've seen those attractions that develop long lines.

## Disney-MGM Studios Backlot Tour

| APPEAL BY AGE | PRE-SCHOOL ★★★ | GRADE SCHOOL ★★★★ | TEENS ★★★★ |
|---|---|---|---|
| YOUNG ADULTS ★★★★ | | OVER 30 ★★★★ | SENIORS ★★★★ |

**What it is** Combination tram and walking tour of modern film and video production. **Scope and scale** Headliner. **When to go** Anytime. **Author's rating** Educational and fun; not to be missed; ★★★★. **Duration of presentation** About 30 minutes. **Special comments** Use the restroom before getting in line. **Preshow entertainment** A video before the special effects segment and another video in the tram boarding area.

**DESCRIPTION AND COMMENTS** About two-thirds of Disney-MGM Studios is a working film and television facility, where actors, artists, and technicians work on productions year-round. Everything from TV commercials, specials, and game shows to feature motion pictures are produced. Visitors to Disney-MGM can take the backstage studio tour to learn production methods and technologies.

Disney periodically changes the name of this tour. At press time, it was called the Disney-MGM Studios Backlot Tour.

The tour begins on the edge of the backlot with the special effects walking segment, then continues with the tram segment. To reach the Disney-MGM Studios Backlot Tour, turn right off Hollywood Boulevard through the Studio Arch into the Animation Courtyard. Bear left at the corner where *Voyage of the Little Mermaid* is situated. Follow the street until you see a red brick warehouse on your right. Go through the door and up the ramp.

The first stop is a special effects water tank where technicians explain the mechanical and optical tricks that "turn the seemingly impossible into on-screen reality." Included are rain effects and a naval battle. The waiting area for this part of the tour displays miniature naval vessels used in filming famous war movies.

A prop room separates the special effects tank and the tram tour. Trams depart about once every four minutes on busy days, winding among production and shop buildings before stopping at the wardrobe and crafts shops. Here, costumes, sets, and props are designed, created, and stored. Still seated on the tram, you look through large windows to see craftsmen at work.

The tour continues through the backlot, where western desert canyons exist side by side with New York City brownstones. The tour's highlight is Catastrophe Canyon, an elaborate special-effects movie set where a thunderstorm, earthquake, oil-field fire, and flash flood are simulated.

**TOURING TIPS** Because the Backlot Tour is one of Disney's most efficient attractions, you will rarely wait more than 15 minutes (usually less than 10). Take the tour at your convenience, but preferably before 5 p.m., when the workday ends for the various workshops.

### Who Wants to Be a Millionaire

| APPEAL BY AGE | PRE-SCHOOL ★★ | GRADE SCHOOL ★★★★ | TEENS ★★★★ |
|---|---|---|---|
| YOUNG ADULTS ★★★★ | | OVER 30 ★★★★ | SENIORS ★★★★ |

**What it is** Look-alike version of the TV game show. **Scope and scale** Major attraction. **When to go** Before noon, or after 4 p.m., or use FASTPASS. **Special comments** Contestants play for points, not dollars. **Author's rating** No Regis, but good fun; ★★★★. **Duration of presentation** 25 minutes. **Preshow entertainment** Video of Regis. **Probable waiting time** 20 minutes.

**DESCRIPTION AND COMMENTS** It's the familiar ABC television game show sans Regis, played on a replica of the real set, including all the snazzy lighting and creepy sound effects. Contestants are selected from among the audience and play for points and prizes. The 600-seat studio is located in Soundstages 2 and 3 on Mickey Avenue. To get there, go to the end of Hollywood Boulevard and turn right through the Studios Arch, then immediately left alongside *Voyage of the Little Mermaid.* The soundstages are about 80 yards down on the right.

**TOURING TIPS** Each member of the audience has a small electronic display and keypad to use for recording answers. The keypad has a key for each letter (A, B, C, and D) representing one of the four multiple-choice answers to a given question. When the keypad lights up, typically just as the last choice (D) is revealed, that's your cue to enter your answer. The faster you enter the answer, the better your score. Most people hold their fingers ready and push the letter key designating their answer as fast as humanly possible. You can't change your answer, so once you push the key, you're committed. Getting an answer right but taking longer is better than registering a wrong answer. Your score is tabulated electronically, with points awarded for being both fast and right.

We recommend catching a *Millionaire* show after you've experienced all of the park's rides.

### One Man's Dream

| APPEAL BY AGE | PRE-SCHOOL ★ | GRADE SCHOOL ★★½ | TEENS ★★★ |
|---|---|---|---|
| YOUNG ADULTS ★★★½ | | OVER 30 ★★★★ | SENIORS ★★★★ |

**What it is** Tribute to Walt Disney. **Scope and scale** Minor attraction. **When to go** Anytime. **Author's rating** Excellent! . . . and about time; ★★★★. **Duration of presentation** 25 minutes. **Preshow entertainment** Disney memorabilia. **Probable waiting time** For film, 10 minutes.

DESCRIPTION AND COMMENTS *One Man's Dream* is a long-overdue tribute to Walt Disney. Launched in 2001 to celebrate the 100th anniversary of Walt Disney's birthday, the attraction consists of an exhibit area showcasing Disney memorabilia and recordings, followed by a film documenting Disney's life. The exhibits chronicle Walt Disney's life and business. On display are a replica of Walt's California office, various innovations in animation developed by Disney, and early models and working plans for Walt Disney World, as well as for various Disney theme parks around the world. The film provides a personal glimpse of Disney and offers insights regarding both Disney's successes and failures.

TOURING TIPS Give yourself some time here. Every minute spent among these extraordinary artifacts will enhance your visit to Walt Disney World, taking you back to a time when the creativity and vision that created Walt Disney World were personified by one struggling entrepreneur. Located to the right of *Millionaire* on Mickey Avenue, *One Man's Dream* will not be difficult to see. Try it during the hot, crowded middle part of the day.

### Playhouse Disney Live on Stage

| APPEAL BY AGE | PRE-SCHOOL ★★★★★ | GRADE SCHOOL ★★★½ | TEENS ★★ |
|---|---|---|---|
| YOUNG ADULTS ★★★ | | OVER 30 ★★ | SENIORS ★★★ |

**What it is** Live show for children. **Scope and scale** Minor attraction. **When to go** Per the daily entertainment schedule. **Author's rating** A must for families with preschoolers; ★★★★. **Duration of presentation** 20 minutes. **Special comments** Audience sits on the floor. **Probable waiting time** 10 minutes.

**DESCRIPTION AND COMMENTS** The show features characters from the Disney Channel's *Rolie Polie Olie, The Book of Pooh, Bear in the Big Blue House,* and *Stanley.* A simple plot serves as the platform for singing, dancing, some great puppetry, and a great deal of audience participation. The characters, who ooze love and goodness, rally throngs of tots and preschoolers to sing and dance along with them. All the jumping, squirming, and high-stepping is facilitated by having the audience sit on the floor so that kids can spontaneously erupt into motion when the mood strikes. Even for adults without children, it's a treat to watch the tykes rev up. If you have a younger child in your party, all the better: just stand back and let the video roll.

**TOURING TIPS** The show is headquartered in what was formerly the Soundstage Restaurant located to the immediate right of the Animation Tour. Because the tykes just can't get enough, it has become the toughest ticket at the Studios. Show up at least 30 minutes before showtime. Once inside, pick a spot on the floor and take a breather until the performance begins.

## The Magic of Disney Animation

| APPEAL BY AGE | PRE-SCHOOL ★★★ | GRADE SCHOOL ★★★ | TEENS ★★★ |
|---|---|---|---|
| YOUNG ADULTS ★★★★ | OVER 30 ★★★★ | | SENIORS ★★★★ |

**What it is** Overview of Disney Animation process with limited hands-on demonstrations. **Scope and scale** Minor attraction. **When to go** Before 11 a.m. or after 5 p.m. **Special comments** Opens an hour later than the rest of the park. **Author's rating** Not as good as previous renditions; ★★½. **Duration of presentation** 30 minutes. **Preshow entertainment** Gallery of animation art in waiting area. **Average wait in line per 100 people ahead of you** 7 minutes.

**DESCRIPTION AND COMMENTS** The consolidation of Disney Animation at the Burbank, California, studio has left this attraction without a story to tell. Park guests can still get a general overview of the Disney animation process but will not see the detailed work of actual artists, as was possible in previous versions.

The revamped attraction starts in a small theater, where the audience is introduced to a cast-member host and Mushu, the dragon from Mulan. Between the host's speech, Mushu's constant interruptions and a very brief taped segment with real Disney animators, guests are hard-pressed to learn anything about actual animation. The audience is shown a plug for current Disney animated releases ("Home on the Range" while we were there), which falls flat.

Next, the audience moves to another room with floor seating, where another cast member gives guests a verbal description of what used to be the walking tour of the actual animation studio. The cast member supplies bits of Disney character trivia (e.g., Buzz Lightyear's original name was Lunar Larry) and fields questions from the audience, but nothing truly enlightening is presented.

Afterwards, guests have the option of exiting the attraction or attending the Animation Academy (space is limited, and is on a first-come, first-served basis). This is by far the most interesting segment of the attraction, but not designed for all guests. The animator works quickly, which seems to frustrate younger guests who need more time or assistance to get their drawing right. For those who do keep up with the animator, this part is interesting and gives a good idea of how difficult hand-drawn animation really is.

**TOURING TIPS** Some days, the animation tour doesn't open until 10 or 11 a.m., by which time the park is pretty full. The tour is a relatively small-volume attraction, and lines can build on busy days by mid- to late morning

# LIVE ENTERTAINMENT *at* DISNEY-MGM STUDIOS

WHEN THE STUDIOS OPENED, LIVE entertainment, parades, and special events weren't as fully developed or elaborate as those at the Magic Kingdom or Epcot. With the introduction of an afternoon parade and elaborate shows at *Theater of the Stars,* the Studios joined the big leagues. These outstanding performances, coupled with the Sorcery in the Sky fireworks spectacular, gave Disney-MGM live entertainment every bit as compelling as that in the other parks. In 1998, Disney-MGM launched a new edition of *Fantasmic!,* a water, fireworks, and laser show that draws rave reviews. *Fantasmic!,* staged in its own specially designed 10,000-person amphitheater, makes the Studios the park of choice for spectacular nighttime entertainment. *Fantasmic!* is profiled on pages 252–253.

*unofficial* **TIP**
Our favorite vantage point for the parade is the steps of the theater next to *Sounds Dangerous.*

**AFTERNOON PARADE** Staged one or more times a day, the parade begins near the park's entrance, continues down Hollywood Boulevard, and circles in front of the giant hat. From there, it passes in front of *Sounds Dangerous* and ends by

Star Tours. An alternate route begins at the far end of Sunset Boulevard and turns right onto Hollywood Boulevard.

The parade features floats and characters from Disney's animated features. Excellent parades based on *Mulan, Aladdin, Toy Story,* vintage automobiles, and *Hercules,* among others, have been produced. The current parade showcases Disney characters in vintage autos. Colorful, creative, and totally upbeat, the afternoon parade is great. It does, however, bring pedestrian traffic to a standstill along its route and hampers crossing the park. If you're anywhere on the parade route when the parade begins, your best bet is to stay put and enjoy it.

**THEATER OF THE STARS** This covered amphitheater on Sunset Boulevard is the stage for production reviews, usually featuring music from Disney movies and starring Disney characters. Performances are posted in front of the theater and are listed in the daily entertainment schedule in the handout *Times Guide.*

**DISNEY CHARACTERS** Find characters at the *Theater of the Stars* and Backlot Theater, in parades, on the Streets of America backlot, in the Animation Courtyard, by Al's Toy Barn, in Backstage Plaza, and along Mickey Avenue. Mickey sometimes appears for autographs and photos on Sunset Boulevard. Times and locations for character appearances are listed in the complimentary *Times Guide.*

**STREET ENTERTAINMENT** Jugglers and other roving performers appear on Hollywood and Sunset boulevards. The Studios' modest marching band and a brass quartet play Hollywood Boulevard, Sunset Boulevard, Studio Courtyard, and the Echo Lake area. Not exactly street entertainment, a piano player performs daily at The Hollywood Brown Derby.

# DISNEY-MGM STUDIOS TOURING PLAN

BECAUSE DISNEY-MGM OFFERS FEWER attractions, touring isn't as complicated as at the Magic Kingdom or Epcot. Most Disney-MGM rides and shows are oriented to the entire family, eliminating disagreements on how to spend the day. Whereas in the Magic Kingdom Mom and Dad want to see The Hall of Presidents, Big Sis is revved to ride Space Mountain, and the preschool twins are clamoring for

Dumbo the Flying Elephant, at Disney-MGM Studios the whole family can pretty much tour together.

Since there are fewer attractions, crowds are more concentrated at Disney-MGM. If a line seems unusually long, ask an attendant what the estimated wait is. If it exceeds your tolerance, retry the attraction while *Indiana Jones* is in progress or during a parade or special event. These draw people away from the lines.

## BEFORE YOU GO

1. Call ☎ 407-824-4321 to verify the park's hours.
2. Buy your admission before arriving.
3. Make lunch and dinner advance reservations or reserve the *Fantasmic!* dinner package (if desired) before you arrive by calling Disney Dining at ☎ 407-WDW-DINE.
4. The schedule of live entertainment changes from month to month and even from day to day. Review the handout daily *Times Guide* to get a fairly clear picture of your options.

## Disney-MGM Studios One-Day Touring Plan

By way of introduction, we didn't believe it when our touring plan software spit out this plan. It requires a fair amount of backtracking and postpones several big attractions until later in the day. Field testing, however, confirmed that it saves about 40 minutes over other plans.

Our touring plan assumes a willingness to experience all major rides and shows. Be aware that the Rock 'n' Roller Coaster, Star Tours, The Great Movie Ride, *The Twilight Zone* Tower of Terror, and the Catastrophe Canyon segment of the tram tour sometimes frighten children younger than 8. Further, Star Tours and the Rock 'n' Roller Coaster can upset anyone prone to motion sickness. When following the plan, skip any attraction you don't wish to experience.

1. Arrive at the park, admission in hand, 30–40 minutes before official opening time.
2. When you're admitted, grab a park map and a daily entertainment schedule, known as a *Times Guide,* from the little round shop straight ahead and just inside the turnstiles. Then blow down Hollywood Boulevard and turn right onto Sunset Boulevard. Stay to the right side of the street and proceed to the Tower of Terror. Ride. If your route is blocked by a rope barrier, position yourself as near the rope as possible and on the right side of the street. When you are allowed to proceed, go directly to the Tower of Terror.

3. After exiting the Tower of Terror, bear right to Rock 'n' Roller Coaster. Obtain FASTPASSes for the Rock 'n' Roller Coaster if the wait is more than 30 minutes, otherwise ride now.

4. Backtrack down Sunset Boulevard and turn right on Hollywood Boulevard. On the far side of the giant hat is The Great Movie Ride. Enjoy.

5. Exit The Great Movie Ride and bear left. Turn left again just past The Great Movie Ride building and walk the stairs to Mickey Avenue. If the next showing of *Who Wants to Be a Millionaire* is less than 20 minutes from now, see *Who Wants to Be a Millionaire.* If the next showing is between 20 and 40 minutes from now, see *One Man's Dream* first, then *Millionaire.* If the next showing of *Millionaire* is more than an hour away, take the Backlot Tour and see *One Man's Dream* first.

6. Exit *Who Wants to Be a Millionaire* and bear left. Take the Backlot Tour.

7. Exit the Backlot tour and turn left. Walk back down Mickey Avenue and see *One Man's Dream* if you have not already done so.

8. Check the daily entertainment schedule for performance times of *Beauty and the Beast, Playhouse Disney Live,* and *Lights! Motors! Action!* Work these shows in around lunch.

9. See *Muppet-Vision 3-D* near the Streets of America Set.

10. Explore the Streets of America Set if you didn't see enough en route to the *Muppets.*

11. Head in the direction of the Echo Lake. Ride Star Tours.

12. See *Sounds Dangerous,* which faces Echo Lake near *Indiana Jones.*

13. Checking the daily entertainment schedule for performance times, see the *Indiana Jones Epic Stunt Spectacular* (FASTPASS), as well as the *Voyage of the Little Mermaid* (FASTPASS). Also take the Magic of Disney Animation tour.

14. Tour Hollywood and Sunset Boulevards. Enjoy *Fantasmic!.*

15. This concludes the touring plan. Eat, shop, enjoy live entertainment, or revisit your favorite attractions.

# PART THIRTEEN

# THE WATER THEME PARKS

DISNEY HAS TWO SWIMMING THEME PARKS, and two more independent water parks are in the area. At Disney World, **Typhoon Lagoon** is the most diverse Disney splash pad, while **Blizzard Beach** takes the prize for the most slides and most bizarre theme. Outside the World, find **Wet 'n Wild** and **Water Mania.**

At all Disney water parks, the following rules and prices apply: one cooler per family or group is allowed, but no glass and no alcoholic beverages; towels $1, locker $5 (plus $2 deposit for lockers), life jacket free with a $25 refundable deposit. Admission to both parks runs about $36 a day for adults and $29 a day for children ages 3 to 9. Children younger than age 3 are admitted free. For current information about water park status, prices, and hours, call ☎ 407-824-4321.

## River Country

The oldest of the Disney swimming parks, **River Country** was closed during 2002 as a consequence of the soft travel market. It now appears that the closure is permanent.

# BLIZZARD BEACH

BLIZZARD BEACH IS DISNEY'S MOST EXOTIC water adventure park and, like Typhoon Lagoon, it arrived with its own legend. This time, the story goes, an entrepreneur tried to open a ski resort in Florida during a particularly savage winter. Alas, the snow melted; the palm trees grew back; and all that remained of the ski resort was its Alpine lodge, the ski lifts, and, of course, the mountain. Plunging off the mountain are ski slopes and bobsled runs transformed into water slides. Visitors to Blizzard Beach catch the thaw: icicles drip and patches of snow remain. The melting snow has formed a lagoon (the wave pool), fed by gushing mountain streams.

In addition to the wave pool, there are 17 slides (2 of which are quite long), a children's swimming area, and a tranquil stream for tubing. Picnic areas and sunbathing beaches dot the park. Summit Plummet, one of the world's longest speed slides, begins with a steep 120-foot descent. The Teamboat Springs slide is 1,200 feet long.

# TYPHOON LAGOON

TYPHOON LAGOON IS COMPARABLE in size to Blizzard Beach. Ten water slides and streams, some as long as 400 feet, drop from the top of a 100-foot-tall, man-made mountain. Landscaping and an "aftermath-of-a-typhoon" theme add adventure to the wet rides.

Typhoon Lagoon provides water adventure for all ages. Activity pools for young children and families feature geysers, tame slides, bubble jets, and fountains. For the older and more adventurous are the enclosed Humunga Kowabunga speed slides, corkscrew storm slides, and three whitewater raft rides (plus one children's rapids ride) plopping off Mount Mayday. Slower metabolisms will enjoy the scenic, meandering, 2,100-foot-long stream that floats tubers through a hidden grotto and rain forest. And, of course, the sedentary will usually find plenty of sun to sleep in. Typhoon Lagoon's surf pool and Shark Reef are unique, and the wave pool is the world's largest inland surf facility, with waves up to six feet high. Shark Reef is a saltwater snorkeling pool where guests can swim among real fish.

# WHEN *to* GO

THE BEST WAY TO AVOID STANDING IN LINES is to visit the water parks when they're less crowded. Because the parks are popular with locals, weekends can be tough. We recommend going on a Monday or Tuesday, when most other tourists will be visiting the Magic Kingdom, Epcot, the Animal Kingdom, or Disney-MGM Studios and locals will be at work or school. During summer and holiday periods, Typhoon Lagoon and Blizzard Beach fill to capacity and close their gates before 11 a.m.

If your schedule is flexible, a good time to visit the swimming parks is midafternoon to late in the day when the weather has cleared after a storm. The parks usually close during bad weather. If the storm is prolonged, most guests leave for their hotels. When Typhoon Lagoon or Blizzard Beach reopen after inclement weather has passed, you almost have a whole park to yourself.

# PART FOURTEEN

# BEYOND *the* PARKS

# DOWNTOWN DISNEY

DOWNTOWN DISNEY IS A SHOPPING, DINING, and entertainment development strung out along the banks of the Buena Vista Lagoon. On the far right is the Downtown Disney Marketplace (formerly known as the Disney Village Marketplace). In the middle is the gated (admission-required) Pleasure Island nighttime entertainment, and on the far left is Disney's West Side.

## DOWNTOWN DISNEY MARKETPLACE

ALTHOUGH THE MARKETPLACE OFFERS interactive fountains, a couple of playgrounds, a Lagoon-side amphitheater, and watercraft rentals, it is primarily a shopping and dining venue. The centerpiece of shopping is the **World of Disney,** the largest Disney trademark merchandise store in the world. If you can't find what you are looking for in this 38,000-square-foot Noah's Ark of Disney stuff, it probably doesn't exist. Another noteworthy retailer is the **LEGO Imagination Center,** showcasing a number of huge and unbelievable sculptures made entirely of LEGO "bricks." Almost worthy of a special trip, spaceships, sea serpents, sleeping tourists, and dinosaurs are just a few of the sculptures on display. **Once Upon a Toy** is a toys, games, and collectibles superstore. Rounding out the selection are stores specializing in resort wear, athletic attire and gear, Christmas decorations, Disney art and collectibles, and handmade craft items. Also located in the Marketplace is **Disney Tails,** where guests can buy Disney themed clothing and other oddities for their pets.

Rainforest Café is the headliner restaurant at the Marketplace. There is also Cap'n Jack's Oyster Bar, Wolfgang Puck pizza kitchen, a soda fountain, a deli and bakery, and a McDonald's.

## PLEASURE ISLAND

PLEASURE ISLAND IS A NIGHTTIME ENTERTAINMENT complex featuring eight nightclubs. Shops and restaurants, formerly open throughout the day with no admission charge, are now open exclusively in the evening. Pleasure Island's shops offer more Disney art, casual fashions, Disney character merchandise, movie collectibles, and music memorabilia. **Superstar Studios** is a recording studio where you can make your own music video. There are several full-service restaurants at Pleasure Island.

*unofficial* **TIP**
Fulton's Crab House and the Portobello Yacht Club can be accessed at any time without paying admission to Pleasure Island.

## DISNEY'S WEST SIDE

THE WEST SIDE IS THE NEWEST ADDITION to Downtown Disney and offers a broad range of entertainment, dining, and shopping. Restaurants include the House of Blues, which serves Cajun specialties; Planet Hollywood, offering movie memorabilia and basic American fare; Bongo's Cuban Cafe, serving Cuban favorites; and Wolfgang Puck Cafe, featuring California cuisine. West Side shopping is some of the most interesting in WDW. For starters, there's a **Virgin** (records and books) **Megastore**. Across the street is the **Guitar Gallery by George's Music,** specializing in custom, collector, rare, and unique guitars. Other specialty shops include a cigar shop, a rock-and-roll and movie memorabilia store, and a western apparel boutique.

In the entertainment department, there is **DisneyQuest,** an interactive theme park contained in a building; the **House of Blues,** a concert and dining venue; and a 24-screen AMC movie theater. The West Side is also home to **Cirque du Soleil,** a not-to-be-missed production show with a cast of almost 100 performers and musicians. The House of Blues concert hall and Cirque du Soleil are described in Part Fifteen, Nightlife in Walt Disney World. DisneyQuest is described below.

## DISNEYQUEST

DISNEYQUEST, IN CONCEPT AND ATTRACTION mix, is aimed at a youthful audience, say 8–35 years of age, though younger and older patrons will enjoy much of what it offers. The feel is dynamic, bustling, and noisy. Those who haunt the video arcades at shopping malls will feel most at home at DisneyQuest. And like most malls, when late afternoon turns to evening, the median age at DisneyQuest rises toward adolescents and teens who have been released from parental supervision for awhile.

You begin your experience in the Departure Lobby, adjacent to admission sales. From the Departure Lobby you enter a "Cyberlator," a sort of "transitional attraction" (read elevator) hosted by the genie from *Aladdin,* that delivers you to an entrance plaza called Ventureport. From here you can enter the four zones. Like in the larger parks, each zone is distinctively themed. Some zones cover more than one floor, so, looking around, you can see things going on both above and below you. The four zones, in no particular order, are Explore Zone, Score Zone, Create Zone, and Replay Zone. In addition to the zones, DisneyQuest offers two restaurants and the inevitable gift shop.

# DISNEY'S WIDE WORLD *of* SPORTS

DISNEY'S WIDE WORLD OF SPORTS COMPLEX is a 200-acre, state-of-the-art competition and training complex consisting of a 7,500-seat ballpark, a fieldhouse, and dedicated venues for baseball, softball, tennis, track and field, beach volleyball, and 27 other sports. From Little League Baseball to rugby to beach volleyball, the complex hosts a mind-boggling calendar of professional and amateur competitions, with one or more events scheduled nearly every day.

Counter-service and full-service dining are available at the sports complex, but there's no on-site lodging. Disney's Wide World of Sports is off Osceola Parkway, between World Drive and where the parkway crosses I-4 (no interstate access). The complex has its own parking lot and is accessible via the Disney Transportation System.

# THE DISNEY WILDERNESS PRESERVE

LOCATED ABOUT 40–60 MINUTES SOUTH of Walt Disney World is the Disney Wilderness Preserve, a real wetlands restoration area operated by the Nature Conservancy in partnership with Disney. At 12,000 acres, this is as real as Disney gets. There are hiking trails, an interpretive center, and guided outings on weekends. Trails wind through grassy savannas, beneath ancient cypress trees, and along the banks of pristine Lake Russell. It's open daily from 9 a.m. to 5 p.m., and general admission is $3 for adults and $2 for children ages 6–17. Guided trail walks are offered on Saturday at no extra cost, and "buggy" rides are available on Sunday afternoon. The buggy in question is a mammoth amphibious contraption, and the rides last a few hours. The buggy ride is $10 for adults and $5 for children ages 6–17; reservations are highly recommended. For information and directions, call the preserve directly at ☎ 407-935-0002.

# WALT DISNEY WORLD SPEEDWAY

ADJACENT TO THE TRANSPORTATION AND Ticket Center parking lot, the one-mile tri-oval course is host to several races each year. Between competitions, it's home to the Richard Petty Driving Experience, where you can ride in a two-seater stock car for $99 or learn to drive one. Courses are by reservation only and cost between $379 (8 laps), $749 (18 laps), and $1,249 (30 laps). You must be age 18 or older, have a valid driver's license, and know how to drive a stick shift to take a course. For information, call ☎ 800-BE-PETTY or check out **www.1800bepetty.com**.

# WALT DISNEY WORLD RECREATION

MOST WALT DISNEY WORLD GUESTS never make it beyond the theme parks, the water parks, and Downtown Disney. Those who do, however, discover an extraordinary selection of recreational opportunities ranging from guided fishing expeditions and water skiing outings to hayrides, horseback riding, fitness center workouts, and miniature golf. If it's something you can do at a resort, it's probably available at Walt Disney World.

Boat, bike, and fishing equipment rentals are handled on an hourly basis. Just show up at the rental office during operating hours and they'll fix you up. The same goes for various fitness centers in the resort hotels. Golf, tennis, fishing expeditions, water ski excursions, hayrides, trail rides, and most spa services must be scheduled in advance. Though every resort features an extensive selection of recreational options, those resorts located on a navigable body of water offer the greatest variety. Also, the more upscale a resort, the more likely it is to have such amenities as a fitness center and spa. In addition, you can rent boats and other recreational equipment at the Marketplace in Downtown Disney.

# WALT DISNEY WORLD GOLF

WALT DISNEY WORLD HAS SIX GOLF COURSES, all expertly designed and meticulously maintained. The **Magnolia,** the **Palm,** and the **Oak Trail** are across Floridian Way from the Polynesian Resort. They envelop the Shades of Green recreational complex, and the pro shops and support facilities adjoin the Shades of Green hotel. **Lake Buena Vista Golf Course** is at the Saratoga Springs Resort, near Walt Disney World Village and across the lake from Pleasure Island. The **Osprey Ridge** and **Eagle Pines** courses are part of the **Bonnet Creek Golf Club** near the Fort Wilderness Campground. In addition to the golf courses, there are driving ranges and putting greens at each location.

*unofficial* **TIP**
To avoid the crowds, play on a Monday, Tuesday, or Wednesday, and sign up for a late-afternoon tee time.

Oak Trail is a nine-hole course for beginners. The other five courses are designed for the mid-handicap player and, while interesting, are quite forgiving. All courses are popular, with morning tee times at a premium, especially January–April.

Peak season for all courses is September–April; off-season is May–August. Off-season and afternoon twilight rates are available. Carts are required (except at Oak Trail) and are included in the greens fee. Tee times may be reserved 60 days in advance by Disney resort guests, 30 days in advance for day guests with a credit card, and 7 days in advance without guarantee. Proper golf attire is required: collared shirt and Bermuda-length shorts or slacks.

Besides the ability to book tee times farther in advance, guests of Walt Disney World–owned resorts get other benefits that may sway a golfer's lodging decision. These include discounted greens fees, charge privileges, and the shipping of your clubs between facilities, if, say, you are playing the Lake Buena Vista course one day and a course at one of the other two golf facilities the next. The single most important, and least known, benefit is the provision of free round-trip taxi transportation between the golf courses and your hotel, which lets you avoid moving your car or dragging your clubs on Disney buses. The cabs, which make access to the courses much simpler, are paid by vouchers happily supplied to hotel guests.

For complete details about Walt Disney World golf courses and packages, call ☎ 407-WDW-GOLF.

# MINIATURE GOLF

FANTASIA GARDENS MINIATURE GOLF is an 11-acre complex with two 18-hole dink-and-putt golf courses. One course is an "adventure" course, themed after Disney's animated film *Fantasia*. The other course, geared more toward older children and adults, is an innovative approach-and-putt course with sand traps and water hazards.

**Fantasia Gardens** is on Epcot Resort Boulevard, across the street from the Walt Disney World Swan. To reach Fantasia Gardens via Disney transportation, take a bus or boat to the Swan resort. The cost to putt at this course is $10.65 for adults and $8.50 for children. If you arrive hungry or naked, Fantasia Gardens has a snack bar and gift shop. For more information, call ☎ 407-WDW-GOLF.

*unofficial* **TIP**
The Winter Summerland courses are much easier than the Fantasia courses, making them a better choice for families with preteen children.

In 1999, Disney opened **Winter Summerland,** a second miniature golf facility located next to the Blizzard Beach water park. Winter Summerland offers two 18-hole courses—one has a blizzard in Florida theme, while the other sports a tropical holiday theme. It's open daily, 10 a.m.–11 p.m., and the cost is the same as for Fantasia Gardens.

# PART FIFTEEN

# NIGHTLIFE *in* WALT DISNEY WORLD

## WALT DISNEY WORLD *at* NIGHT

### IN THE THEME PARKS

EPCOT'S MAJOR EVENING EVENT IS *IllumiNations,* a laser and fireworks show at World Showcase Lagoon. Show time is listed in the daily entertainment schedule *(Times Guide).*

In the Magic Kingdom are the popular evening parade(s) and *Wishes* fireworks. Consult the daily entertainment schedule *(Times Guide)* for performances.

On nights when the park is open late, Disney-MGM Studios features a fireworks presentation called *Fantasmic!,* a laser, special effects, and water spectacular. The daily entertainment schedule *(Times Guide)* lists times.

At present there is no nighttime entertainment at the Animal Kingdom.

### AT THE HOTELS

THE FLOATING ELECTRICAL PAGEANT IS A sort of Main Street Electrical Parade on barges. Starring King Neptune and creatures of the sea, the nightly pageant (backed by Handel played on a doozie of a synthesizer), is one of our favorite Disney productions. The first performance of the short but captivating show is at 9 p.m. off the Polynesian Resort docks. From there, it circles around and repeats at the Grand Floridian at 9:15 p.m., heading afterward to Fort Wilderness Campground, Wilderness Lodge and Villas, and the Contemporary Resort.

For something more elaborate, consider a dinner theater. If you want to go honky-tonkin', several hotels at the Disney Village Hotel Plaza have lively bars.

## AT FORT WILDERNESS CAMPGROUND

THE NIGHTLY CAMPFIRE PROGRAM AT Fort Wilderness Campground begins with a sing-along led by Disney characters Chip 'n' Dale and progresses to cartoons and a Disney movie. Only Disney lodging guests may attend. There's no charge.

## AT DISNEY'S BOARDWALK

JELLYROLLS AT THE BOARDWALK FEATURES dueling pianos and sing-alongs. The BoardWalk has Disney's first and only brew pub. A sports bar, Atlantic Dance Hall, a dance club, and several restaurants complete the Board-Walk's entertainment mix. Access is by foot from Epcot, by launch from Disney-MGM Studios, and by bus from other Disney World locations.

Taste varies, of course, but the *Unofficial Guide* research team rates Jellyrolls as their personal favorite of all the Disney nightspots, including the clubs at Pleasure Island. It's raucous, upbeat, frequently hilarious, and positively rejuvenating. The piano players are outstanding, and they play nonstop with never a break. Best of all, it's strictly adult.

## AT DOWNTOWN DISNEY

**PLEASURE ISLAND** Pleasure Island, Walt Disney World's nighttime entertainment complex, offers eight nightclubs for one admission price. Dance to rock, soul, or Celtic; take in a comedy show; or listen to some rock oldies. Pleasure Island is in Downtown Disney next to Downtown Disney Marketplace and is accessible from the theme parks and the Transportation and Ticket Center by shuttle bus. For details on Pleasure Island, see pages 278–280.

**DOWNTOWN DISNEY MARKETPLACE** It's flog your wallet each night at the Marketplace, with shops open until 11:30 p.m.

**DISNEY'S WEST SIDE** Disney's West Side is a 70-acre shopping, restaurant, and nightlife complex situated to the left of Pleasure Island. Not to be confused with the West End Stage at nearby Pleasure Island, this latest addition to Downtown Disney features a 24-screen AMC movie complex, Disney-Quest pay-for-play indoor theme park (see page 268), a permanent showplace for the extraordinary Cirque du Soleil, and a 2,000-capacity House of Blues concert hall. Dining options include Planet Hollywood, a 450-seat Cajun restaurant at House of Blues, Wolfgang Puck (serving California fare), and Bongo's (Cuban cuisine), owned by Gloria and Emilio Estefan. The complex can be accessed via Disney buses from most Disney World locations.

## Cirque du Soleil's *La Nouba*

| APPEAL BY AGE | UNDER 21 ★★★★ | 21–37 ★★★★★ | 38–50 ★★★★★ |
|---|---|---|---|
| 51 AND UP ★★★★½ | | | |

☎ **407-939-7719**

**Type of show** Circus as theater. **Admission cost with taxes** Category 1: $92 adults, $69 children (ages 3–9); Category 2: $80 adults, $59 children; Category 3: $63 adults, $47 children. **Cast size** 72. **Night of lowest attendance** Thursday. **Usual show times** Thursday–Saturday, 6 p.m. and 9 p.m. **Smoking allowed** No. **Author's rating** ★★★★★. **Duration of presentation** An hour and a half (no intermission) plus pre-show.

**DESCRIPTION AND COMMENTS** Cirque du Soleil's *La Nouba* is a far cry from a traditional circus but retains all the fun and excitement. It is whimsical, mystical, and sophisticated, yet pleasing to all ages. The action takes place on an elaborate stage that incorporates almost every part of the theater. The original musical score is exotic, like the show.

**TOURING TIPS** Be forewarned that the audience is an integral part of *La Nouba* and that at almost any time you might be plucked from your seat to participate. Our advice is to loosen up and roll with it. If you are too rigid, repressed, hungover, or whatever to get involved, politely but firmly decline to be conscripted. Then fix a death grip on the arms of your chair. Tickets for reserved seats can be purchased in advance at the Cirque box office or over the phone, using your credit card. Oh yeah, don't wait until the last minute; book well in advance from home.

*unofficial* **TIP**
Unless you cancel your tickets at least 48 hours before your reservation time, your credit card will still be charged the full amount.

## House of Blues
☎ **407-934-2222**

**Type of show** Live concerts with an emphasis on rock and blues. **Admission cost with taxes** $10–$60, depending on who is performing. **Nights of lowest attendance** Monday and Tuesday.

**Usual show times** Monday–Thursday, 8:30; Friday and Saturday, 9:30.
**Dark** Sunday.

**DESCRIPTION AND COMMENTS** The House of Blues, developed by original Blues Brother Dan Aykroyd, features a restaurant and Blues Bar, as well as the concert hall. The restaurant serves from 11 a.m. until 2 a.m., which makes it one of the few late-night dining options in Walt Disney World. Live music cranks up every night at 11 p.m. in the restaurant/Blues Bar, but even before then, the joint is way beyond ten decibels. The Music Hall next door features concerts by an eclectic array of musicians and groups. During one visit, the showbill listed gospel, blues, funk, ska, dance, salsa, rap, zydeco, hard rock, groove rock, and reggae groups over a two-week period.

**TOURING TIPS** Prices vary from night to night according to the fame and drawing power of the featured band. Tickets ranged $7–$35 during our visits but go higher when a really big name is scheduled.

The Music Hall is set up like a nightclub, with tables and bar stools for only about 150 people and standing room for a whopping 1,850 people. Folks dance when there's room and sometimes when there isn't. The tables and stools are first-come, first-served, with doors opening an hour before show time on weekdays and 90 minutes before show time on weekends. Acoustics are good, and the showroom is small enough to provide a relatively intimate concert experience. All shows are all ages unless otherwise indicated.

## WALT DISNEY WORLD DINNER THEATERS

SEVERAL DINNER THEATER SHOWS PLAY each night at Walt Disney World, and unlike other Disney dining venues, they make hard reservations instead of advance reservations. You must guarantee advance dinner-show reservations with a credit card. You will receive a confirmation number and be told to pick up your tickets at a Disney hotel Guest Services desk. Dinner-show reservations can be made up to two years in advance; call ☎ 407-939-3463. While getting reservations for *Spirit of Aloha* isn't too tough, booking the *Hoop-Dee-Doo Revue* is a trick of the first order. Call as soon as you're certain of the dates of your visit. The earlier you call, the better your seats will be. If you can't get reservations and want to see one of the shows:

1. Call ☎ 407-939-3463 at 9 a.m. each morning while you're at Disney World to make a same-day reservation. There are three performances each night, and for all three combined,

only 3 to 24 people total will be admitted with same-day reservations.

2. Arrive at the show of your choice 45 minutes before show time (early and late shows are your best bets) and put your name on the standby list. If someone with reservations fails to show, you may be admitted.

## Hoop-Dee-Doo Revue
### Pioneer Hall, Fort Wilderness Campground; ☎ 407-939-3463

**Usual show times** 5, 7:15, and 9:30 p.m. nightly. **Cost** $50; $26 ages 3–11. **Discounts** Seasonal; American Express discount at 9:30 show only. **Type of seating** Tables of various sizes to fit the number in each party, set in an Old West–style dance hall. **Menu** All-you-can-eat barbecue ribs, fried chicken, corn-on-the-cob, and strawberry shortcake. **Vegetarian alternative** On request (at least 24 hours in advance). **Beverages** Unlimited beer, wine, sangria, and soft drinks.

**DESCRIPTION AND COMMENTS** Six Wild West performers arrive by stagecoach (sound effects only) to entertain the crowd inside Pioneer Hall. There isn't much plot, just corny jokes interspersed with song or dance. The humor is of the *Hee-Haw* ilk but is presented enthusiastically.

Audience participation includes sing-alongs, hand-clapping, and a finale that uses volunteers to play parts onstage. Performers are accompanied by a banjo player and pianist who also play quietly while the food is being served. The fried chicken and corn-on-the-cob are good, but the ribs are a bit tough, though tasty. With the all-you-can-eat policy, at least you can get your money's worth by stuffing yourself silly.

## Mickey's Backyard Barbecue
### Fort Wilderness Campground; ☎ 407-939-3463

**Show times** Tuesday and Thursday, 6:30 p.m. **Cost** $39; $25 ages 3–11. **Type of seating** Picnic tables. **Menu** Baked chicken, barbecued pork ribs, burgers, hot dogs, corn, beans, vegetables, salads and slaw, bread, and watermelon and marble cake for dessert. **Vegetarian alternatives** On request. **Beverages** Unlimited beer, wine, lemonade, and iced tea.

**DESCRIPTION AND COMMENTS** Situated along Bay Lake and held in a covered pavilion next to the now-closed River Country swimming park, *Mickey's Backyard Barbecue* features Mickey, Minnie, Chip 'n' Dale, and Goofy, along with a live country band and line dancing. Though the pavilion gets some breeze off Bay Lake, we recommend going during the spring or fall if possible. The food is pretty good, as is, fortunately, the insect control.

Because the barbecue is seasonal, dates are usually not entered into the WDW-DINE reservations system until late February or early March. Once the dates are in the system, you can make advance reservations for anytime during the dinner show's nine-month season.

The easiest way to get to the barbecue is to take a boat from the Magic Kingdom or from one of the resorts on the Magic Kingdom monorail. Though getting to the barbecue is not nearly as difficult as commuting to the *Hoop-Dee-Doo Revue,* give yourself at least 45 minutes if you plan to arrive by boat.

### *Spirit of Aloha*
### Disney's Polynesian Resort; ☎ 407-939-3463

**Show times** Tuesday–Saturday, 5:15 and 8 p.m. **Cost** $49; $25 ages 3–11. **Discounts** Seasonal. **Type of seating** Long rows of tables, with some separation between individual parties. The show is performed on an outdoor stage, but all seating is covered. Ceiling fans provide some air movement, but it can get warm, especially at the early show. **Menu** Tropical fruit, roasted chicken, island pork ribs, shrimp, mixed vegetables, rice, and pineapple cake; chicken tenders, mini–corn dogs, and mac and cheese are also available for children. **Vegetarian alternative** On request. **Beverages** Beer, wine, and soft drinks.

DESCRIPTION AND COMMENTS Formerly the *Polynesian Luau,* this show features South Sea–island native dancing followed by a "Polynesian-style," all-you-can-eat meal. The dancing is interesting and largely authentic, and dancers are attractive though definitely PG in the Disney tradition. We think the show has its moments and the meal is adequate, but neither is particularly special.

# █ PLEASURE ISLAND

PLEASURE ISLAND IS A SIX-ACRE NIGHTTIME entertainment complex on a man-made island in Downtown Disney. It consists of eight nightclubs, restaurants, and shops. A few of the restaurants and shops are open during the day, but the nightclubs don't start opening until 7 p.m. Some of the clubs may not open until 8 p.m. or later, and Pleasure Island doesn't fully come alive until after 9 or even 10 p.m.

**ADMISSION OPTIONS** One admission (about $22) entitles a guest to enjoy all eight nightclubs. Guests younger than 18 years must be accompanied by a parent after 7 p.m. Unlimited eight-day admission to Pleasure Island is included in All-in-

One passes. In addition to the Multi-Club admission, a Single-Club Ticket is available for about $11. The Single-Club Ticket, introduced in 2005, is good for visiting one club only. Participating clubs are Rock 'n' Roll Beach Club, BETSound-Stage (for those 21 and older), Mannequins Dance Palace (for those 21 and older), Motion, and 8TRAX. Excluded are the Comedy Warehouse and the Adventurers Club. The eighth club, the Raglan Road Irish Pub, does not require admission to Pleasure Island. You can only purchase Single-Club Tickets at Pleasure Island or Downtown Disney Guest Services.

If you just want to shop, dine, or see what's going on, admission is not required. One club, Raglan Road, will admit you at no charge, and you can also enjoy the live music on the West End Stage. Wristbands are issued to those buying Multi- or Single-Club Tickets to distinguish them from the shoppers and rubberneckers.

**ALCOHOLIC BEVERAGES** Guests not recognizably older than 21 must provide proof of their age if they wish to buy alcoholic beverages. To avoid repeated checking as the patron club-hops, a color-coded wristband indicates eligibility. All nightclubs serve alcohol. Those under 21, while allowed in all clubs except Mannequins, Rock 'n' Roll Beach Club, and the BET Soundstage, aren't allowed to buy alcoholic beverages. Finally, and gratefully, you don't have to order drinks at all. You can enjoy the entertainment at any club and never buy that first beer. No server will hassle you.

**DRESS CODE** Casual is in, but shirts and shoes are required.

**IT'S POSSIBLE TO VISIT ALL THE CLUBS IN ONE NIGHT** Whereas performances in nightclubs elsewhere might be an hour or more in duration, at Pleasure Island shows are shorter but more frequent. This allows guests to move among clubs without missing much. Since you can catch the essence of a club pretty quickly, there's no need to hang around for two or three drinks to see what's going on. This format enables guests to have a complete and satisfying experience in a brief time, then move to another club if they want.

The music clubs (Rock 'n' Roll Beach Club, 8TRAX, Motion, BET Soundstage, Mannequins, and Raglan Road) go nonstop. Sometimes, there are special performances within the ongoing club entertainment. The Adventurers Club and the Comedy Warehouse offer scheduled shows.

**PARKING IS A HASSLE** Pleasure Island's parking lot often fills up. On the bright side, the lot is now well marked. If you jot down the location of your space, you'll be able to find your car when it's time to leave. A good strategy is to park in the lot adjacent to the movie theaters and Disney's West Side and enter via the bridge connecting the West Side to Pleasure Island. Because there's an admission booth at the bridge, there's no need to enter through Pleasure Island's main gate.

# INDEX